DATE DUE

Primary Prevention of Psychopathology
Volume II: Environmental Influences

Primary Prevention of Psychopathology

VOLUME II:

ENVIRONMENTAL INFLUENCES

EDITOR

Donald G. Forgays

Published for the University of Vermont
by the University Press of New England
Hanover New Hampshire 1978

The University Press
of New England

Brandeis University
Clark University
Dartmouth College
University of New Hampshire
University of Rhode Island
University of Vermont

This volume is dedicated to those who work hard to develop primary prevention of psychopathology, knowing that success in this venture will put many of them out of their customary work.

Contents

Preface by Donald G. Forgays   ix

PART I
INTRODUCTION   1

1. What is Positive Mental Health?   3
    HEINZ L. ANSBACHER

2. Demystifying Primary Prevention   7
    EMORY L. COWEN

3. A National Perspective   25
    STEPHEN E. GOLDSTON

PART II
RESEARCH APPROACHES TO PREVENTION   37

4. Sociocultural Mental Retardation: A Longitudinal
    Study   39
    F. RICK HEBER

5. Plasticity in the Rates of Achieving Cognitive and
    Motivational Landmarks   63
    J. McV. HUNT
    DISCUSSANT: ROBERT SOMMER

6. Marital Disruption as a Stressor   81
    BERNARD L. BLOOM
    DISCUSSANTS: STEPHEN E. GOLDSTON, IRWIN ALTMAN

PART III
THEORETICAL APPROACHES TO MENTAL
HEALTH   113

7. Strange Bedfellows: The Yogi and the Commissar   115
    ROBERT SOMMER

8. Privacy and Mental Health   133
    IRWIN ALTMAN
    DISCUSSANT: BERNARD L. BLOOM

PART IV
ENVIRONMENTAL PSYCHOLOGY AND
PREVENTION   157

9.   Research Strategies in Environmental Psychology   159
        JONATHAN L. FREEDMAN

10.   Utility of the Behavior Settings Approach   164
        PHIL SCHOGGEN
        DISCUSSANT: F. RICK HEBER

        PART V
        INTEGRATION

11.   Conference Integration   183
        M. BREWSTER SMITH

12   Epilogue   201
        DONALD G. FORGAYS

        APPENDIX
        Report of the Task Panel on Prevention   205

        Name Index   251

        Subject Index   257

Preface

The First Vermont Conference on the Primary Prevention of Psychopathology took place in June 1975, and the proceedings were published by the University Press of New England in 1977.* The theme of that conference was the identification of basic issues in the area, and more than twenty experts in the field were invited to make formal presentations. Their reports covered, among other topics, definitional problems; genetic, prenatal, and perinatal factors of concern; identification of high risk persons; and interventions for primary prevention. The meeting was planned by a group of faculty members of the Department of Psychology, University of Vermont, and underwritten financially by the Waters Foundation.

It was decided to institutionalize the Vermont Conference as an annual meeting dealing separately each year with one of the important issues identified during the first conference and at subsequent meetings.

The theme selected by the Planning Committee for the second conference, in 1976, was the environment—more specifically, environmental factors contributing to the development of psychopathology and environmental manipulations which may effectively prevent psychopathology. Speculation about these areas was invited, though VCPPP continues the tradition of the first year in being action-oriented and in emphasizing reports of hands-on research and community programs.

It is apparent to us all that such environmental factors as the

*George W. Albee and Justin M. Joffe, eds., *Primary Prevention of Psychopathology*. Volume I: The Issues. Hanover, N.H.: University Press of New England, 1977.

the stresses of modern living, urbanization, and poverty are intimately involved in the development of psychopathology. It is also apparent that interventional methods involve manipulations of environmental variables. It has been difficult, however, to specify which environmental factors cause or contribute to the development of psychopathology and how they do so; it has been equally difficult to specify which environmental variables are manipulated in interventional attempts and how they relate to ensuing changes in behavior.

One of the difficulties is that behavioral scientists who are most knowledgeable about the environment and expert in the relationships between environmental dimensions and human behavior are not usually those who make the environmental manipulations as interventional attempts. It would be desirable, perhaps, both to enhance the environmental sophistication of the interventional people and to get the environmental experts more interested in the problems of psychopathological prevention than they have appeared to be in the past.

The Planning Committee for the Second Vermont Conference decided to include people with internationally recognized competence in environmental areas significant to issues of primary prevention. It was our wish to bring two groups together: those who have been actively involved in manipulating environmental variables as attempts to prevent or alleviate behavioral disorder, and experts in the field of the environment in its various forms. Bringing together such persons for several days of intensive communication could provide the arena for the coalescence of individual creative research and theorizing into more effective plans for social-action intervention programs.

Volume I of the Vermont Conference was the first full-length book in the field of primary prevention; the present book, Volume II, is still one of the very few available in the area. But interest appears to exist, and more research is being done on prevention variables. Relevant publications are appearing, and we hope that greater financial support of demonstration studies and fundamental research in the field will be forthcoming. At the time of this writing, the Third Vermont Conference has been held, on the theme of Promoting Social Competence and Coping in Children.

The Second Conference, held June 23–26, 1976, was opened

by Heinz L. Ansbacher, whose paper urged that primary prevention be identified with a concept of positive mental health, for which he supplied a definition. In the keynote address, Emory L. Cowen spoke out for clarifying the scope and sharpening the focus of the broad area of primary prevention by analyzing and modifying important social systems and initiating competence training programs. A conceptual framework was presented by Stephen E. Goldston, who also summarized what had—and had not—been accomplished in the field during 1976 by federal contributions, meetings and conferences, and program development.

Part II papers report research in the area of primary prevention. F. Rick Heber makes the first public written report of the well-known Milwaukee Project, which attempts to prevent mental retardation through environmental manipulation. J. McV. Hunt compares Heber's work with what he himself accomplished over a long period in Iran and in this country. His evidence supports the Heber conclusions and adds some detail on the cognitive areas which may be most susceptible to environmental impact. Generalizing prevention research to an older population, Bernard L. Bloom describes a new program investigating marital disturbance as an important social stressor.

Robert Sommer and Irwin Altman present in Part III different theoretical approaches to important mental health issues. Sommer suggests that we must work on both the environment and the individual at the same time. Altman believes that privacy is so critical to mental health that it is a pancultural variable.

In Part IV Jonathan L. Freedman and Phil Schoggen develop the relationships between environmental psychology and primary prevention. Freedman discusses research strategies available in the area; Schoggen describes the work he did with Roger Barker and others leading to the important and relevant concepts of undermanning and overmanning.

In the last section, Part V, M. Brewster Smith provides a summary and integration of all of the papers presented earlier. Donald G. Forgays evaluates the conference in terms of its successes and failures.

In each section of the conference, time was provided for discussion among speakers, other participants, and audience members. The discussions, either edited or summarized, appear at the end of each Part.

Like the first conference, the second was organized with support from and with the collaboration of James and Faith Waters and the Waters Foundation. Both have attended every session of the first three conferences; at each of the first two, James Waters made a welcoming address. At the 1976 conference he stated that the Waters Foundation, although it has a business background, had developed a keen interest in human behavior and, more specifically, in contributing to the alleviation of human misery and the improvement of mental health; this concern led to the foundation's interest in primary prevention of psychopathology. The VCPPP conferences could not be held without the active support of the Waters Foundation.

The Planning Committee of the 1976 Vermont Conference consisted, in addition to the editor of this volume, of Dr. George Albee, Dr. Lawrence Gordon, and three advanced graduate students in the Department of Psychology, University of Vermont: Janet W. Forgays, Robert A. Lubin, and Frank Petho.

Special thanks are due Mrs. Hildegarde Bolsterle, who worked patiently on the transcripts and the manuscript over many months.

D.G.F.

Burlington, Vermont
February 1978

I
Introduction

1

What is Positive Mental Health?

HEINZ L. ANSBACHER

Heinz L. Ansbacher received his Ph.D. degree in Psychology from Columbia University in 1937, having left a budding business career. He was Assistant Editor of Psychological Abstracts *for three years. During World War II he worked as a psychological warfare specialist with the Office of War Information, then taught briefly at Brooklyn College and Duke University. In 1946 he came to the University of Vermont, where he is presently an Emeritus Professor of Psychology and where he has spent virtually his entire professional career.*

Well known as one of the more influential supporters and interpreters of Adlerian psychology in the world today, Ansbacher has been equally well known as editor of the Journal of Individual Psychology *for nearly twenty years. He has published prodigiously over the years and still continues this activity.*

The need for a definition of positive mental health is greatest in *primary* prevention; in a well population we want to prevent mental disorders from ever developing. In *secondary* prevention, on the other hand, we want "to prevent [existing] mild disorders from becoming acute or prolonged," while in *tertiary* prevention our goal is to prevent "consequences of mental illness" (Sanford, 1965, p. 1389). In both of the latter, we want to do away with a negative factor: we want to prevent an undesirable state from getting worse and, if possible, change it for the better.

In primary prevention, by contrast, we would like to make certain that persons who are already enjoying mental health continue to do so. Yet in the absence of a workable positive definition of mental health, primary prevention, too, has concentrated on changing known negative environmental factors. Zax and Cowen

(1976) say: "We have made a strong case for . . . modifying social systems as a way of preventing behavior disorders" (p. 403). This is all to the good, but it is limited and implies environmental determinism. All social, historical, and biological determinants, however, provide only probabilities. They only provide raw data fed into the computer of the human brain—which differs fundamentally from the ordinary computer in that it additionally feeds into the mix spontaneous ideas of its own. If this were not the case, human culture, history, and progress would be inconceivable. Thus, even under good conditions some individuals will be mentally disturbed, while even at worst some will remain mentally healthy.

We need, then, the positive definition of mental health to provide guidelines for positive further development of those who are growing up under relatively favorable home and school conditions, because these alone are no guarantee. Actually, a positive definition is already implied when we speak of favorable home and school conditions. These are educational endeavors, and in all educational endeavors the problem of the goal to be attained has to be faced. If in the mental health field, and primary prevention in particular, we wish to replace the medical model with the educational model, we must define a positive goal, to provide guidelines for our actions as groups and institutions as well as individuals.

The problem of defining positive mental health is not solved, even though books have been written on it; there is no agreement among psychologists and professionals on how to define it. But fortunately we need only a workable definition, not an absolute definition. All the various theories seem to agree that mental disorder is related to immaturity and positive mental health is related to maturity.

The greatest divergence in almost anything related to mental health and mental disorder is between Freud and Adler, not because of their personalities, but because they represent extreme opposites in philosophy of science. Yet, interestingly, they agree that to be mentally healthy is to be mature. In his metapsychological language Freud (1933) formulated the objective of his therapeutic efforts as "Where id was, there shall ego be" (p. 112). Since id stands for immaturity and ego for maturity, the objective is to establish maturity. Freud also disguised this thought in sexual metaphors by associating desirable adjustment with the genital stage of psychosexual development—the mature stage—and describing neurosis as partly a fixation on one of the three less mature childhood stages of sexual development. So, to be mentally healthy is to have reached the mature stage. Adler (1956) made the association explicit: "The cure of mental disorder is brought about by a correction of the faulty picture of the world [which is the picture of a pampered child] and the unequivocal acceptance of a mature picture of the world" (p. 333).

To leap to the present scene, the National Institute of Mental Health (1969) also associates mental health with maturity, and extends this thinking to society: "In the final analysis, the mental health of each citizen is affected by the maturity and health of our society, from the smallest unit to the largest" (p. 120).

Now to the definition of maturity. Good data are available through the Vineland Social Maturity Scale (Doll, 1965, based on his research during the 1940's), a scale designed to measure maturity as distinct from intelligence in children. It consists of 117 items grouped into age levels and ranging from birth to 25 years. At birth, the individual is almost completely dependent, but with increasing age he is able to move by himself, feed himself, dress himself, help in the household, look after younger children, and so on. At the highest level he is capable of advancing general welfare. The psychological maturation process is thus represented as development from being a complete social burden or liability into being an individual of social usefulness who is a support to others and a social asset. From this, maturity can be defined as social usefulness and immaturity as social uselessness.

On the Strong Vocational Interest Blank (Strong, 1943), we find that younger people have more interests in common with persons in such occupations as pilot, policeman, or worker in the forest service, whereas somewhat older people share more interests with persons in occupations involving service to other people, such as minister and social worker. Thus in the Strong Blank maturity also involves greater social usefulness—meaning more to others in a constructive sense.

Finally, one obtains a similar definition by interviewing any group of students. The immature person will be described as self-centered, unreliable, burdensome, and having characteristics of mental disorder, while the mature person will be described as responsible, reasonable, helpful, and so on.

Mental health, then, can be equated with maturity, and maturity in turn with social usefulness. On this basis I propose the following definition of positive mental health (adapted from Adler, 1956, pp. 157–159): an orientation or striving on the socially useful side of life, a sense of ultimate usefulness to humanity rather than conformity to existing norms. As a definition of mental disturbance, I propose: a striving on the socially useless or harmful side.

Mental health so defined would be a suitable objective for primary prevention. No longer would primary prevention have to concentrate almost exclusively on changing undesirable social environments (important as this is), but could also work out programs directed at individuals, guiding them toward maturation not as an end condition to be reached at a single time but as a continuous movement. It is relative social usefulness that counts: a five-year-old can be relatively very mature and sensible and useful within his capabilities, while many adults are immature in that they direct their striving toward goals that are objectively useless or even harmful.

REFERENCES

Adler, A. *The Individual Psychology of Alfred Adler*. Edited by H. L. and R. R. Ansbacher. New York: Basic Books, 1956.

Doll, E. A. *Vineland Social Maturity Scale: Manual of directions*. (Rev. ed.) Minneapolis, Minn.: Educational Test Bureau [now American Guidance Service], 1965.

Freud, S. *New introductory lectures on psycho-analysis*. New York: Norton, 1933.

National Institute of Mental Health. *The mental health of urban America*. Washington, D.C.: Government Printing Office, 1969.

Sanford, N. The prevention of mental illness. In B. B. Wolman (Ed.), *Handbook of clinical psychology*. New York: McGraw-Hill, 1965. Pp. 1378–1400.

Strong, E. K., Jr. *Vocational interests of men and women*. Stanford, Calif.: Stanford University Press, 1943.

Zax, M., and Cowen, E. L. *Abnormal psychology: changing conceptions*. (2nd ed.) New York: Holt, Rinehart and Winston, 1976.

2

Demystifying Primary Prevention

EMORY L. COWEN

Emory L. Cowen received the Ph.D. degree in Psychology from Syracuse University in 1950. Upon finishing his graduate training he went to the University of Rochester, where he has been ever since, presently as Professor of Psychology, Director of the Center for Community Study, Professor of Psychiatry, and Professor of Education.

He has been a consultant to several federal, state, and local agencies, including the Veterans Administration, the National Science Foundation, and the American Psychological Association. At present he is serving as Advisory Editor of the Journal of Consulting and Clinical Psychology *and Associate Editor of the* American Journal of Community Psychology.

A career-long researcher and writer, Cowen has published over 100 articles and several books and has contributed sections to many more books. His research over the years has included problem-solving rigidity, aspects of manifest anxiety, trait description, and community psychology. He is well known for his studies of the early identification of emotional disorder in young children. For over ten years he has been vitally concerned with the prevention of psychopathology on all three levels.

These days, writers treat the concept of primary prevention with reverence. Kelly (1975) says: "In my opinion the topic of primary prevention is a most exciting and overdue challenge for psychology." I feel that way, too.

This paper was written with support from an NIMH grant (MH 11820–06, Experimental and Special Training Branch) for which I express my appreciation. I also thank my colleagues Ellis L. Gesten and James G. Kelly for suffering through an earlier draft and for their many constructive inputs and suggestions. I retain full claim to all flaws and imperfections.

Although there is some difference of opinion about exactly how to define the concept (Kessler & Albee, 1975) there is enough agreement about its main abstract thrust. Caplan (1964) offers a representative definition:

> *Primary prevention . . . involves lowering the rate of new cases of mental disorder in a population, over a certain period by counteracting harmful circumstances before they have had a chance to produce illness. It does not seek to prevent a specific person from becoming sick. Instead, it seeks to reduce the risk for a whole population so that, although some may become ill, their number will be reduced. (p. 26)*

Sanford (1972) is briefer and more direct. He speaks of it simply as preventing the *development* of disorder. Another definition (Zax & Cowen, 1976) emphasizes three elements: (1) reducing new instances of disorder, (2) reducing irritants to dysfunction before they exact their toll, and (3) building psychological health.

If most people agree on an abstract definition of primary prevention and put it in the same league as God, motherhood, flag, and apple pie, we should be way ahead. But we aren't! Several vexing subsurface problems thwart applications of primary prevention in mental health and keep us from reaping its benefits. Identifying these problems explicitly may help to free up the considerable potential of the approach. Let me temporarily label two such groups of problems as: (a) "slippage" between abstract definitions and concrete illustrations of primary prevention and (b) what mental health people are, and are not, competent to do.

Slippage Problems

There seems to be a bumpy, tortuous road between consensually validated abstract definitions of primary prevention and the concrete instances cited to document them. More than once in recent years, after having read a clear definition of primary prevention, I have found the specific program examples cited subsequently by the author to be basically unrelated to it. The first few times I attributed the gap to my own lack of sophistication. But it has happened too often now for me to continue to dismiss it so simply. Without "fingering" specific author-culprits, I can offer several examples from what is potentially a long list. One author, writing about primary prevention, cites suicide clinics and suicide prevention programs. Others talk about counseling programs for parents of disturbed children, newly married couples and parents of college freshmen, or the role of child guidance clinics in primary prevention.

The issue hits even closer to home. For many years my associates and I have been developing a school mental health program based on early detection and intervention for school maladaptation (Cowen, Trost, Lorion, Dorr, Izzo, and Isaacson, 1975). It is a nice program—a genuine alternative to past traditional delivery systems—that gets to children in need at an early stage and then geometrically expands the reach of helping services (Cowen, Lorion, Kraus, and Dorr, 1974). It is a demonstrably useful alternative to past ways and I do not apologize for it. But it is *not* primary prevention: it is ontogenetically early secondary prevention, focusing on children who are experiencing visible adaptive problems. Yet more than once it has been cited as a shining example of primary prevention.

There must be reasons why people identify our project as primary prevention, even though we ourselves have never made such a claim. I can only guess at them. Some people may just be careless in their use of words; having defined an abstract "good," they may not worry sufficiently about whether their concrete examples match the definition. Others perhaps are fuzzy about precise applications. But the most likely explanation, in my opinion, stems from the fact that mental health has done so little of anything palpable in primary prevention. Subscribing (sometimes with zeal) to a valued "in"-concept for which there are a few good examples creates dissonance. One way to reduce the dissonance is to latch onto concrete instances that depart from traditional ways in a generally preventive direction, even if they do not approximate the ideal, and to proclaim these to be primary prevention, by fiat. As a result, the number of projects cited as examples of primary prevention in mental health exceeds by a major mutiple the number of projects that actually *are* primary prevention.

What Mental Health People Can and Cannot Do

My second concern is a by-product of the fact that primary prevention's abstract definition is, indeed, so broad and vague. Caplan

(1964) likens it to a motorist's large-scale road map that provides only the grossest directions. The term's connotative meaning ("good") is far clearer than its specific denotative meanings, seen in its actual operations. Things are murkier at the latter level: primary prevention touches many aspects of life; it seeks to improve the quality of life; it requires new combinations of expertise from many fields to be brought off successfully (Zax and Cowen, 1976).

Fortunately or otherwise, people's psychological well-being is not a reified entity, divorced from the rest of their existence. To the contrary, "virtually anything done to improve man's life can also be viewed as primary mental health prevention" (Zax and Cowen, 1976, p. 479). Kessler and Albee (1975) in a recent *Annual Review* chapter on primary prevention provide a tongue-in-cheek rendition of the same point:

> *During the past year we found ourselves constantly writing references and ideas on scraps of paper and emptying our pockets each day of notes on the primary prevention relevance of children's group homes, titanium paint, parent effectiveness-training, consciousness raising, Zoom, Sesame Street, the guaranteed annual wage, legalized abortion, school integration, limits on international cartels, unpolished rice, free prenatal clinics, antipollution laws, a yoghurt and vegetable diet, free VD clinics, and a host of other topics. Nearly everything, it appears, has implications for primary prevention, for reducing emotional disturbance, for strengthening and fostering mental health. (p. 560)*

The statement, incredibly, is absolutely correct. But mental health professionals are limited enough in their own mandated sphere; they are hardly equipped to tackle the "nearly everything" that seems to feed into primary prevention (Bloom, 1965). Sarason, Levine, Goldenberg, Cherlin, and Bennett (1966) inveigh against professional "preciousness"—i.e., the belief of certain groups (take mental health professionals as a random example) that they, and they alone, stand as God's chosen people for stamping out the woes of civilization. We are *not* architects, engineers, nutrition specialists, recreation experts, politicians, or urban planners, nor can we assume a near infinity of such roles. If we are to gain ground in primary prevention, some of the fuzz and mystery must be removed from the concept to provide sharper, more operational answers to the question of what we as mental health specialists are best equipped to contribute to, in the quest for this Holy Grail. Such contributions, we can hope, will go beyond heartfelt vocal support for the platitude of improving the "quality of life."

In sidling up to this challenge, it helped me to dredge up several elemental concepts (dependent and independent variables) from my earlier formation and training. Mental health comes together as a field because of a shared emphasis on certain dependent variables. Although people might quibble a bit about their exact nature, we are talking essentially about such variables as adjustment, adaptation, security, happiness, and self-image—a person's "well-being," if you will. Various people in the extended mental health family engage these dependent variables differently. Historically, the clinical role has been to undo deficit in these states— a casualty-repair orientation. Community mental health (CMH) accepts some of that emphasis, but seeks to streamline the repair process by identifying problems sooner and in more natural settings, and by engaging them more flexibly and realistically. This set moves CMH people away from classic repair institutions (hospitals, clinics, private consulting suites, and so on) into new, community settings (schools, storefronts, and the like).

Although community psychology is oriented to the same dependent measures as traditional clinical practice and community mental health, it seeks to prevent rather than to repair—to build strengths rather than to counterpunch against deficit. That sounds like primary prevention and, indeed, philosophically, it is. But to date it has been a concept in search of operational practices. Troubles start at the level of independent variables. We have already suggested that the answer to the question "Which independent variables materially shape outcomes on mental health's prime dependent measures?" is "Virtually any!" Indeed Kessler and Albee's facetious list of prospective independent variables is far less facetious than it is incomplete. And most of those variables are so far removed from mental health's knowledge and experience bases that we are incapable of engaging them.

There are two ways in which groping, floundering, and probably failure—the failure of trying to shovel water—may be reduced. One, more obvious and hence more often proposed (Kelly, 1973), is that mental health people should strengthen their contacts and collaborative working relationships with specialists who are charged with responsibility for areas (independent variables) that are likely to affect mental health outcomes significantly. These are the same architects, policy-makers, urban planners, and so on who we said above we could not ourselves *be*. Doubtless, much can be done with such people to clarify obscure linkages between decisions and actions in seemingly "remote" areas and mental health outcomes. Indeed, the argument has been carried a step further (Vallance, 1976) with the suggestion that training should be broadened to produce people capable of using psychological knowledge to deal with live social problems as they occur, rather than people who are discipline-bound.

A second, less apparent tack has thus far attracted less attention. From among the multitude of independent variables that have an impact on adjustment, several rather important clusters are *relatively* closer to existing knowledge and competence bases of mental health people. We need to ask which these are, and how their manipulation might promote more positive mental health outcomes. That can be done now; doing so would help both to demystify and to further primary prevention in mental health.

Two broad areas strike me as prime candidates for such a thrust: the analysis and modification of social environments, and competence building. Both exemplify primary prevention in that they are targeted to people-in-general rather than to individuals at known risk.

Social environments

People's (especially children's) development and adaptation are significantly shaped by a limited number of high-impact social environments: communities, churches, schools, and families. In the past we have tended to take properties of these systems for granted and, except for so intimate a system as the family, to overlook their shaping impact. There are, to be sure, exceptions. Barker and Gump (1964) studied the predispositional properties of one significant dimension of physical environment: a school's size. They found that youngsters from small schools. compared to those from large schools, participated in more, and more diverse, activities; were less aware of individual differences; had clearer self-identities; and were more visible. Although Barker and Gump's dependent measures were not all centrally relevant to mental health, the basic question of whether aspects of physical and, more importantly, social environments shape adaptive-adjustive outcomes in people is legitimate and important. Thus, Moos (1974a) says:

"the social climate within which an individual functions may have an important impact on his attitudes and moods, his behavior, his health and overall sense of well-being and his social, personal and intellectual development." (p.3)

Several developments are needed to reap full benefit from a social-environment approach to primary prevention. First, we must better understand how to assess social environments; we must also understand their key impact dimensions and how they vary with respect to them. We then need to establish more clearly how environmental attributes relate to people's personal development and behavior, both generally and in terms of specific person-environment matches. This orientation assumes that social systems are not neutral in their effects on people: they either contribute to development or impair it. If the whys and wherefores of these relations can be charted, such information could be harnessed to engineer health promoting environments (Coelho and Rubenstein, 1972). That seems much preferable to allowing rutted practice to reign by default.

Rudolf Moos and his co-workers in the Social Ecology Laboratory at the Stanford University Medical School have pioneered this area. They (Moos, 1973, 1974b) have identified six broad methodologies (for example, ecological analysis, analysis of behavior settings, study of psychosocial characteristics) for conceptualizing environmental variables and relating them to behavior. With much perseverance they (Moos, 1974a) have developed a series of parallel social climate scales, each with 7 to 10 dimensions and 84 to 100 items, to assess nine different types of social environments ranging from hospital-based treatment programs on the one hand to correctional and educational settings, work milieus, family environments, and military companies on the other. These scales have been used to assess multiple examples of each of the nine types of settings.

Several fascinating findings emerged from that work. First, three social climate clusters—relational, personal development, and system maintenance qualities—have faithfully recurred in describing seemingly diverse environments. Relational factors describe the nature of interpersonal relations, such as how people affiliate and the support they provide each other. Personal development dimensions indicate how people's personal growth and enhancement takes place in terms of such variables as autonomy, amount of competition, and task-orientation. And system maintenance dimensions assess the extent to which environments are orderly, controlling, change-oriented, etc. Moos et al.'s findings suggest that: (a) social climate factors can be reliably measured; (b) a small number of common dimensional clusters well describe superficially different social environments; (c) the scales discriminate well among multiple instances of various environments; and (d) the scales reflect enduring environmental qualities.

Although such information has considerable instrumental value, it is not yet primary prevention. A bridge to the latter is built by considering environmental consequences. That is a challenging area and, as Moos (1974a) points out, one about which we still know very little. But some encouraging, if only suggestive, findings are available. For example, Moos et al.'s data indicate that such social environments as therapy groups and hospital and educational settings, which score high in relational qualities like involvement and support, have occupants who are not irritable and depressed, are satisfied and comfortable, and have high self-esteem (Moos, 1974a, 1974b). Similar early returns suggest that environments high on personal development dimensions, such as autonomy and problem orientation, have positive effects. Trickett and Moos (1974) found that students were happy in classes with high student involvement and a close student-teacher relation. By contrast, some system maintenance dimensions—for example, high control—seem to have negative effects. But the matter may be more complex. Trickett and Moos (1974) found that students from school environments high in competition—a personal development dimension with a negative aura—learned more than students from school environments lower in competition.

Although Moos et al. have been conceptual and methodological leaders in the study of environment effects, others have joined the fray, sometimes defining environmental variables in more macromolar, less operational ways. For example, a group at the Bank St. College of Education (Minuchin, Biber, Shapiro, and Zimiles, 1969; Zimiles, 1967) has examined some personal correlates of modern versus traditional educational environments. Modern

environments were defined as those that encouraged the development of thought and learning process; traditional environments
were oriented more to the acquisition of facts. Children educated
in modern environments were found to (a) be more identified as
children; (b) have greater acceptance of negative impulses; (c) have
more differentiated self-concepts; and (d) pursue learning more
seriously and analytically. Reiss and Martell (1974) found that
children from open-space educational environments surpassed
demographically comparable peers from self-contained classes in
oral fluency, persistence, and imaginativeness. In a broader,
literary way Kozol (1967) describes the disastrously negative
consequences of the school environment on slum children in
Boston.

Each of the above examples can be thought of as a main-effect
consequence of environmental properties. It is insufficient, however, to speak of environmental effects independent of people. A
facilitating environment for one person can restrict another. Several
examples amplify the point. A study by Allinsmith and Grimes
(1961) showed that whereas anxious-compulsive children fared
poorly in loosely structured school environments, peers without
such characteristics did very well in them. Reiss and Dyhdalo
(1975) as part of the research program cited above found that,
overall, children from open-space classes compared to those from
self-contained environments persisted more on difficult tasks and
showed a stronger relation between persistence and academic
achievement. On the other hand, nonpersistent (distractible) children from self-contained classes had significantly higher educational achievement scores than those from open environments.

Kelly and his colleagues (Kelly, 1968, 1969; Kelly et al., 1971,
1976) have long stressed the need for this type of ecological
orientation, i.e. an emphasis on the person-environment fit. They
have focused on the types of adaptations that are encouraged by
fluid and stable high school environments (defined by annual
pupil turnover rates). They found, for example, that new students
were more readily accepted in a fluid, as compared to a stable,
environment. Whereas personal development was highly valued
in the former, status and achievement were respected in the latter.
The same exploratory behaviors that could be adaptive in one
environment could be maladaptive in another. Insel and Moos
(1974) take the ecological-match question a step closer to mental

health: "A source of distress and ill health is the situation in which a person attempts to function within an environment with which he is basically incompatible" (p. 7).

Thus, the evidence suggests not only that social environments can be reliably described and that they vary, but also that these variations relate to person-outcomes on variables important to the mental health domain and, potentially, in different ways for different people. Though we have a long way to go in dotting all the i's and crossing all the t's for these complex relationships, at least this is a brand of knowledge from which bona fide primary prevention efforts can be fashioned. The independent variables involved—system properties—have a high probability for impacting states with which mental health must be concerned. Some mental health professionals already have skills, competencies, and tools to pursue such work. As the knowledge base in the area expands, the pot of gold at the end of the rainbow is the possibility of engineering systems—be they new communities (Barker and Schoggen, 1973; Price and Blashfield, 1975), well-baby clinics, or schools that can build health and resources in people—a true primary prevention.

Several reality constraints, however, bear mention. One is that primary prevention calls for an expanded time perspective. As Kelly (1975) says, "If we wish to understand behavior in relation to primary prevention we will do more work with people over time" (p. 3). There are several reasons why this is so. The manipulations and processes of primary prevention are intrinsically complex, their means-end contingencies are less than immediate, and the target behaviors in question are often ones that change only slowly, over time. Several major studies have been reported recently (Kelly et al., 1976; Hartley, 1972) in which anticipated preventive effects failed to appear initially but became clearer and clearer as time passed.

A second limiting factor is that knowing how to build health facilitating systems and actually being able to build them are two different matters. The latter entails severe practical problems. Once established, systems resist change. Power structures form, vested interests are protected, and system occupants are threatened by the prospect of change. Thus, rooted systems may not be expected to yield passively or graciously to change and, even if we clearly understood the theory and practice of system-change, such change would not be easy. Important economic, psychological, and political determinants quite beyond cold scientific facts influence the social change processes (Sarason, 1972; Fairweather, Sanders, and Tornatzky, 1974; Rothman, 1974; Rothman, Erlich, and Teresa, 1976).

Competence and Adjustment

A second pathway, different but very attractive, can also be followed in the service of primary prevention. It can be argued that the best possible defense against problems is to build resources and adaptive strengths in people from the start (Murphy and Chandler, 1972). This broad orienting set has been applied at several levels, with instructive findings.

The view assumes that people often become maladjusted because they lack specific skills needed to resolve personal problems. If such skills could truly be taught from the outset there would be less need ever to engage maladjustment. The thrust of this approach is educational rather than restorative, and mass-oriented rather than individual-casualty-oriented. Its key questions are: (1) What core skills undergird positive adjustment? (2) Can curriculum be developed to teach young children these skills? (3) Does acquiring a given competence lead to improved interpersonal adjustment? (4) Do adjustive gains, so acquired, endure? Positive answers to these questions would markedly advance de facto primary prevention.

Ojemann's long-term effort (1961, 1969) to develop causal teaching curricula was an early move in this direction. Although children exposed to this approach, compared to the traditionally educated, were better able to generalize knowledge, weigh alternatives, and understand factors underlying behavior, the program's main thrust has been more toward educational processes and outcomes than toward personal ones (Zax and Specter, 1974).

Recently, through Spivack and Shure's (1974) work, the approach has been brought closer to mental health. These investigators, based on extensive prior research with patients and clinical groups, concluded that social problem-solving skills (for example, sensitivity to human problems, the ability to perceive alternatives and means-end relations, and awareness of the effects of one's behavior on others) critically mediated sound personal adjustment.

They reasoned that if they could teach such skills to young children, it would lead to improved behavioral adjustment.

They developed a social problem-solving curriculum for 4-year-old Head-Start children. The curriculum included prior instrumental training in listening and attending skills and in the acquisition of basic building concepts such as negation and similarity, as well as the actual social problem-solving skills. This was done in the form of brief, interesting games and dialogues, covering 10 weeks of daily 5-to-20-minute lessons. After teachers were trained in the approach, they taught the skills directly to the children. Comparisons were made between the experimental group and demographically similar nonprogram control children.

Program children learned these social problem-solving skills readily and were much superior to controls at the end of the program. Their use of irrelevant and forceful problem solutions also decreased significantly. These changes were maintained at follow-up during the next (kindergarten) school year (Shure and Spivack, 1975a). And a parallel program (Shure and Spivack, 1975b) showed that inner-city mothers could successfully teach social problem-solving skills to their own children.

Among other criterion measures, classroom teachers submitted behavioral and adjustment ratings for all children before the training program started. Some of the study's most significant findings, from the standpoint of primary prevention, came from these data. For example, initially maladjusted program children gained the most in social problem-solving skills. Moreover, there was a direct relation between gain in social problem-solving skills and reduction in maladjustment. Program children also improved significantly on such dimensions as concern for others, ability to take the initiative, and autonomy, with the initially most maladjusted showing the greatest gains. None of these things happened with control children. Implanting social problem-solving skills apparently established a competence beachhead that radiated positively to a cluster of variables that we think of as good mental health.

Spivack and Shure's findings are not isolated. Allen, Chinsky, Larcen, Lochman, and Selinger (1976), as part of a comprehensive three-tiered preventive school mental health program, also did social problem-solving training with fourth-grade children, as their primary prevention component. They too found that the training succeeded and that there were positive spill-over effects: children became more internally oriented and developed more positive expectancies about the school experience.

Although social problem-solving seems to be an important mediating skill for good adjustment, it is not the only one. How important is it to adjustment to know how to be able to plan ahead, make decisions, take roles, and assert oneself when appropriate? Illustratively, Stamps (1975) used self-reinforcement methods to teach goal-setting skills to deprived inner-city fourth-graders. As a result of this training the children did, indeed, learn to set more accurate goals. Simultaneously, their overall achievement scores improved significantly. These cognitive gains were paralleled by behavioral and personality improvements. Thus, teachers rated program children as having significantly fewer problem behaviors than controls. On test measures, they showed increases in openness, awareness, and self-acceptance and a greater willingness to assume responsibility for negative outcomes on a locus of control measure. Again, rooting a gut competency radiated positively to adjustment.

A child's ability to ask questions, i.e. curiosity behavior, is widely accepted as a positive value (Susskind, 1969). Yet studies of the spontaneous occurrence of curiosity behavior, often measured in terms of children's question-asking behaviors in class, show that it is far less common than what people consider ideal, or estimate to be occurring. Thus, Susskind (1969), using 30-minute classroom observation units, found that teachers on the average asked 20 to 25 times as many questions as an entire class combined. This type of observation lies behind several studies designed both to help teachers augment children's question-asking behavior (Susskind, 1969) and to evaluate approaches (for example, social reinforcement, auto-instruction) designed to increase children's question-asking (Blank and Covington, 1965; Evans, 1971). In one such study (Blank and Covington, 1965) using auto-instruction, not only did children learn to ask more questions, but they also had higher achievement test scores and participated more in class discussions, in comparison to controls who were not so trained.

The primary preventive strategy of enhancing competencies (Riessman, 1967) has been applied at levels that are socially more macromolar. Thus Rappaport, Davidson, Wilson, and Mitchell (1975) developed a setting called the Community Psychology Action Center (CPAC) with the black inner-city poor. CPAC seeks to identify existing competence bases in the community and to support their further development. This program in no way tries to reshape people to conform to regnant systems or to modify people's styles or values. Rather, it takes strength where and as it is, and builds on it, thus enhancing the community's competence base and broadening it to new areas. It is not an anti-problem program. Its goals are to foster independence and positive behaviors, based on the belief that developing resources and competencies is the best way to engage problems and to meet adversity.

The work cited in this section suggests that several pivotal competencies, on the surface removed from the dependent variables of prime concern to mental health, can be taught to people, or strengthened where they already exist. Acquiring these competencies is accompanied by positive radiating effects to adaptations and behaviors squarely related to mental health. That message should not be repressed. Symptoms, or problem behaviors, have been reduced without ever engaging them, through direct training of the critical competencies. Health has been engineered, so to speak, indirectly through skill acquisition. Oriented to people in general, not just troubled people, such efforts model a promising type of primary prevention.

At least one point needs clarification. Up to now, I must confess, I have cheated a bit in suggesting that mental health people already have the wherewithal to bring off these new developments. A few do, perhaps, but the implication that all do is more than charitable. Sociologists and social and organizational psychologists know much more than we about social system analysis and modification, just as developmentalists and educational psychologists may be better versed in competence training. Yet these groups are less knowledgeable about the prime dependent variables of concern. Hence some new marriages are called for, if the chase is to proceed judiciously and efficiently. And, for the future, new training combinations will be needed to produce people genuinely qualified to enrich these areas.

SUMMARY

Nothing in this paper is to suggest that primary prevention is either simple or straightforward. Indeed, what was said earlier about its devilish complexity still holds. The core dilemma is that virtually any manipulation imaginable can affect people's well-being and the so-called quality of life. If we let the matter go at that, the temptation for mental health people will be either to throw up their arms in despair or to traffic in gushy, impalpable platitudes. If as mental health specialists we want a piece of the action, now, we must separate the near-infinity of manipulations and independent variables that could potentially affect well-being into those for which we do, and do not, have a knowledge-and-competence base. If we lack the knowledge base (that is the case for most areas), we shall be limited either to learning more or to working in closer collaboration with people who know more. Where we possess or can readily acquire the necessary competence and technology, we should be getting on with the show.

A major thesis of this paper is that there are at least two broad, very important areas that meet the latter criterion: (a) the analysis and modification of impactful social systems; and (b) competence training. Examples of recent work in these areas have been cited, and linkages have been reported between system qualities and competence as independent variables and criteria of adjustment and well-being. Work in both areas is targeted impersonally to large numbers of people, not to individuals at risk—a desideratum of primary prevention.

Notions of system analysis and modification and competence training are far from new. One difference today is that people are beginning to do things with them concretely rather than just worshiping them from afar. A second difference is that linkages have been found between qualities of social environments and/or the skills people have, and adjustment. These important developments suggest exciting possibilities for restructuring mental health's classic, tunnel-visioned, definition of mandate—to combat pathology. As concrete, operational steps toward primary prevention, which tap skills that are reasonably close to the special backgrounds and training of mental health people, they can help immeasurably to demystify what has always been a deliciously attractive, but very slippery, concept.

REFERENCES

Allen, G. J., Chinsky, J. M., Larcen, S. W., Lochman, J. E., and Selinger, H. V. *Community psychology and the schools: A behaviorally oriented multilevel preventive approach.* Hillsdale, N.J.: Lawrence Erlbaum Associates, 1976.

Allinsmith, W., and Grimes, J. W. Compulsivity, anxiety, and school achievement. *Merrill-Palmer Quarterly,* 1961. *7,* 247–261.

Barker, R. G., and Gump, P. *Big school, small school.* Stanford, Ca.: Stanford University Press, 1964.

Barker, R. G., and Schoggen, P. *Qualities of community life.* San Francisco: Jossey-Bass, 1973.

Blank, S. S., and Covington, M. Inducing children to ask questions in solving problems. *Journal of Educational Research,* 1965, *59,* 21–27.

Bloom, B. L. The "medical model," miasma theory and community mental health. *Community Mental Health Journal,* 1965, *1,* 333–338.

Caplan, G. *Principles of preventive psychiatry.* New York: Basic Books, 1964.

Coelho, G. V., and Rubenstein, E. A. (Eds.). *Social change and human behavior: Mental health challenges of the seventies.* Washington, D.C., U.S. Government Printing Office, DHEW Publication No. (HSM) 72–9122, 1972.

Cowen, E. L., Lorion, R. P., Kraus, R. M., and Dorr, D. Geometric expansion of helping resources. *Journal of School Psychology,* 1974, *12,* 288–295.

Cowen, E. L., Trost, M. A., Lorion, R. P., Dorr, D., Izzo, L. D., and Isaacson, R. V. *New ways in school mental health: Early detection and prevention of school maladaptation.* New York: Human Sciences, Inc., 1975.

Evans, D. R. Social reinforcement of question asking behavior. *Western Psychologist,* 1971, *2,* 80–83.

Fairweather, G. W., Sanders, D. H., and Tornatzky, L. G. *Creating change in mental health organizations.* New York: Pergamon Press, 1974.

Hartley, W. S. *An epidemiologic follow up of a cohort of school children: The Kansas City Youth Development Project experiment in preventive psychiatry.* Kansas City, Kansas: University of Kansas Medical Center, Department of Human Ecology and Community Health, 1972.

Insel, P. M., and Moos, R. H. The social environment. In P. M. Insel and R. H. Moos (Eds.), *Health and social environment.* Lexington, Mass.: Lexington Books, 1974. Pp. 1–12.

Kelly, J. G. Towards an ecological conception of preventive interventions. In J. W. Carter (Ed.), *Research contributions from psychology to community mental health.* New York: Behavioral Publications, 1968. Pp. 75–97.

Kelly, J. G. Naturalistic observations in contrasting social environments. In E. P. Willems and H. L. Raush (Eds.), *Naturalistic viewpoints in psychological research.* New York: Holt, Rinehart and Winston, 1969. Pp. 183–199.

Kelly, J. G. Qualities for the community psychologist. *American Psychologist,* 1973, *26,* 897–903.

Kelly, J. G. The search for ideas and deeds that work. Burlington, Vt., Keynote Address at Vermont Conference on the Primary Prevention of Psychopathology, 1975.

Kelly, J. G., Edwards, D. W., Fatke, R., Gordon, T. A., McGee, D. P., McClintock, S. K., Newman, B. M., Rice, R. R., Roistacher, R. C., and Todd, D. M. The coping process in varied high school environments. In M. J. Feldman (Ed.), *Studies in psychotherapy and behavior change, No. 2: Theory and research in community mental health.* Buffalo, N. Y.: State University of New York, 1971. Pp. 95-166.

Kelly, J. G., et al. *The high school: An exploration of students and social contexts in two midwestern communities.* Community Psychology Series, No. 4. New York: Behavioral Publications, Inc., 1976.

Kessler, M., and Albee, G. W. Primary Prevention. In M. R. Rosenzweig and L. C. Porter (Eds.), *Annual Review of Psychology,* 1975, *26,* 557-591.

Kozol, J. *Death at an early age.* Boston, Mass.: Houghton Mifflin, 1967.

Minuchin, P., Biber, B., Shapiro, E., and Zimiles, H. *The psychological impact of school experience.* New York: Basic Books, 1969.

Moos, R. H. Conceptualizations of human environments. *American Psychologist,* 1973, *28,* 652-665.

Moos, R. H. *The social climate scales: An overview.* Palo Alto, Ca.: Consulting Psychologists Press, Inc., 1974 (a)

Moos, R. H. *Evaluating treatment environments: A social ecological approach.* New York: John Wiley & Sons, 1974. (b)

Murphy, L. B., and Chandler, C. A. Building foundations for strength in the preschool years: Preventing developmental disturbances. In S. E. Golann and C. Eisdorfer (Eds.), *Handbook of community mental health.* New York: Appleton-Century-Crofts, 1972. Pp. 303-330.

Ojemann, R. H. Investigations on the effects of teacher understanding and appreciation of behavior dynamics. In G. Caplan (Ed.), *Prevention of mental disorders in children.* New York: Basic Books, 1961. Pp. 378-397.

Ojemann, R. H. Incorporating psychological concepts in the school curriculum. In H. P. Clarizio (Ed.), *Mental health and the educative process.* Chicago: Rand-McNally, 1969. Pp. 360-368.

Price, R. H., and Blashfield, R. K. Explorations in the taxonomy of behavior settings: Analysis of dimensions and classification of settings. *American Journal of Community Psychology,* 1975, *3,* 335-357.

Rappaport, J., Davidson, W. S., Wilson, M. N., and Mitchell, A. Alternatives to blaming the victim or the environment: Our places to stand have not moved the earth. *American Psychologist,* 1975, *30,* 525-528.

Reiss, S., and Dyhdalo, N. Persistence, achievement, and open-space environments. *Journal of Educational Psychology,* 1975, *67,* in press.

Reiss, S., and Martell, R. Educational and psychological effects of open space and education in Oak Park, Ill.: Final Report to Board of Education, District 97, Oak Park, Illinois, 1974.

Riessman, F. A neighborhood-based mental health approach. In E. L. Cowen, E. A. Gardner, and M. Zax (Eds.), *Emergent approaches to mental health problems*. New York: Appleton-Century-Crofts, 1967. Pp. 167–184.

Rothman, J. *Planning and organizing for social change: Action principles from social science research.* New York: Columbia University Press, 1974.

Rothman, J., Erlich, J. L., and Teresa, J. G. *Promoting innovation and change in organizations and communities: A planning manual.* New York: John Wiley and Sons, 1976.

Sanford, N. Is the concept of prevention necessary or useful? In S. E. Golann and C. Eisdorfer (Eds.), *Handbook of community mental health.* New York: Appleton-Century-Crofts, 1972. Pp. 461–471.

Sarason, S. B. *The creation of settings and the future societies.* San Francisco: Jossey-Bass, 1972.

Sarason, S. B., Levine, M., Goldenberg, I. I., Cherlin, D. L., and Bennett, E. M. *Psychology in community settings.* New York: Wiley, 1966.

Shure, M. B., and Spivack, G. A preventive mental health program for young "inner city" children: The second (kindergarten) year. Paper presented at the American Psychological Association, Chicago, 1975. (a)

Shure, M. B., and Spivack, G. Training mothers to help their children solve real-life problems. Paper presented at the Society for Research in Child Development, Denver, Colo., 1975. (b)

Spivack, G., and Shure, M. B. *Social adjustment of young children.* San Francisco: Jossey-Bass, 1974.

Stamps, L. W. Enhancing success in school for deprived children by teaching realistic goal setting. Paper presented at Society for Research in Child Development, Denver, Colo., 1975.

Susskind, E. C. Questioning and curiosity in the elementary school classroom. Unpublished Ph.D. dissertation, Yale University, 1969.

Trickett, E. J., and Moos, R. H. Personal correlates of contrasting environments: Student satisfaction in high school classrooms. *American Journal of Community Psychology,* 1974, *2,* 1–12.

Vallance, T. R. The professional nonpsychology graduate program for psychologists. *American Psychologist,* 1976, *31,* 193–199.

Zax, M., and Cowen, E. L. *Abnormal Psychology: Changing conceptions.* 2nd Edition. New York: Holt, Rinehart, and Winston, 1976.

Zax, M., and Specter, G. A. *An introduction to community psychology.* New York: Wiley, 1974.

Zimiles, H. Preventive aspects of school experience. In E. L. Cowen, E. A. Gardner, and M. Zax (Eds.), *Emergent approaches to mental health problems.* New York: Appleton-Century-Crofts, 1967. Pp. 239–251.

3

A National Perspective

STEPHEN E. GOLDSTON

Stephen E. Goldston received the M.S. degree in Public Health in 1953 from the Columbia University School of Public Health and Administrative Medicine, and the Ed.D. degree in 1958 from Columbia University. He was a Lecturer and an Instructor in Mental Health at Columbia from 1956 to 1958. For two years thereafter he served as Assistant to the Director, Westchester County (N.Y.) Community Mental Health Board, and from 1960 to 1962 he was Chief, Mental Health Education Unit, and Director, Mental Health Consultation Program to the Aged, New York City Community Mental Health Board. Ever since, he has been associated with the National Institute of Mental Health in Extramural Programs, Training and Manpower Resources, Experimental and Special Training Branch, and finally in Preventive Programs. In 1972 he became Coordinator of Primary Prevention Programs for NIMH, a position he continues to fill today.

Goldston has written extensively in the area of public health, with special focus on health training—sixteen articles, three monographs, three books, and six chapters in as many books. One of the latter appears in Primary Prevention of Psychopathology, *the first volume in this series.*

A CONCEPTUAL FRAMEWORK FOR PRIMARY PREVENTION

Considerable confusion prevails about primary prevention. A good part of the misunderstanding stems from the absence of a conceptual framework. I suggest that there are four specific,

This paper was prepared in the author's private capacity, and the views expressed are not necessarily official positions of the National Institute of Mental Health or the Alcohol, Drug Abuse, and Mental Health Administration.

distinct frameworks for conceptualizing and classifying primary prevention efforts.

(1) Primary Prevention of Mental Illnesses of Known Etiology

This framework involves a medical approach focused on conditions of *known* etiology which it is possible to prevent by "specific protection" interventions. The aim is to avoid the onset of mental disorders by intercepting the causes of disease before people become exposed. In the medical psychiatric sphere there is enough scientific evidence to prevent some mental disorders, including both acute and chronic brain syndromes resulting from (a) poisoning by certain substances, such as lead-based paints; (b) infections, such as encephalitis, rubella, syphilis; (c) genetic diseases, such as PKU and galactosemia; (d) nutritional deficiencies, such as pellegra and beri-beri; (e) general systemic diseases, such as erythroblastosis fetalis and cretinism; and (f) accidents and other physical traumas. The monograph *Mental Disorders, A Guide to Control Methods* (American Public Health Association, 1962) lists 83 poisons, 20 infectious diseases, 9 genetic diseases, 5 nutritional deficiencies, and 12 general systemic diseases that produce mental disorders.

Operationally, primary prevention of the mental illnesses of known etiology has become the responsibility of public health and environmental protection agencies; by and large, mental health workers are not involved in programs for this kind of primary prevention, nor are they generally aware of the multiple opportunities—buttressed by incontestable research findings—to prevent many conditions which result in diagnosable mental illness. If the unique contribution of mental health workers—their expert knowledge of human behavior—were applied to such public mental health functions as community poison control programs and communicable disease immunization programs, incidence of new cases of those disorders which can result in mental illness might well be reduced.

(2) Primary Prevention of Mental Illnesses of Unknown Etiology

For most mental health workers, this category is not merely the most familiar conceptual framework of primary prevention: it is the totality of their understanding of primary prevention. It is the framework most frequently evoked by skeptics who maintain that it is impossible, if not absurd, to pursue primary prevention activities without clear knowledge of the etiology of the major mental illnesses, such as the schizophrenias and the depressions. Current knowledge of the etiology of the *major* mental illnesses is limited; consequently, generalized, nonspecific efforts purported to be aimed at their primary prevention merit considerable suspicion. This key guideline in planning and conducting primary prevention efforts needs to be observed: all primary prevention activities must be characterized by *specific* actions directed at *specific* populations for *specific* purposes.

(3) Primary Prevention of Emotional Distress, Maladaptation, Maladjustment, Needless Psychopathology, and Human Misery

This framework is characterized by a psycho-socio-cultural educational approach in which crisis theory, crisis intervention, and anticipatory guidance are major constructs. Counseling, mental health consultation, community organization, training of vital community care-givers, and mental health education serve as the major forms of professional mental health activity. The objective is to reduce or obviate unnecessary emotional distress when possible.

(4) Promotion of Mental Health

This framework is also characterized by a psycho-socio-cultural educational approach. The objective is to promote social and functional competence, coping capacities, ego strengths, and "positive mental health." Crisis theory, along with the mastery of developmental tasks, are basic constructs which are augmented by other theoretical orientations. Consultative, training, educational, and organizational modalities are of major significance. Illustrative areas are family life education, including parent education, sex education, and death education, as well as affective education at home and in the schools.

Bernard L. Bloom has identified marital disruption as an area for primary preventive interventions.* His work encompasses and

*See below, pp. 81 ff.

demonstrates the applicability of all four conceptual frameworks. First, with respect to the primary prevention of the mental illnesses of known etiology, Bloom observes poisoning associated with suicidal behaviors; accidents and physical trauma, especially automobile accidents among persons experiencing marital disruption; nutritional deficiencies when diets change; and infections, as a consequence perhaps of greater vulnerability or susceptibility to some diseases. Regarding primary prevention of the mental illnesses of unknown etiology, he also touches on marital disruption as a precipitant of depressive states or of a mental illness. The major part of his paper deals with preventing needless psychopathology and human misery, but he touches on promoting mental health—the need for ego strengths and competencies to cope with crises—and points out implications for anticipatory guidance approaches through family life education programs, premarital counseling, and divorce counseling. He thus unites the four principles of the conceptual framework.

THE PRIMARY PREVENTION HIGHLIGHTS OF 1976

What kind of year has it been for primary prevention in Washington? Progress has been made, though short of what many of us would like. There is some good news and some bad.

First the good news—the highlights, the achievements. These are most meaningful when one understands that the Federal Government not only provides financial support, but also supplies technical assistance, coordinates information, and stimulates the development, application, and sharing of knowledge. It provides this assistance through conferences, workshops, publications, and policy formation.

I have divided my review of the highlights into three broad categories.

(1) *Within the Federal Bureaucracy: National Institute of Mental Health/Alcohol, Drug Abuse, and Mental Health (NIMH/ ADAMHA), Department of Health, Education, and Welfare (DHEW).* A major highlight is that primary prevention is receiving attention from top-level staff within the National Institute of Mental Health. Second, because an inventory of NIMH primary

prevention projects has been performed, we now know what is being supported and, equally important, we can identify the gaps.

Another highlight is that DHEW's forward planning document for the period 1978 to 1982 (DHEW, 1976) again lists prevention as one of six major program emphases. The Department has accepted (a) our definition of primary prevention, (b) the concept of crisis approaches as a major theme, and (c) our program guidelines (to be indicated later).

An additional achievement is that a second full-time professional mental health worker has been hired; there are now two of us working full-time on primary prevention program development.

Lastly, at the Department level, concept clearance was obtained for initiating a Primary Prevention Publication Series—a new mechanism for information-sharing. We plan to issue monographs, conference proceedings, commissioned papers, and bibliographies to provide authoritative information about primary prevention to the field, thereby meeting a long-standing need. The new series may in time help to short-circuit the present journal jam-up; there is now a two-year lag period from manuscript acceptance to its appearance in print.

(2) *Constituency-Building.* A second major category of activity this past year has been constitutency building. As one important event, in April 1976 a model conference on primary prevention was convened, sponsored by the National Association for Mental Health, in cooperation with NIMH and the National Council of Community Mental Health Centers. Through the mechanism of the conference, these three powerful national mental health organizations have taken steps toward a commitment to primary prevention. Both the American Orthopsychiatric Association and the American Public Health Association had special sessions on primary prevention during their annual meetings. Discussions are being held presently with staff of the American Psychiatric Association in response to their expressed interest in primary prevention. And there have been interactions with the State and Territorial Mental Health Authorities about primary prevention.

(3) *Meetings on Primary Prevention.* Earlier this month, there was a gala gathering at the White House on the Prevention of Psychosocial Disabilities in Infancy, at which the work of Elsie

Broussard, Marshall Klaus, Selma Fraiberg, and others was presented before a prestigious group of persons from government and the major mental health foundations. In July 1975 a work conference was held on parent-child communications about death. Another focused on the mental health aspects of the Sudden Infant Death Syndrome. Last fall, the State of Michigan held a seminar on primary prevention program development. Other meetings on primary prevention include the Great Lakes Forum on Primary Prevention in 1976; the Milwaukee Conference on the Delivery of Mental Health Services to the Black Consumer in April 1976 which devoted much of the program to primary prevention; a one-day training institute on primary prevention at the annual meeting of the American Psychiatric Association; and, of course, the Vermont Conference on the Primary Prevention of Psychopathology, a meeting which now is institutionalized with a tradition, a history, and a future.

All these highlights have involved, by necessity, considerable planning, action, and politics—and, I might add, pain; the phrase "biting the bullet" has been mentioned. At this stage, we are legitimizing primary prevention through informing, educating, and enlisting the support of key decision-makers in the mental health establishment.

So much for the good news.

IV. GAPS, DEFICITS, AND PROBLEM AREAS

The bad news is the gaps that remain. First, we still lack a commitment at the policy and operating levels to provide support, encouragement, resources, and a clear mandate for prevention activities. This is evidenced by the insufficient budgetary allocations and by the fact that there is no organizational structure with visible responsibility and authority for programming in primary prevention. Priorities must be reoriented so that we can initiate planned programming rather than merely responding to projects suggested by workers in the field. Regrettably, mental health continues conceptually and operationally separate and distinct from health. Not enough resources are devoted to studying ways of helping people deal with real-life problems, the ever-recurring life crises. An information and retrieval system is needed to identify prevention activities; we hope to deal with one aspect of this need through the Primary Prevention Publication Series. Few training oportunities exist for mental health workers to become familiar with public health principles, epidemiology, and primary prevention content. Only four states have primary prevention units within their departments of mental health. Little money is going into research on new techniques and approaches in primary prevention. All these gaps have to be addressed.

V. PROGRAM DEVELOPMENT

Now, a glance at the year ahead. Our activities will be based on three guidelines:

(1) Mental health is not synonymous with mental illness. The scope of the mental health field extends beyond exclusive concern with the psychiatrically ill and the emotionally disturbed into virtually all areas of human behavior.

(2) Problem areas which are fundamentally public health matters but have mental health components offer significant opportunities for mental health workers to implement the principles and practices of community mental health, particularly reaching out and collaborating with other community agencies around a specific issue.

(3) Crisis theory and crisis intervention approaches provide a relevant foundation for developing programs to help people deal with real life problems: that is, the ever-occurring life crises which require specific coping capacities and ego strengths in order to maintain physical and mental health.

During the year ahead, funds will be available for the following activities. (1) A work conference will be held on the state of the art of primary prevention, dealing with conceptualizations, research strategies and methodologies, and models of practice; perhaps we can put to rest, once and for all, the myths that primary prevention cannot be conceptualized, that research cannot be done in this area, and that there are no models for practice. (2) On the Sudden Infant Death Syndrome, efforts will be made to involve community mental health centers in health service networks that have been developed in various communities and states throughout the United States. (3) We expect to produce documents in the Primary Prevention Publication Series, some on the conferences that have been held, in addition to a monograph by Phyllis Silverman on mutual-help groups.

Other subject areas which have been proposed for exploration include maternal-infant affectional bonding, mental health needs of children in the hospital, family planning and mental health, children of divorce, postpartum disturbances, mutual-help groups, primary prevention in state mental health departments, nutrition and mental health (particularly anorexia nervosa), a life-crisis film series, developing school mental health advocates, research into the epidemiology of healthy coping behaviors, training needs, and an information clearinghouse. This is an agenda for years to come!

And there will be more meetings. In September the Tripartite International Conference on Prevention will be held—a small work conference attended by representatives from the United Kingdom, Canada, and the United States; the State and Territorial Mental Health Authorities are meeting in Denver in October, with one-third of the program devoted to primary prevention; and in June 1977 will be the Third Annual Vermont Conference.

To summarize, there is cause for a measure of hope, and perhaps cautious optimism; there is much to be done. We at NIMH have a greal deal to learn about primary prevention, and we welcome your input on priorities, strategies, and programs.

REFERENCES

American Public Health Association Program Area Committee on Mental Health, *Mental disorders: A guide to control methods.* New York: American Public Health Association, 1962.

APA Task Force on Health Research. Contributions of psychology to health research: Patterns, problems, and potentials. *American Psychologist,* 1976, *31,* 263-274.

Tyhurst, J. S. The role of transition states—including disasters—in mental illness. In Walter Reed Army Institute of Research, *Symposium on preventive and social psychiatry,* April 15-17, 1957. Washington, D.C.: U.S. Government Printing Office, 1957.

U.S. Department of Health, Education, and Welfare, Public Health Service. *Forward plan for health, FY 1978-82.* Washington, D.C.: U.S. Government Printing Office, 1976.

SELECTED DISCUSSION:

Dr. Cowen was asked to comment on primary prevention issues in adults.

Dr. Cowen: One can think of many important issues at the adult level. The whole concept of treatment during crisis, for instance, is built around the notion that people can be influenced and helped much more at certain critical periods in their development. But I would prefer to stay away from this question, because I am convinced that you get more mental health mileage from a five-year old than from a ten-year-old and more from a two-year-old than from a five-year-old and more from at any age from building than from repairing. In our school project (which I have not spoken about), we stop our concern for the children subjects when they are eight years old. The real challenge in such research is developing and hierarchizing a set of priorities; and my personal priorities are very much with young children and their environment.

Several questions were asked about the priority of working with high-risk children in contrast to promoting better mental health in other children.

Dr. Cowen: The question is, where would you target a primary prevention effort? As an analogy, if one were applying to the Law Enforcement Assistance Administration to do a competence-building program for young children, it would make sense to target the project to a high crime risk area, rather than to the affluent suburbs. There may be some parsimony in focusing primary prevention efforts on groups that have a high probability for serious disorder: that's a personal value judgment I'd feel comfortable with if I were in control of a hundred-million-dollar budget.

Dr. Cowen was asked by several persons to comment on the political aspects of instituting primary prevention programs.

Dr. Cowen: There are some political strikes against some of the types of programs that I've been talking about. We mental health people have tended to operate like the emergency room of a hospital. The hospitals I have been associated with respond quickly only to blood; we mental health professionals have tended to respond only to psychic blood and vocal constituencies. The types of programs I have suggested involving social system changes and competence training do not speak directly to palpable visible problems, nor are they likely to have vocal constituencies.

Prevention is something you cannot see; it is in the future, in contrast to other more visible ailments. In a scarce economy with much competition for funds and resources, it will not be easy to get that type of program funded or supported. There is a finite limit on resources, and hard decisions will have to be made about how those resources are going to be allocated. If we continue to allocate them in the repair mold, we will wipe out the possibility for developing a viable approach to prevention.

Dr. Altman: With respect to assessing the effectiveness of primary prevention programs, when one is dealing with people who aren't reflecting any kind of crisis or symptomatology, does one *know* that a certain approach to the problem is better than another approach?

Dr. Cowen: If, for example, I wished to assess the effectiveness of competence training in social problem solving and were looking for some kind of experimental design, I would probably do as Spivak and Shure did: set up a social problem-solving group and a control group. To make it more sophisticated, I might set up multiple interventions, including some that would be theoretically inert, such as movie-going.

Dr. Altman: Since you're concerned with overall functioning of people in a long-term sense, doesn't this require extensive longitudinal analyses that go beyond questions of competency and problem solving and into general matters of psychological functioning?

Dr. Cowen: Long-term perspectives are important; I am not just interested in the question of how far a particular social competence develops but also when it develops and how it radiates to variables and measures that others will agree relate to adjustment and enduring effects.

Dr. Hunt: Shouldn't your main measure be the percentage of people in both groups who show various types of adjustment?

Dr. Cowen: There are short-term criteria, behavioral criteria, and bell-weather criteria showing when people appear in delinquency registers, addiction registers, state hospitals, or mental health centers.

Dr. Hunt: You could use those social system criteria in a certain kind of study. Hopefully, you could also do a finer grain assessment. In either case you will have longitudinal problems; in the mental health field you can never be sure that the client will not be worse later on because of your intervention.

Dr. Cowen: The Spivak and Shure book reports one of the best known studies in this connection. They followed up the children in the year after the intervention and found that the early results in terms of both competence acquisition and radiation to adjustment endured over that short period. This, of course, does not answer the question of what kind of erosion may take place ten years from now, but it is relevant.

Dr. Hunt: Would you tell us what radiation means in concrete operational terms?

Dr. Cowen: Consider that a group of children are trained in a specific skill which is, on the surface, removed from any criterion measure of adjustment. It is established that the children acquire the skill on some test performance measure. In a separate series of data collections, tapping behavioral and adjustive measures (presumably as a consequence of the skill acquisition since it doesn't happen in control children), the experimental children show either an improvement in adjustment or a reduction in problem behavior, or both.

Several questions were asked of Dr. Cowen whether it is adequate to define adjustment as the absence of pathology.

Dr. Cowen: I am unhappy with such a definition. One of my colleagues, Ellis Gesten, who is doing social systems research, has developed a fairly comprehensive measure of competence behavior in children—a positive indication of adjustment which includes five components. Criteria in our earlier work included primarily symptomology, maladjustment, and problem behavior. Through this recent methodological development, we are now in a position to examine not only problem reduction, but also the acquisition of competence. Gesten found that maladjustment and competence are not precisely correlated inversely, nor are they quite the opposite of each other. Envision a number of children who share the fact of having many problems and symtoms but who differ in their types and numbers of competencies. One may have symptomology and very few competencies, and another symptomology and some reasonably solid base of competence. This picture is likely to mean two different things prognostically.

The question of initiating a community primary prevention program outside of an academic setting was raised.

Dr. Goldston: There are many like-minded people in communities who need some form of catalytic agent to bring them together. One of our problems has been our presumptive, if not arrogant, attitude that we, as mental health workers, have such a comprehensive bag of tricks that we can take on virtually everything and do it successfully. Of course we cannot. The notion of mutual self-help groups in which mental health people are consultants—back-up personnel—is going to be the wave of the future, and mental health people have a great deal to learn about them. We must recognize the catalytic function we play in bringing these groups together, and realize that we must relate to them on an equal-status basis; they are not inferior or subordinate in any sense.

One problem in providing adequate preventive services is that no specific professional person is responsible for primary prevention at the state level except in Ohio, Kentucky, Michigan, and Massachusetts. The role of such a person is to mobilize the resources in the community to primary prevention acitvities.

M. Brewster Smith responded to a number of questions and comments on how to instigate things in a bureaucratic society, as follows.

Dr. Smith: This problem is more difficult than it needs be. Getting the right kind of administrative support falls in the area of community organization and especially social work. Community psychology seems to have felt the need to re-invent the whole area of social work. What we need is more interdisciplinary and professional collaboration. Specific local roles are community organization roles—getting the volunteer groups formed. There really is a profession that thinks it knows how to do this, and we psychologists shouldn't think we have to do it all ourselves.

II
Research Approaches to Prevention

4

Sociocultural Mental Retardation: A Longitudinal Study

F. RICK HEBER

Rick Heber received the Ph.D. degree in Psychology from George Peabody College in 1957. Between his undergraduate training at the University of Arkansas and his graduate work, he taught and acted as principal at the Manitoba School for Mental Defectives in Canada. He spent two years as Research Associate with the American Association on Mental Deficiency, working on the Project on Technical Planning in Mental Deficiency, and in 1959 he went to the Waisman Center on Mental Retardation and Human Development at the Rehabilitation Research and Training Center in Mental Retardation at the University of Wisconsin, where he is presently professor in the Department of Studies in Behavioral Disabilities. In 1961 he spent a year on leave from Wisconsin as Research Director of President Kennedy's Panel on Mental Retardation.

He has written extensively in the field of mental deficiency and presented papers in the field throughout this country and in several others. His book Epidemiology of Mental Retardation *was published in 1970, and since then he has contributed chapters to several other books.*

Heber's pioneering work on the prevention of mental retardation has brought him many honors, including the National Leadership Award in Education from the American Association on Mental Deficiency. The "Milwaukee Project," which he directs, is well known in this country and abroad.

Research supported in part by Grant 16–P–56811/5–11, from the Social and Rehabilitation Services of the Department of Health, Education, and Welfare.

Dr. Heber has produced a thirty-minute color film showing the interaction patterns between his trainees and the children in the experimental group of the Milwaukee Project, described in this paper. Inquiries should be directed to Dr. Heber at the University of Wisconsin, Waisman Center on Mental Retardation and Human Development, Madison, Wisconsin.

For the past ten years I have participated in research that grew out of my concern over the fact that virtually the total national research effort in the field of mental retardation was being directed toward that aspect of the problem associated with gross pathology of the central nervous system. Before that time, little effort had been directed toward so-called sociocultural or cultural-familial mental retardation—mental retardation which exists in the absence of demonstrable pathology of the central nervous system, shows a high within-family incidence, and is concentrated in the economically depressed areas of our nation. This neglect of the most significant aspect of the problem (from the point of view of the numbers involved) was attributable to the long-held and widely accepted view that cultural-familial mental retardation was genetic in origin and therefore nonpreventable except through socially unacceptable measures to limit reproduction.

A little over a decade ago, however, there occurred a massive awakening of America's conscience concerning the plight of the "poor" and those racial and ethnic minorities so heavily represented among the poverty-stricken. With this stirring of conscience there arose, particularly within the social professions, a sometimes blind and uncritical acceptance of the view that the high frequency of mental retardation found among the poverty-stricken is directly attributable to deprivation of opportunities available to the nonpoor to learn and practice intellectual skills. These two divergent, often passionately held views of the etiology of cultural-familial mental retardation aroused a debate over the past decade which has often resembled a street brawl more than scholarly conversation.

Our research, which has come to be known as the Milwaukee Project, was designed to add to our factual knowledge of the etiology of cultural-familial mental retardation and its susceptibility to preventive measures. Those adhering to either the hereditary or the social deprivation hypothesis have cited virtually the same data in support of their respective positions: principally epidemiological data on population and family group incidence frequencies of mental retardation.

It should be obvious, however, that simple awareness of the high frequency of mental retardation in areas where the economically or otherwise disadvantaged are concentrated is sufficient neither to validate the prepotence of genetic determinants nor to conclude that social deprivation in the slum environment causes the retardation encountered there. Such a generalization ignores the fact that most children reared by economically disadvantaged families are by no means mentally retarded. In actual fact, a majority of children reared in city slums grow and develop and learn relatively normally in the intellectual sense.

Before we could begin any prospective research it was necessary to learn more about the distribution of cultural-familial mental retardation. We conducted a series of surveys in a residential section of Milwaukee, a city of 800,000, characterized by census data as having the lowest median family income, the greatest population density per living unit, and the greatest rate of dilapidated housing in the city. For the United States it was a typical urban slum of the 1960's and it yielded by far the highest prevalence of identified mental retardation among school children in the city. In our first survey, all of the families who had a newborn infant and at least one other child of up to the age of six were selected for study.

The major finding relevant to this discussion is that the variable of maternal intelligence proved to be by far the best single predictor of the level and character of intellectual development in the offspring. Mothers with IQ's of less than 80, although comprising less than half the total group of mothers, accounted for almost four-fifths of the children with IQ's below 80 (see Table 1).

It has been generally acknowledged that slum-dwelling children score lower on intelligence tests as they grow older; as Figure 1

Table 1
Distribution of Child IQ's as a Function of Maternal Intelligence

Mother's IQ	Percent of Mothers	Children's IQ		
		%>90	%80–90	%<80
>80	54.6	65.8	47.3	21.9
<80	45.4	34.1	52.7	78.2

> = greater than   < = less than

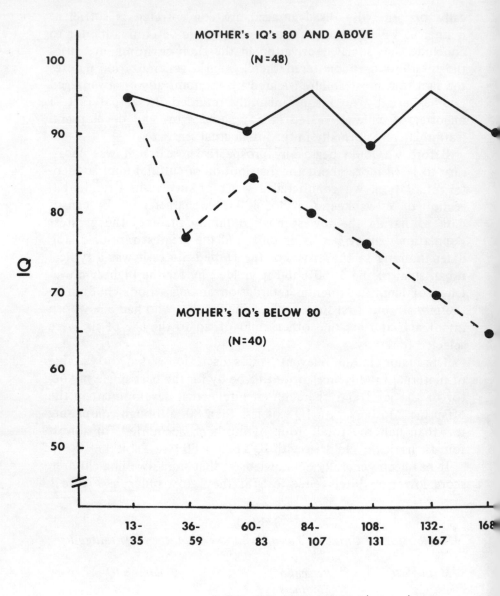

Figure 1. Source: F. R. Heber, R. B. Dever, and J. Conry, "The influence of environmental and genetic variables on intellectual development," in H. J. Prehm, L. A. Hamerlynck, and J. E. Crosson (Eds.), *Behavioral Research in Mental Retardation* (Eugene, Oregon: University of Oregon, 1968), p. 9.

Table 2
Probability of Child IQ Following Within IQ Ranges
As a Function of Maternal IQ

		Mother IQ		
Child IQ	>100	84-99	68-83	52-67
>100	1	.98	.67	.25
84-99	1	1.02	.95	.93
68-83	1	1.57	1.24	2.20
52-67	1	2.36	3.70	14.20

shows, however, the mean measured intelligence of offspring of mothers with IQ's above 80 is relatively constant. And it is only the children of mothers with IQ's below 80 who show a progressive decline in mean intelligence as age increases.

Further, the survey data showed that the lower the maternal IQ, the greater the probability of offspring scoring low on intelligence tests. For example, as Table 2 shows, the mother with an IQ below 67 had roughly a fourteen-fold increase in the probability of having a child test below 67 as compared with the mother whose IQ fell at or above 100.

In our first survey, the fathers were not evaluated. In a second survey of 519 consecutive newborns in our study area, however, fathers, mothers, and all children over the age of two were given an intelligence test. The results added further to our knowledge of the distribution of intellectual functioning within a slum population (see Table 3). First, there was a striking congruence of maternal and paternal IQ. Of mothers below 70, 61 percent had husbands who also scored below 70 and only 14 percent had husbands who scored above 100. By contrast, not a single mother scoring above 100 had a husband who scored below 80, as seen in Table 4, which also shows that the percentage of absent fathers was approximately the same irrespective of the measured intelligence of the mother. Further, there were almost twice as many mothers under 20 and over 35 in the below 70 group as compared with mothers above 100 (see Table 5). This was reflected in a substantially greater number of offspring in families where both mother and father tested below 70 (see Table 6): the average

Table 3
*Percentage of Fathers in PQ Groupings
As a Function of Maternal PQ Level*

			Father PQ	
		<70	70-99	100+
	<70	.61	.25	.14
Mother	70-99	.27	.50	.23
PQ	100+	.00	.42*	.58

*No fathers in 70-79 range

Table 4
*Mean Maternal Age and Percent of Absent
Fathers As a Function of Maternal IQ*

Maternal PQ	<70	70-99	100+
% Fathers Absent	34.5	38.6	35.0
Mean Maternal Age	25.4	25.8	25.1
N	119	280	120

Table 5
*Percent of Mothers of Newborns in Various Age Groups
As a Function of Peabody Quotient*

			Maternal PQ	
		<70	70-99	100+
	20	.17	.16	.11
Maternal Age	20-34	.68	.77	.82
	35+	.15	.07	.07
	N	119	280	120

Table 6
Mean Number of Offspring

		Father PQ				
		<70	70–99	100+	None	Mean
Mother PQ	70	4.63	2.95	1.5	4.24	3.41
	70–99	3.42	3.39	3.21	3.65	3.50
	100+	–	3.06*	3.43	3.05	3.20
	Mean	4.02	3.25	3.14	3.64	

*No fathers in 70–79 range

difference was 1.2 children. Considering that these families were estimated to be about halfway through their child-bearing years, the mean difference in the final number of offspring, when the families were completed, might be around 2.5. The adverse consequences of this differential in reproductive activity are of great social concern irrespective of one's views of the etiology of the intellectual deficiency in the parents.

These surveys convinced us that the prevalence of mental retardation associated with the slums of American cities is not randomly distributed but, rather, is strikingly concentrated within individual families who can be identified on the basis of maternal intelligence. In other words, the source of the excess prevalence of mental retardation appeared to be the retarded parent residing in the slum environment, rather than the slum itself.

These population survey data have been taken by some as support for the prepotence of hereditary determinants of cultural-familial mental retardation. Our simple casual observation, however, suggested that the mentally retarded mother residing in the slum creates a social environment for her offspring which is distinctly different from that created by her next-door neighbor of normal intelligence.

Most importantly, these survey data suggested that it would be feasible to conduct the longitudinal, prospective research essential to achieving a more adequate understanding of what determines the kind of retardation that perpetuates itself from parent to child in the economically deprived family. That is, the survey data suggested that parental intelligence could be utilized as a tool to select a sample which would be small enough for practical experimental manipulation but would still yield a sufficient number of cases who would later become identifiable as mentally retarded.

As a consequence of the survey data, we took maternal IQ as a basis for selecting a group of newborns, confident that a substantial percentage would be identified as mentally retarded as they grew older. By screening all mothers of babies born in our survey area over a period of a little over a year, we identified mothers of newborns with IQ's less than 75. Forty of these mentally retarded mothers were assigned to either an experimental or a control group.

Although our geographic study area was racially mixed, our sample was confined to black families because of the substantially lower mobility of the black population in that section of Milwaukee. Obviously, a longitudinal study is seriously weakened when its test sample is decimated by attrition.

The 20 Experimental families were entered into an intense rehabilitation program with two primary emphases: (1) education, vocational rehabilitation, and home and child care training of the mother; and (2) an intense, personalized intervention program for their newborn infants which began in the first few weeks of life. The objective of the intervention was to displace all of the presumed negative factors in the social environment of the infant being reared in the slum by a mother who is herself retarded. Our goal was to test the social deprivation hypothesis of etiology by attempting to determine whether it is possible to prevent retardation in the offspring of these retarded mothers.

It was our contention that if the experimental children should reach school age and exhibit normal intelligence, we would know that it is indeed possible to prevent mental retardation from occurring at the present high frequency in this group. Should they exhibit a retarded level of functioning, at least we would know that their intensive exposure to learning experiences of the type we provided was not sufficient to displace their genetic or other biologic predispositions for intellectual functioning.

Initially, each experimental family was assigned one special teacher whose responsibility was to establish rapport, gain the family's confidence, and work with both the mother and the newborn child in the home.

Once the mother trusted the teacher, the infant began to attend our infant center every day from 9 until 4, five days a week, on a year-round basis. The mother began her own rehabilitation program when the child began participation in our infant intervention program.

One of the major purposes of the maternal program was to alter the manner in which the economically and intellectually disadvantaged mother interacted with her children and operated within the home and within the community. At the outset, a major obstacle was the attitude of many of the mentally retarded mothers themselves: they were hostile and suspicious toward social agencies and had a sense of economic despair. It was hoped that as the mother's rehabilitation proceeded, her improved employment potential and increased earnings and self-confidence would bring about positive changes in the home.

Over the course of the maternal rehabilitation program, the emphases changed. At the beginning, the focus was on the mother's vocational adjustment. Since a number of the families did not have a stable income-producing father, occupational training and placement was of major importance. After formal vocational training and placement was completed, increased emphasis was given to remedial education and homemaking and child-care skills. As we established rapport with the parents, they called on us increasingly to intervene and assist in internal family crises and, not uncommonly, in conflicts with the community.

The occupational training program used two large private nursing homes in Milwaukee. These were chosen because of the appropriate job skill areas they offered, the availability of professional staff with some understanding of rehabilitation programs, and the employment opportunities available in nursing homes and other chronic care facilities. The basic remedial academic curriculum emphasized reading, writing, and arithmetic— that is, basic literacy training. In addition, the curriculum included child care techniques, home economics, community oriented social studies, interpersonal relations, and home management.

Although our maternal efforts were a success in many dimensions, they by no means put an end to all of the mother's internal family and community conflicts. We attempted to evaluate the effectiveness of the maternal program through a number of measures.

The Experimental mothers showed some significant changes

in behavior and attitude in dealing with their children. On experimental task measures of mother-child interaction, they encouraged reciprocal communication with their children; that is, given a behavior by one, there was a greater certainty of the behavior of the other. This relationship did not occur within the Control families. Also, this behavior change was reflected in the Experimental mother's greater tendency to engage in verbally informative behaviors as compared to the non-task-oriented physical behaviors shown by the Control mothers and by the Experimental mothers at the beginning of the program.

On the Wechsler Adult Intelligence Scale (WAIS) eight years after their initial testing, there was no significant change for either Experimental or Control groups.

The Experimental mothers are significantly superior to the Control mothers in basic literacy but remain relatively low—roughly at fourth-grade level.

By every measure, the most effective component of our maternal program was the vocational one. We succeeded in placing all mothers in employment where the family situation made this feasible. And their record of job stability and work performance is distinctly superior to that of the Controls. For mothers in both groups who are presently working, salary favors the Experimental mother by an average of $40 per week.

Our direct infant intervention program was initiated when the children were about three months of age and continued, on an all-day 5-day-a-week year-round basis, until the children entered public school. The general goal was to provide an environment and a set of experiences which would foster the acquisition of cognitive skills and allow each child to develop socially, emotionally and physically. The program focused heavily on developing language and cognitive skills and on maintaining a positive and responsive learning environment for the children.

Throughout the intervention program, the curriculum was concerned with three main areas of growth: perceptual-motor development, cognitive-language development, and social-emotional development. During infancy (0–2), a period characterized by the rapid development of perceptual-motor skills, we provided a wealth of varied experiences designed to enable the child to refine his perceptual acuity, especially the ability to differentiate between visual and auditory stimuli. At the same time, attention was given to developing motor behavior by providing considerable opportunity for the children to practice newly developing skills and explore their environment.

Because infancy is a crucial time for laying the foundations of cognitive and language development, the program made use of the rapidly developing perceptual-motor skills as a vehicle through which cognitive and language experiences (size, color, relations) could be systematically introduced. We attempted to meet the social-emotional needs of the developing infant by providing a consistent one-to-one teacher-child relationship throughout the child's first year in the program. During the preschool years (2–6), the educational program continued to focus upon the same three areas of growth, but increased emphasis was placed on the cognitive-language area—gradually broken down into the three traditional academic areas of reading, language, and math/problem-solving. By this time, groups of 10 to 12 children had come together with three teachers into a more traditional classroom setting. Within the classroom, there were three learning areas and a free-flowing or free-choice area. At specified intervals during the day, small groups of children would meet with teachers to engage in teacher-planned activities at each of the three learning centers. In addition, there was opportunity for science, art, music, and gross motor activities in the free-choice area.

The general intervention program is best characterized as having a cognitive-language orientation implemented through a planned environment utilizing informal prescriptive teaching techniques. By this latter we mean that in planning appropriate activities, each teacher would (1) make direct observation of the child's strengths, weaknesses, preferences; (2) gear tasks and experiences specifically for this child; and (3) evaluate the effect of the task or experience on the child.

Most importantly, the program gave major emphasis to the social and emotional development of the children. Although language and cognitive development were the foundation, it was recognized that motivation—the child's desire to utilize these skills—was essential to making the system work. We attempted to develop achievement motivation by designing tasks and creating an atmosphere which would maximize interest and provide success experiences and supportive and corrective feedback from responsive adults, and which would gradually increase the child's responsibility for task completion.

ASSESSMENT OF DEVELOPMENT

In order to assess the effects of this six-year comprehensive intervention in the natural environment of the infant and his retarded mother, we undertook an ambitious schedule of measurements consisting of medical evaluations, standardized and nonstandardized tests of general intelligence, experimental learning tasks, measures of mother-child interaction, and various measures of language development.

Both the Experimental and Control subjects were on an identical measurement schedule keyed to each child's birth date. Assessments were carried out every two months from age 6 months to 24 months, and then monthly through age 6. The particular measure administered at a given session depended upon the predetermined schedule of measures for that age level. Each test or task was administered to both the Experimental and Control subjects by the same persons. The testers, who were both men and women, white and black, were not involved in any component of the maternal or child intervention program.

Medical evaluations of our research children have shown no significant differences in height, weight, or other specific medical tests (See Fig. 2). Gesell data illustrate some of the earliest differences between Experimental and Control infants. Though reasonably comparable through the fourteenth month of testing, the Control group fell three to four months below the Experimental group, although still performing close to test norms. At 22 months, the Experimental group was 4½ to 6 months in advance of the Control group on all four Gesell schedules and the Control group had fallen below Gesell norms on the Adaptive and Language schedules.

On Z transformations of scores from a number of measures, administered at varying age levels, there is a sustained differential in performance in favor of the Experimental children.

In the learning-performance tasks, such as color-form, probability matching, and oddity discrimination, the Experimental

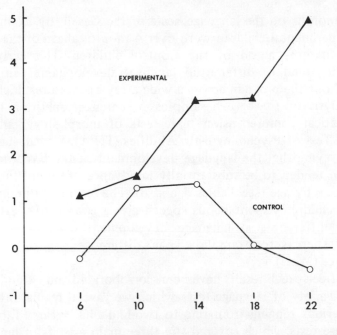

Figure 2. Comparison of experimental and control children on Gesell growth norms.

group was superior to the Control group on all tasks and all testings between 2½ and 6 years of age. The important aspect of the differential in performance, however, was the development of more sophisticated and more consistent response behaviors by the Experimental children. Generally, the Experimental children's responses demonstrated that they tended to use strategies or hypothesis-testing behavior and were sensitive to feedback information from their responses. The Control children, on the other hand, showed a marked tendency to response stereotypy, often perseverating in their responses with no attempt to use a strategy. They also tended to be passive and unenthusiastic in their response behavior. This early learning performance had potential implications for future development: the Experimental child's approach to problem-solving could be facilitative, while the Control child's behavior style could interfere with the ability to learn and perform.

The first significant difference in language performance appeared at 18 months on the language scale of the Gesell. By 22 months the Experimental children were over 4 months ahead of the norm and 6 months ahead of the Control children. This early and dramatic trend of differential language development continued throughout the program across a wide array of measures, including an analysis of free-speech samples, a sentence repetition test, a grammatical comprehension test, tests of morphology, and the Illinois Test of Psycholinguistic Abilities (ITPA). We can summarize by saying that the language development of the Experimental children tended to be substantially in advance of that of the Control group by age (see Tables 7 and 8). The results of our analysis of the children's spontaneous speech give a conservative estimate of the differences in language development between the two groups. There is, for example, a year's difference in mean length of utterance (MLU).

Our free-speech results have been corroborated and extended by a wide variety of language tests which we gave at regular intervals over periods ranging from one to two-and-a-half years (Table 8). On these tests, which covered the three main aspects of language acquisition—comprehension (The Grammatical Comprehension Test), imitation (Sentence Repetition Tests I and II), and production (The Picture Morphology and Berko Morphology tests)—there was as much as two years' difference in age between Experimental and Control group children. Levels achieved by the Experimental children at age 3½ years on the Grammatical Comprehension Test, for instance, were reached by the Control children only at age 5½ years.

We have been careful to ensure that we are not merely measuring differences resulting from different degrees of dialect usage. Our tape recordings of their conversational speech show that the children from both groups speak the dialect referred to as "Black English"; where there was any possibility, however, that test scores could be influenced by dialect patterns, we devised alternative scoring systems to reduce the possibility. One such system was used in the Sentence Repetition Tests to arrive at the "Structures Preserved" measure. This measure makes allowances for errors in repetition resulting from such dialect patterns as the omission of past tense and plural markers and of the copulative verb *be*—recognized features of Black English. As Table 8 shows, the two groups differed in the same manner and to the same degree on this

Table 7

Free-speech Analysis for the Experimental (E) and Control (C) Children for the First Five Years

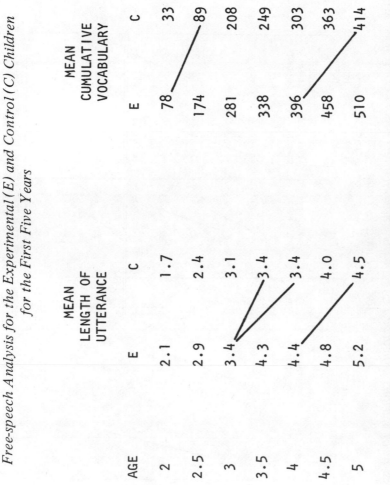

AGE	MEAN LENGTH OF UTTERANCE		MEAN CUMULATIVE VOCABULARY	
	E	C	E	C
2	2.1	1.7	78	33
2.5	2.9	2.4	174	89
3	3.4	3.1	281	208
3.5	4.3	3.4	338	249
4	4.4	3.4	396	303
4.5	4.8	4.0	458	363
5	5.2	4.5	510	414

The diagonal lines represent the age differential between groups achieving similar performance levels.

Table 8
The Results of Various Language Tests for the Experimental (E) and Control (C) Children for the First 6½ Years

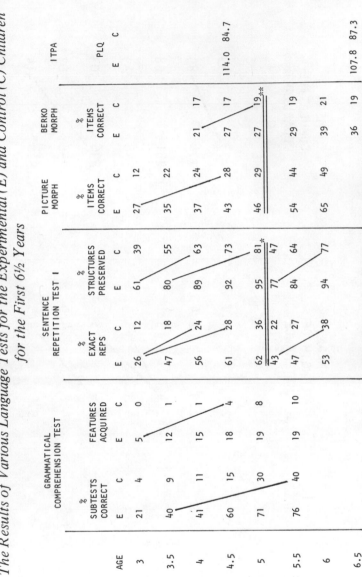

AGE	Grammatical Comprehension Test				Sentence Repetition Test I				Picture Morph		Berko Morph		ITPA	
	% Subtests Correct		Features Acquired		% Exact Reps		% Structures Preserved		% Items Correct		% Items Correct		PLQ	
	E	C	E	C	E	C	E	C	E	C	E	C	E	C
3	21	4	5	0	26	12	61	39	27	12				
3.5	40	9	12	1	47	18	80	55	35	22				
4	41	11	15	1	56	24	89	63	37	24	21	17		
4.5	60	15	18	4	61	28	92	73	43	28	27	17		
5	71	30	19	8	62	36	95	81*	46	29	27	19**	114.0	84.7
5					43	22	77	47						
5.5	76	40	19	10	47	27	84	64	54	44	29	19		
6					53	38	94	77	65	49	39	21		
6.5											36	19	107.8	87.3

*SENTENCE REPETITION TEST II GIVEN AT AGE 5 AND AFTER

**REVISED TESTS GIVEN AFTER AGE 5

measure as on all the other language measures used. Our findings indicate that it is not dialect usage that underlies the difference in performance levels between the two groups, but rather a difference in the grasp of the concepts and relationships that are expressed or implied in syntactic structures.

The ITPA was administered to all children when they were 4½ and again when they were 6½. The results are consistent with our experimental measures of language. At 6½, the difference between the groups found at 4½ had been maintained: the Experimental subjects performed six months above their mean CA, while the Control subjects performed 11 months below their mean CA. The mean Psycholinguistic Quotient (PLQ) for the Experimental group was 108.3, that for the Control group was 86.3—a difference of 22 points. In Figure 3 we have derived the distribution for the performance of the two groups on the ITPA. The difference between groups is quite apparent: there is virtually no overlap between distributions.

As a group, the Experimental children have an aptitude for language substantially greater than that of their counterparts in the Control goup. The readiness with which they grasped and acquired new linguistic structures appeared to be a manifestation of their readiness to learn structures in general, and suggested enhanced awareness of their surroundings and of their ability to express themselves in relation to these surroundings. What is perhaps more important is that they entered school with the language skills and aptitudes needed for further learning.

We attempted (perhaps somewhat feebly) to measure mother-child interactions, using Hess and Shipman (1968) techniques. In the mother-child interaction, most of the sophisticated behavior is done by the mother—initiating problem-solving by verbal clues and verbal prods, organizing tasks with respect to goals in problem-solving situations, and so on. Where the mother has a low IQ, the interaction is often more physical and less organized, and less direction is given to the child. Such was the case in the Control group mother-child dyads. The Experimental dyads transmitted more information than the Control dyads, but this appeared to be a function of the quality of the Experimental child's verbal behavior. The Experimental children supplied more information verbally and initiated more verbal communication than Controls. The children in the Experimental dyads took responsibility for guiding the

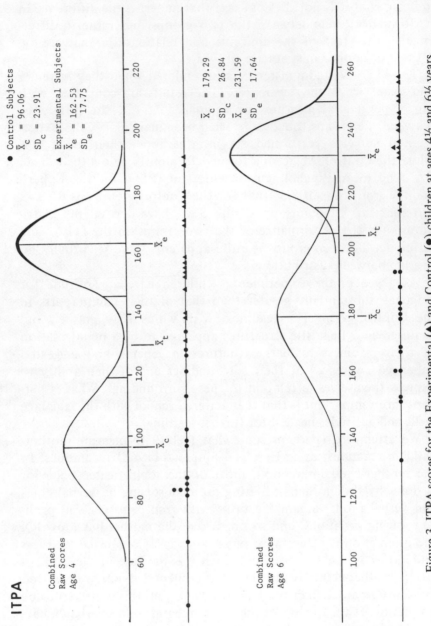

Figure 3. ITPA scores for the Experimental (▲) and Control (●) children at ages 4½ and 6½ years.

flow in information, providing most of the verbal information and direction. Experimental and Control mothers showed little difference in their teaching ability during the testing session. However, in the Experimental dyads the children structured the interaction session either by their questioning or by teaching the mother. The Experimental mothers appeared to model some of the behaviors of their children and, consequently, used more verbal positive reinforcement and more verbal responses. This finding suggested that, in fact, our Experimental children, rather than their mothers, may have assumed the role of "educational engineer."

Those much maligned standardized tests of intelligence have been employed throughout our study to the present time, at which we have just completed follow-up evaluations of subjects at the nine-year level (see Figure 4).

From 24 months to 72 months the Experimental group has maintained better than a 20-point difference over the Control group on the Cattell and Stanford-Binet, and at the mean age of 72 months the Experimental group's mean IQ is 120.7 (SD = 11.2) compared to the Control group mean IQ of 87.2 (SD = 12.8), a difference of over 30 IQ points. These levels have been substantiated by an independent testing service using a "double blind" procedure.

One should be cautioned not to overinterpret these IQ values. There is without doubt an effect of undetermined magnitude of repeated practice on the Binet under conditions of maximum motivation and where test-taking skills for both groups have been enhanced. What is to be viewed as of significance is the differential in performance between the two groups.

Recall that our intervention program terminated at school entry. Figure 5 presents post-intervention performance on the Wechsler Intelligence Scale for Children (WISC) at roughly one, two, and three years after school entry. One major question is the extent to which the gains of intervention will be maintained as time goes on. It is apparent that up to this point, at least, the WISC differential of around 20 IQ points has been maintained over a three-year follow-up to age nine.

We are asked repeatedly about any diffusion effects on siblings of our Experimental children. There is, in fact, a small but significant difference between Experimental and Control sibling IQ's in favor of the Experimentals. The Control group of siblings shows

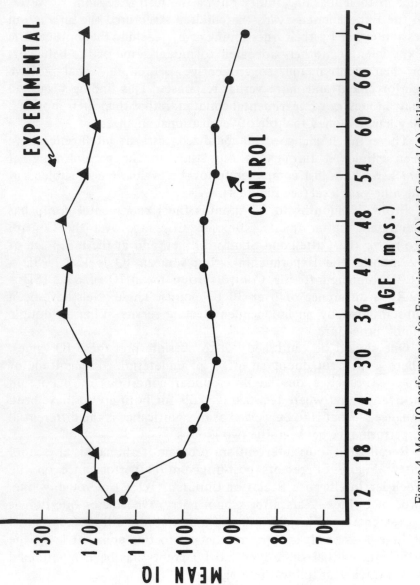

Figure 4. Mean IQ performance for Experimental (▲) and Control (●) children.

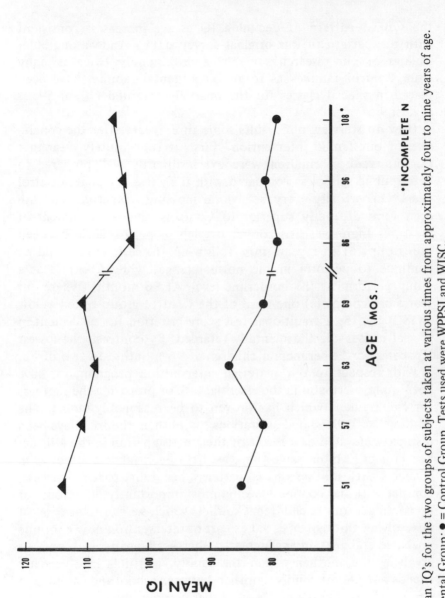

Figure 5. Mean IQ's for the two groups of subjects taken at various times from approximately four to nine years of age.
▲ = Experimental Group; ● = Control Group. Tests used were WPPSI and WISC.

the typical pattern of declining IQ as age increases (consistent with the pattern of our original survey data.) And among older siblings of our research subjects, approximately twice as many from Control families as from Experimental families have been placed in special classes for the mentally retarded (17 of 59, as against 9 of 68).

How do we view our results some three years after the conclusion of our family intervention? First, it is absolutely clear that our intervention children were extraordinarily well prepared to enter public school as compared with their less fortunate Control peers. On virtually every behavioral measure, Experimental children were distinctly superior to Controls, and in a number of measures there was little or no overlap in performance between the groups. Three years into follow-up, Experimental children continue to perform in the normal range, while Controls as a group perform at the borderline level. At 96 months (where our scores are complete) one-third of the Control group tested below (WISC) IQ 75, a traditional test score criterion for placement in special classes for the mentally retarded. By contrast, the lowest IQ scores for Experimental children at 96 months are two of 88.

With respect to our maternal intervention program, we have been quite successful in the essential task of preparing the mothers for employment which has proven to be reasonably stable. The mothers' verbally stated aspirations for all their children have been distinctly elevated as a result of their participation in the Milwaukee Project. At the same time, we have been far less effective in changing each mother's social patterns, her ability to remain free of conflict with her community, and most importantly, her modes of interacting with her children. Conflicts which we were able to assist in resolving through crisis aid as part of intervention now continue unabated and are perhaps increased. By these I mean social conflicts involving the mother within the family, conflicts involving her friends outside the family, conflicts between school and parent, and conflicts involving the police and other community agencies.

For example, while children attended the intervention center, they were given breakfast, lunch, and an afternoon snack. Some of the children now report going to school hungry or inappropriately dressed. Where the parent has become aware of minor school adjustment problems, she may respond by physical beatings or by threatening to "send him south to live with his father."

Based on comments teachers have written on report cards, one-third of our Experimental children have some social or behavioral difficulty in the school setting. Often these difficulties can be translated to mean "the child talks too much." The Experimental children display the same behavioral problems as their Control counterparts but in addition are able to confront the teacher and their classmates verbally. Above all else, the Milwaukee Project children were given confidence, skill, and practice in the use of language as an effective tool for interacting with the adults in their lives. Whether this will be seen as an asset or a liability to the children is yet to be determined.

But we have seen geniune problems of adjustment emerge as well. With frequently poor communication between school and parent, simple problems are exaggerated to the detriment of the children. For example, notes are frequently sent home requesting a meeting and our mothers often do not respond; the public school teacher is inclined to believe the mother is not interested, rather than understanding that she may be unable to read or that the note's request is not clearly stated. On the mother's part, unquestioning attitudes of "schools know best" have led to decisions of placement for the children with no parental input.

For example, one little girl of the Experimental group tested at the 96th percentile in reading on a pre-first-grade achievement test. During her first two months of school she decided that she did not want to speak. Possibly she was angry about no longer being with her preschool teachers. Her teacher had decided to place her back in kindergarten because her parents offered no support for the first grade adjustment problem she was having. Luckily, just before the change was to be made, the child walked up to the teacher's desk, opened a book, and fluently read from it. A shocked teacher called in her supervisors to witness the event. From then on she has been a model student.

It is our subjective judgment that parent-school incompatibilities and disrupted family living environments will continue to erode the high hopes engendered by our Experimental childrens' performance at the end of our intervention effort. Nevertheless, the performance of our Experimental children three years into follow-up is such that it is difficult to conceive of their ever dropping to the performance standards of the Control group. Those of us who have participated in this experience have witnessed a capacity for learning on the part of these children dramatically in excess of their epidemiologically based expectations. At the same time, we are rapidly approaching the view that intervention and support for children reared with the intellectually inadequate parent and living in a disrupted family environment must continue throughout the child's school as well as preschool years. Nevertheless, our data to this time do nothing to inhibit the hope that it may indeed prove possible to prevent the high frequency of mental retardation among children reared by parents of limited intellectual competence under circumstances of severe economic deprivation.

5

Plasticity in the Rate of Achieving Cognitive and Motivational Landmarks

J. McV. HUNT

Joseph McVicker Hunt received the Ph.D. degree in Psychology in 1933 from Cornell University. He was a National Research Council Fellow for one year at New York Psychiatric Institute and for a second year at Columbia University and at Worcester State Hospital and Clark University. Thereafter he served as Research Consultant to, and later Director of, the Institute of Welfare Research of the Community Service Society of New York. He taught briefly at the University of Nebraska and then for ten years at Brown University, where he was also a Research Associate at Butler Hospital. After other teaching engagements at Teacher's College, Columbia University, and at the Graduate College of New York University, in 1951 he became Professor of Psychology at the University of Illinois, where he remained until he became Emeritus Professor of Psychology in 1974.

Hunt has written over 150 papers and eight books, including the classic two-volume work Personality and the Behavior Disorders *(Ronald Press, 1944). His primary interests have been in the areas of early education, intelligence and experience, experiential bases of incompetence, and the effects of poverty.*

The many honors he has received for his contributions include Honorary Sc.D. degrees from Brown University and the University of Nebraska.

I have known about the Milwaukee Project for seven or eight years. From my perspective, educational intervention in infancy and the other preschool years is unique in the behavioral sciences, though the idea of starting with a group of newborn infants at risk for experientially based mental retardation is not unique. Even before World War II, Skeels and Dye (1939) happened onto such an investigative strategy as a consequence of their earlier observations. A number of others, including myself, have utilized this strategy.

But it is the combination of tactics used by Heber and his collaborators that makes their work unique. These include taking an IQ of 75 or less to define the population of mothers whose infants served as his subjects; sustaining the educational intervention through home visits and then educational day care from shortly after birth until the infants were 66 months old and ready for school; and following them for another three years in school. I very much hope that Heber and his team will continue to follow the school progress of the subjects up to or into high school, if support can be found.

While the avowed aim of the Milwaukee Project is to prevent mental retardation, and while the tactics of the intervention fit nicely with Emory Cowen's definition of primary prevention (above, p. 8), I believe the intervention must also be said to encourage positive mental health, for several reasons.

First, the effort at prevention is indeed primary. Since Heber's intervention begins shortly after the birth of his subjects, it would be hard to conceive of any approach more primary without intervening in the gestation process or reverting to the eugenics of Sir Francis Galton. Although it may become feasible to diagnose a few forms of pathology in utero in order to intervene with chemical therapies or to abort them, it is highly unlikely that interuterine interventions will ever become a major means of preventing mental retardation. Perhaps, moreover, the incidence of very serious forms of pathology with known hereditary mechanisms can be reduced through genetic counseling. Yet the eugenic approach is not likely to become an effective strategy. It is based on the notion that human characteristics are fixed at the time of conception by heredity—a notion that has already caused untold damage. Beginning with Parson Malthus in the late eighteenth century and continuing with the Social Darwinism of Herbert Spencer and the eugenics movement inaugurated by Galton in England, with Gobineau in France, and with C. B. Davenport, Henry Goddard, Madison Grant, and many others (including a great many psychometricians) in the United States, belief in hereditary predeterminism was used to account for all forms of defects in man, including poverty and ethnic and racial differences in test scores. Scientific racism led to Hitler's death camps (see Allan Chase, 1977). Galton chose eugenics as the means of improving man's lot because he (quite wrongly) considered hereditary predeterminism to be a necessary implication of the theory of evolution formulated by his cousin, Charles Darwin; but the evidence, combined with the history of the past 150 years, forces us to the opposite conclusion. With minor exceptions, euthenics must be the means of improving man's lot. And in euthenics, one cannot begin before infancy.

Second, Heber's work appears to foster Ansbacher's "positive mental health." Mental health demands productive participation in one's culture. Productivity, in turn, depends upon competence. Thus, insofar as competence is reflected in scores on tests of intelligence, educational interventions in infancy and early childhood are means of advancing something of social and personal value that one can measure in positive terms as well as in the negative terms of preventing mental retardation. Even though mental retardation has not traditionally been considered a part of the mental health arena, competence and what we assess as intelligence are both essential aspects of mental health. Such quandaries derive from our historical division of mind into cognition, conation, and affection. Plato probably did us a great disservice when he promulgated the division of things mental into intellect or ability on one hand, the motivational aspect on another, and the affective or emotional area on a third. These are tightly bound up together, and the separation is for the most part an abstraction that people make in order to simplify it. The trouble is, Plato's separation has come to have counterparts in our social institutions. Thus, matters concerned with ability, information, and intellect get supported through the Office of Education, whereas those concerned with the motivational or affective parts get their support chiefly from the National Institute of Mental Health; and what started out to be a simplification becomes a conflictful obfuscation.

Ansbacher also contended that "maturity" is what we are seeking in positive mental health. Competence, I contend, is a major aspect of maturity. The mental ages from which IQ's derive increase with age. Insofar as competence is reflected in such tests, there is no semantic violence involved in saying that Heber's interventions are fostering maturity.

Despite the positive things to be said about it, the Milwaukee Project has been looked upon with a great deal of suspicion. Ellis Page (1972) of the University of Connecticut, for instance, in a critique whose title refers to the "Miracle of Milwaukee," argues as follows. Since there is a statistically significant difference between the birth weights of the experimental and control children, the selection of subjects cannot be viewed as random; and since the selection is not random, the difference between the two distributions of IQ's need be considered nothing more than a reflection of this genetic selection. In view of Heber's claim that the effectiveness of his intervention lies in the significant superiority of the mean IQ score for his treated group over that for his control group, I would like to hear his reply to Page.

I myself am as much impressed with the generational change in IQ from mothers to children as I am by the difference between the means for the treated and control children. The gain extends from a mean IQ of no more than 75 for the mothers up to a mean IQ of 125 for the children in the treated group at 66 months of age. This is a change in mean IQ of roughly 50 points, a very substantial gain. Even the children in Heber's control group show a mean IQ that is 15 or 20 points above that of their mothers. For such between-generation comparisons, Heber is properly concerned about the fact that he gives the same test over and over, so the scores of the children can be expected to show a good deal of practice gain. Such practice may indeed be a factor. Yet IQ scores do not measure inherent ability to learn or what Hebb (1949) termed "Intelligence I"; rather, they are measures of achieved phenotypic ability that has emerged in the course of life from the interaction of genotypic potential with the environmental circumstances encountered (what Hebb termed "Intelligence II"). Insofar as repeated encounters with tests improve test performance, they should be expected also to improve performance in other situations for which test scores are valid contemporary predictors—not of future IQ, but rather of performance at about 66 months, when the children are entering school. But parenthetically, from the standpoint of the ethics of such research, it is reassuring to find that repeated testing contributes to measured competence and is thereby something of an educational device. We have found it wherever we have compared the performance on our ordinal scales (Uzgiris and Hunt, 1975) of orphanage-reared children in a cross-sectional study with performance of those in a longitudinal study. Those in the longitudinal studies who were tested repeatedly achieved the landmarks at younger ages. To be sure, competence that is limited to the test situation is part of this picture. As Ed Zigler (1966) has emphasized in his studies of testing, such evidence of competence may be chiefly motivational.

Let us now return to the critique of Ellis Page by asking if the findings in the Milwaukee Project do imply a miracle or if they call for a modification of the theoretical position held by a good many psychometricians. Although Heber and his collaborators employed other tests, such as those of color-form matching and field independence, I shall confine my remarks to the findings obtained from the tests of intelligence, because the notion of a miracle stems from theoretical beliefs about intelligence tests. I call your attention to three findings. First, there are increases in the mean IQ scores between the generations. That between the mothers and their treated children is around 50 points—that is, from below 75 to 124 at age 66 months; that between the mothers and the control children is around 20 points. Second, the children treated with educational day care show a mean IQ at age 66 months that is 30 points higher than that shown by the controls. Third, Heber found that the standard deviation for the distribution of IQ's from the treated group is smaller—in some testings by half—than that for the control group; in other words, a third effect of the educational day-care is a decrease in the heterogeneity of IQ's. This suggests that a portion of that heterogeneity must derive from differences in the development-fostering quality of experiences within families.

My question concerns whether other evidence exists to confirm each of these three kinds of findings. First, for the intergenerational effect, other confirmatory evidence does exist. Albizu-Miranda (1966), for instance, has reported that since the industrial revolution that came to Puerto Rico after World War II, it is common to find children 7 or 8 years old who have higher level ages (as measured by the Spanish version of the Stanford-Binet) than their parents. Yet these parents manage to function fairly successfully. Such is the limited import of the test scores: the test-defined retardates earn their living fairly well. Wayne Dennis has investigated the effects of modernization in the Middle East on the Draw-A-Man IQ's of children whose parent-generation he studied some 20 years ago.*

*I hope the findings from Dennis's work will be published despite his untimely death as a consequence of a rear-end collision in the summer of 1976.

Still other evidence of large intergenerational effects comes from the work of Scarr-Salapatek. Like myself, Sandra Scarr was brought up to believe that intelligence tests measure fundamental, inborn ability.* She started out with the notion that the basis for race differences must reside largely in heredity (Scarr-Salapatek, 1971). Recently, Scarr and Weinberg (1976) have reported the IQ scores for a group of black children who were adopted by white parents. White parents who adopt black children are well above average, not financially, but in education, social concern, and social status. From all that Scarr could learn, the biological parents of her adopted black children were typical of black people in the United States and would have had a mean IQ of about 85, one standard deviation below the mean of white people. The question is, what happens to the level of performance by these adopted black children on tests of intelligence and on school performance? Her principal finding is that their mean IQ is between 106 and 107—an intergenerational gain of 21 or 22 points. This is considerably short of the 50 points obtained by Heber and his colleagues; but Heber has chosen parents who are a standard deviation below the average for black people and he employed a deliberate educational intervention. In my book *Intelligence and Experience* (Hunt, 1961), I hazarded the guess that if we knew how to foster development in the young, we could probably raise the level of intelligence in the population, as now measured, by at least 30 points. Merely moving black children into white families appears to achieve about two-thirds of that in intergenerational gain; but Heber's educational intervention from infancy to 66 months achieves *five*-thirds of it. Who knows what these children

*We psychologists are strange people. If we had ever noticed and taken into account the concept of the range of reaction from genetics, we would never have considered that tests of intelligence measure inborn ability. But this concept that Woltereck set forth in 1909 has been exceedingly slow to find its way into the thought and writing of those who study individual differences. When it has found its way, it has until recently been estimated only indirectly by subtracting empirical estimates of the percentage of variance attributable to heredity (heritability) from 100, the total variance. Had we understood the concept of the norm or range of reaction and its implication for psychological development, we would have recognized long ago that innate ability can exist only as potential, and that the tests measure only what has been realized or achieved in the course of a lifetime sequence of successive interactions between infants and their environmental cirumstances.

in Heber's treated group might achieve in the way of mean IQ by adulthood if the high development-fostering quality of their experience were continued to adulthood?

Let us turn now to the second kind of finding—the increased mean IQ of the treatment group. Among the pioneers of educational intervention was Rowena Ripin (now Mrs. Heinz Ansbacher), who published a report in 1933 on the effect of nursery-schooling on the test performance of three-year-olds being reared in an orphanage in New York. The gains in IQ as well as definite changes for the better in behavior, were quite substantial in these children. This kind of investigation became the stock in trade of the Child Welfare Research Station at the University of Iowa, and Marie Skodak Crissey reported some results at the First Vermont Conference on Primary Prevention of Psychopathology in 1975.* I would like to discuss some findings from our own interventions in child-rearing as it is handled at the Orphanage of the Farah Pahlavi Charity Society in Tehran, Iran.

I had long been intrigued by the role of intrinsic motivation in children's psychological development. Then in 1958 I learned of Wayne Dennis's work in an orphanage in Tehran. In a single week there, he had done a significant piece of horseback research. Going through the wards crib by crib and baby by baby, he asked (through an interpreter) how old each child was and observed and asked about posture and locomotion. He found that of those in their second year, about 60 percent could not yet sit up alone, and none could walk alone. Of those in their fourth year, 85 percent were still not walking alone. Hoping to achieve a dramatic demonstration of the role of early experience in sensorimotor development, I located an appropriate Iranian collaborator and established a laboratory in the Tehran orphanage.

Our methodological strategy is what I have called "wave design." We make no attempt to obtain simultaneous treatment and control groups. Our subjects have been foundlings without evidence of pathology who were obtained from the Municipal Orphanage of Tehran during their first month of life. The first wave of 15 infants constitutes the control group, and each successive wave was started about a year after the preceding one. The only intervention

*See Albee and Joffe, eds., *Primary Prevention of Psychopathology*, I, 187–202.

in the control wave consisted of repeated examinations with ordinal scales of sensorimotor development inspired by the work of Jean Piaget (Uzgiris & Hunt, 1975), which were made every other week during the first year and every fourth week thereafter. For the second wave, we attempted audio-visual enrichment of experience in which the infant could first look at and then activate mobiles and also first hear music and mother-talk and later obtain it at will by moving his arm or leg to turn on a speaker attached to his crib. Later, after I learned about Leon Yarrow's finding of a correlation of nearly 0.6 between the amount of responsiveness in inanimate materials available to an infant and the length of time that the infant persists in trying to achieve a goal at age six months, we added a variety of such responsive inanimate materials. Wave 2, however, was abortive because the local worker in charge of the project in Tehran failed to keep things going. For Wave 3, we employed untutored human enrichment by simply reducing the infant-caretaker ratio from 10/1 to 10/3. These three caretakers had charge of all 10 infants—that is, all were equally in charge of any one of them; and we made no attempt to teach the caretakers what to do. For Wave 4, we had the audio-visual enrichment done essentially as it was intended to be done in Wave 2.

For Wave 5—started about the middle of 1972 and completed in the spring of 1975—we used tutored human enrichment and reduced the infant caretaker ratio to 3/1 or 2/1. This meant that each caretaker had special responsibility for the infants in her care. Moreover, the caretakers were taught to use Earladeen Badger's (1971a, 1971b) learning programs for infants and toddlers. When these learning programs were used with educational day care for children of the poverty sector served by the Parent and Child Center of Mt. Carmel, Illinois, the mean age at which the children achieved top-level object permanence advanced some six months ahead of that for home-reared children from predominantly professional families in Worcester, Massachusetts, but their vocal imitation did not advance. In our project, we taught our caretakers how to foster vocal imitation and how to foster semantic mastery for objects and events regularly encountered in caretaking operations. To foster vocal imitation, we had the caretakers imitate the cooing and babbling of the infants in their charge until the infants responded; then vocal games followed. Once an infant had mastered several babbling patterns, the caretaker proceeded to play "follow the leader" by changing this vocal play from one babbling pattern to another. When the infant had become adept at this, the caretaker introduced novel phonemic patterns which she had never heard the infant utter—a procedure based upon the hypothesis that the phonemic repertoire comes largely through imitation. To foster semantic mastery, the caretakers talked about each operation as they conducted it, sharpening the relationship between the vocal signs and what they signified. Thus, as a caretaker washed the infant's ears, she would say, "Now I am going to wash your *ear.*" At the word *ear*, her washcloth was to make contact with the anatomical ear.

This procedure is derived from my theory of intrinsic motivation. According to the theory, objects and events that are in the process of becoming recognitively familiar are the ones that are attractive and motivate interest through a process that appears to be true imitation but is in reality pseudo imitation. Interest in what is novel or unfamiliar in a familiar context comes later, and motivates genuine imitation. Early language is a coordination of phonemic combinations with objects that have become recognizable and permanent. The first phase of language acquisition concerns the phonemic component, acquired through imitation. The second phase involves semantic mastery and is based upon association between phonemic combinations and recognizable objects and events. Syntactics, the segment of language acquisition to which most attention has been given, is the third phase.

For this phase, I am inclined to accept Jerome Bruner's (1975) account of the acquisition of spoken acts, namely that they represent—at least initially—a semanticization of the child's purposive actions.

The dependent variables in this series of interventions consist of our seven ordinal sensorimotor scales (Uzgiris & Hunt, 1975) plus posture and locomotion. The scales are Object Permanence, the Development of Means for Obtaining Desired Environmental Events, Vocal Imitation, Gestural Imitation, Operational Causality, the Construction of Object Relations in Space, and the Development of Schemes for Relating to Objects. What we measure is the age at which the various steps on these ordinal scales are achieved by the children living under the conditions of the various interventions.

What is most relevant in our findings to Heber's study is the mean ages at which the children in these five waves achieve the top steps on the seven scales. For Object Permanence, the mean ages range from a maximum of 141 weeks for Wave 2 to a minimum of 93 weeks for Wave 5—a difference of more than 11 months, or nearly a year. For the Development of Means, the range is 56 weeks: from 150 weeks for Waves 1 and 2 combined to 94 weeks for Wave 5. For Vocal Imitation, the range is 64 weeks: from a maximum of 157 weeks for Waves 1 and 2 combined to a minimum of 93 weeks for Wave 5. For Gestural Imitation, the range of means goes from 162 weeks for the control wave to 71 weeks for Wave 5—a range of 91 weeks, or about a year and three-quarters. For Operational Causality, the range in mean ages is 55 weeks, from 140 to 85. For Object Relations in Space, the range is from 145 to 88 weeks, or 57. For Schemes of Relating to Objects, the top step consists of spontaneously naming one of the objects or toys thoroughly familiar to the child. It is meaningless to specify the range in weeks of mean age because only one child in either Wave 1 or Wave 2 ever spontaneously named an object during the bi-monthly testing which continued until, at about three and a half years of age, they were transferred to another orphanage. On the other hand, all 11 infants in Wave 5 spontaneously named objects and did so at a mean age of 90 weeks. The innovation in each successive wave (except for Wave 2, which got the abortive attempt at audio-visual enrichment) achieved the top steps on nearly all of these scales at mean ages younger than did the preceding wave. Moreover, the children in Wave 5 who had had the tutored human enrichment actually achieved the top steps on five of these scales at mean ages younger than did twelve home-reared infants from mainly professional families in Worcester, Massachusetts.

I have presented these achievement advances in the unfamiliar terms of difference between the two mean ages, but for communicative purposes it may be worthwhile to transform them into the differences between the means of the IQ ratios for each of the scales. This is done by using the mean age at which home-reared children at Worcester, Massachusetts, and Athens, Greece, had achieved the top steps on these scales: one can consider their mean age as the mental age, and simply divide it by the mean ages for Waves 1 and 2 combined and for Wave 5. For Object Permanence, the mental age determined in this fashion is 110 weeks. Following the procedure with 141 weeks for Wave 2 and 93 weeks for Wave 5 and multiplying by 100 yields the IQ ratios of 78 for the former and 118 for the latter, a range of 40 points. The same procedure applied to vocal imitation results in IQ ratios of 65 for Waves 1 and 2 combined versus 110 for Wave 5, a range of 45 points. These are sufficient, I believe, to indicate that the 30 or so points of difference between the treated children and the control children in Heber's study involve no miracle. No one can tell, of course, what the IQ's of these foundlings in Wave 5 of Tehran may be when they are 66 months old without knowing the conditions under which they will live.

There are other differences. Outstanding among them is charm. The children of Wave 5 were as noted for attractiveness as those of Waves 1 and 2 were for lack of it. This judgment of mine, and of others concerned with the project, gets a certain validation from the adoption records. Of the 55 in the first four waves, only two were ever adopted, and these were taken when they were less than six months old because they were pretty babies. Of the 11 infants in Wave 5, on the other hand, seven had been adopted according to my last information, and they were adopted because they were active and attractive two-year-olds. According to Miss Sakhai, the chief of the examiners, the adoptive parents were "very high people." If we were to follow up these children 25 years hence as Skeels (1966) followed up those studied by Skeels and Dye, I suspect the difference in mean IQ would amount to more than 30 points, perhaps more than the intergenerational difference of 50 points.

Clearly, unless one holds that the sequence of experiences through life can account for no more than 20 percent of the variance in IQ scores (and this involves a completely unjustified generalization of obtained indices of heritability beyond the samples of genotypes and environmental circumstances from which they were derived), such confirmative evidence indicates that no miracle need be involved to obtain the findings that Heber has reported.

Finally, I want to note that our work also contains evidence corresponding to Heber's finding of less variance among the IQ's of children in his treated group than in his control group. For instance, the means of the standard deviations at which the children in our several waves at Tehran achieved both an intermediate step and the top steps on the seven scales is perfectly correlated with the degree to which the environmental circumstances for the various individuals in each wave are standardized. Least standardized were the environmental conditions in Waves 1 and 2; next were those for Wave 3; next were the conditions of the 20 children in Wave 4, who received audio-visual enrichment; and the most standardized were those for Wave 5. The means of the standard deviation in age of achievement for the seven scales by the children in Wave 5 (6.0 weeks) was only slightly over a third of that for Wave 2 (17.0 weeks) on the intermediate steps on the scales and less than half that (7.0 vs. 16.0 weeks) for achieving the top steps. Again, in a cross-sectional study of the ages of children drawn chiefly from the working class in Athens, Paraskevopoulos and I (1971) found the standard deviations in weeks of age for home-reared children at the top level of Object Permanence to be 43 weeks, whereas that for the children of Metera Center, where the conditions of rearing were highly standardized, was only 12 weeks. This suggests that the variation in the development-fostering quality in working-class homes in Athens is slightly more than three and a half times as great as that in Metera Center, where the caretakers were trained and strictly supervised in their care of the three infants they each had charge of. Moreover, the standard deviation for the home-reared children was even greater than that for the children in the Municipal Orphanage, where the infant-caretaker ratio was around 10/1 and where there were outstanding variations in care given to favorites and nonfavorites. The same rule holds for vocal imitation. Whereas the standard deviations of those home-reared at the top level was 30 weeks, that for the children of Metera Center was only 9.4 weeks. Moshe Smilansky (1977) has also reported that growing up on a kibbutz in Israel has the effect of reducing the variance in measured intelligence for the children of parents coming from diverse social classes ranging from professional to unskilled labor. Our findings and those of Smilansky indicate that Heber's result—that there is less variance in his tutored children than in his control—is a genuine effect of reducing the variations in the development-fostering quality of the children's experiences. Such findings strongly suggest that a great deal of the variation in measures of intellectual competence is a function of the variations in the development-fostering quality of experience in different families.

The work of Heber and his collaborators is like our work in that we have both assessed the outcomes of educational interventions. Our findings and those of Heber differ, however, in that his primary dependent variable has been the IQ, while our findings are based on measures along seven branches of sensorimotor development. The IQ is based upon the mental age that involves a substitutive averaging across the various branches of psychological development; our approach involves equal attention to each of the seven branches in our Piaget-inspired ordinal scales. Accordingly, we have uncovered a great deal of specificity between kinds of experience and kinds of developmental advance that is invariably hidden by substitutive averaging to obtain the mental age. For instance, the same intervention that served to advance the achievement of top-level object permanence in one group of children—those of parents of poverty served by the Parent and Child Center of Mt. Carmel, Illinois—about six months ahead of the mean age at which another group—home-reared children of middle class (predominantly professional) families—achieved this landmark, left the children of the first group approximately 5 months behind those of the second in achieving top-level vocal imitation. Similarly, the untutored human enrichment offered to the Wave 3 infants at the Tehran orphanage served to advance the mean age at which they sat up alone by about six months ahead of the age at which those in Waves 1 and 2 sat up, and it advanced the mean age at which they stood and cruised about their cribs by nearly 8 months; yet these advances in posture and locomotion were accompanied by no gains whatever during the first 13 or 14 months of life in achieving landmarks on any of the ordinal scales of sensorimotor development. The generalized advances obtained in the children of Wave 5, moreover, largely dispose of the interpretation that specialized advances represent merely an increased proportion of developmental energy put into them. I believe this finding of specificity between the kinds of experiences and kinds of developmental advance open a new field of investigation which has been largely hidden by the practice of substitutive averaging across items to obtain the mental age. I suspect that knowledge of this specificity is highly important for an educational psychology of infancy and early childhood.

In summary, Heber's work is unique, first for having specified the characteristics of the parents and second in having sustained an educational intervention from shortly after birth until school age. The study represents both primary prevention and concern with positive mental health. Moreover, the outcome need imply no miracle in Milwaukee because other investigators have uncovered intergenerational effects, educational gains, and reductions in the variability of measures of competence comparable in size to his. Heber is to be commended for an outstanding contribution, but I confess to wishing that the relationships between the experiences provided in the educational day care and the nature of the developmental advances were clearer and more specific.

REFERENCES

Badger, E. D. *Teaching guide: Infant learning program*. Paoli, Pa.: The Instructo Corporation, 1971. (a)

Badger, E. D. *Teaching guide: Toddler learning program*. Paoli, Pa.: The Instructo Corporation, 1971. (b)

Bruner, J. S. The ontogenesis of speech acts. *Journal of Child Language,* 1975, *2,* 1-19.

Chase, A. *The legacy of Malthus: The social costs of the new scientific racism.* New York: Knopf, 1977.

Hebb, D. O. *The organization of behavior.* New York: Wiley, 1949.

Hunt, J. McV. *Intelligence and experience.* New York: Ronald Press, 1961.

Page, E. B. Miracle in Milwaukee: Raising the IQ. *Educational Researcher,* 1972, *1,* (10), 8-16.

Paraskevopoulos, J., and Hunt, J. McV. Object construction and imitation under differing conditions of rearing. *Journal of Genetic Psychology,* 1971, *119,* 301-321.

Scarr-Salapatek, S. Race, social class and IQ. *Science,* 1971, *174* (4016), 1285-1295.

Scarr, S., and Weinberg, R. A. IQ test performance of Black children adopted by White families. *American Psychologist,* 1976, *31,* 726-739.

Skeels, H. M. Adult status of children with contrasting early life experiences. *Monographs of the SRCD,* 1966, *31* (3) Serial No. 105, 1-65.

Skeels, H. M., and Dye, H. B. A study of the effects of differential stimulation of mentally retarded children. *Proceedings of the American Association on Mental Deficiency,* 1939, *44,* 114-136.

Smilansky, M. Systems development-planning in education: An Israeli perspective. Chap. 5 in D. A. Wilkerson (Ed.), *Educating all our children.* Wesport, Conn.: Mediax Assoc., Inc. (in press).

Uzgiris, I. C., and Hunt, J. McV. *Assessment in infancy: Ordinal scales of Psychological development.* Urbana: University of Illinois Press, 1975.

Zigler, E. Research on personality structure in the retardate. In N. R. Ellis (Ed.), *International review of research in mental retardation, Vol. 1.* New York: Academic Press, 1966.

DISCUSSION BY ROBERT SOMMER

In discussing the Heber and Hunt presentations, Robert Sommer raised four issues:

1. While he was very impressed by Heber's findings, Sommer is interested in teasing out the reasons for the effect. Since the system dealt with is multicausal, it would be impossible to make only a single change in the system (i.e. the community); therefore, follow-up research would be unproductive.

2. Perhaps Heber's findings could be replicated easily elsewhere in the social system—for example, in schools, if one used there a similarly massive intervention with a one-to-one staff relationship with children.

3. We should not ignore the possibility that institutions can be failures. When we sort and label children by means of mental tests, we absolve the institution or society of responsibility and place the blame on the children. An example of institutional failure is provided in Hunt's research, where orphanages were failures as social institutions. Pertinent research should indicate institutional failure where it exists and be reflected by institutional change, for example doing away with large orphanages.

4. Sommer wondered how the Heber and Hunt results could be generalized to the larger society through the improvement of social institutions, including schools. Simply adding to school budgets and increasing bureaucracy, he felt, was not necessarily a good solution.

SELECTED DISCUSSION

Dr. Hunt: Dr. Heber, would you comment on the criticisms made of your study by Ellis Page?

Dr. Heber: Surprisingly, this is the first time that I have been called upon to answer Page, and I welcome the opportunity.

It is true, indeed, that there was a statistically significant difference in birth weight between the experimental and control groups; we published the data. But the birth weights for both groups, though significantly different, were well within the normal limits for black babies. I am unaware of any substantial correlation between birth weight and subsequent intelligence within normal limits. Page ignored our reported data showing that all other indications of the babies' condition at birth—incidence of prematurity, pregnancy complications, and obstetrical conditions—were equivalent for both groups. Subsequent measures of height, weight, bone age, serum blood levels, and so on are comparable for both groups. Thus, the difference in birth weights was the only indication of physical differences between the groups, and I dismiss it as inconsequential.

Page's second criticism (alluded to by Professor Sommer) is that my treatment was not very specific, so that the results cannot be related to any specific treatment administered. We were well aware of this. At the time we began the study, the research literature described no successful intervention, with any technique, which substantially modified—clinically and educationally—the intellectual competency of these types of children over long periods of time. Most of the data, though tending to produce significant statistical gains, were reduced to inconsequentiality within a few years. So, we deliberately used the strategy of attempting to do everything that might have a positive effect on the children's cognitive development. We found the positive effect, but we cannot specify to which of the treatments the difference is attributable, or at what ages. Our subsequent research will undertake such studies, and I do not regard this criticism as valid.

The third area Page criticized was the public relations releases concerning the Milwaukee Project, even accusing me of having a public relations officer in Washington. In actuality I tried hard to avoid premature publicity and dissemination of findings. Neither I nor any of my research colleagues has ever called a press conference or issued a press release. All of the newspaper accounts referred to by Page were initiated by the Department of Health, Education, and Welfare for general publicity purposes and were based upon my written annual progress reports. Understandably, such releases are likely to extol the virtues of a research project.

Several questioners requested Heber to describe his current research program and to suggest which aspects of his intervention scheme he felt were most likely to produce positive results. Some excerpted replies follow.

Dr. Heber: Our original research design called for us to terminate at age seven, since nonintervened children were testing low at this age in the schools and by then would be placed in separate classes. The decision to continue follow-up results from constructive concern whether the positive effects will continue under circumstances that are less than ideal. We will continue to follow up as long as we have the support; and our funding agency has expressed an interest in continuing it. When the research is completed and published, we will move into another longitudinal and prospective project: a study of adolescent retarded individuals as they move out of the school programs.

Regarding the factors most likely to have been involved in our successful intervention, if I had limited funding I would not hesitate to emphasize the program for child intervention and parental competencies development that I have described. Children of what age? I would guess that about eighteen months would be early enough to start. Continued intervention for the child is essential in school, where he needs support that his parent cannot provide. Another point to keep in mind (though our culture finds the notion distasteful) is that some parents are not sufficiently competent to do an adequate job of rearing their young children and teaching them skills.

Inadequate parents are not necessarily those who score low on tests. Some of our experimental mothers are clearly inadequate and have an adverse effect on the development and the function of their children, and our research indicates that the prospects for these children is extremely limited; other mothers, though, do a fine job and the children have responded well. We were able to identify the bad mothers but not by any of the measures used in the study. It may or may not be relevant that they are the ones who have continued to have a lot of babies. To save money in future programs, one would have to find a good way of differentiating the inadequate mother, and IQ alone is not going to do it.

I suspect that even with far more modest assistance than we provided, some of our mothers would still have done the splendid job they are doing; others, however, were unresponsive, and for that group of extremely high risk children we need to find some alternative.

Several questioners asked Heber to describe more completely the training provided the experimental mothers in the study.

Dr. Heber: We provided vocational guidance, jobs outside the home, and pocket money. These dimensions seem important because the mothers responded so well to them. With respect to the success of the child-care skills training, on the other hand, I have many reservations. As part of this training, a mother was encouraged to observe the teacher interacting with her infant in the center. Mothers were given much relevant classroom-type instruction, but perhaps behavior modeling with the teacher in the home would have been more effective.

6

Marital Disruption as a Stressor

BERNARD L. BLOOM

Bernard L. Bloom received the Ph.D. degree in Clinical Psychology in 1952 from the University of Connecticut. From that time until 1961 he was a clinical psychologist in a Veterans Administration outpatient clinic, Chief Psychologist at the Hawaii State Hospital, and a clinician in a children's clinic, all the while maintaining a private practice. From 1961 to 1962 he worked at the Harvard University School of Public Health and from 1962 to 1965 at the Regional Office of NIMH in Denver, Colorado. In 1965 he became Professor of Psychology at the University of Colorado, a post he still fills.

His research interests are in clinical psychology with especial emphasis on the area of community mental health. He has published extensively in community psychology, including a book in press entitled Community Mental Health: A General Introduction.

The focus of his research and teaching over the past decade has been on the epidemiology of mental disorders. Out of this interest has come his recent emphasis on marital disruption as a source of stress.

Many of the concepts currently employed by mental health professionals interested in the prevention of mental disorders seem analogous to the pre-germ theory view of disease—namely, that diseases are caused by noxious elements in the environment (stresses), and that by the removal of this psychic sewage, much emotional disorder can be eliminated.

Scientists interested in the field of disease prevention have identified three types of prevention. Efforts at *primary prevention* are designed to prevent the disease from ever occurring. Smallpox vaccination is an example. *Secondary prevention* pro-

This paper draws on material copyrighted by the American Psychological Association and published in the *Psychological Bulletin*. Permission to make use of this material is gratefully acknowledged.

grams are designed to develop techniques for early case finding so that treatment can be applied promptly. The "Pap" test for cervical cancer is an example. Finally, the field of *tertiary prevention* is concerned with limiting the disability associated with a disorder after it has run its course. Examples include muscle retraining after a stroke and sheltered workshop programs for rehabilitating discharged chronic psychiatric patients. Thus, the term prevention is actually used in three very different and confusing ways; it might prove better to return to the older terms prevention, treatment, and rehabilitation.

A very large proportion of psychopathology, particularly the milder forms, seems to be brought about as a consequence of psychological rather than biological factors, and a variety of psychological strategies for preventing emotional disorders are currently being developed and tested. The efforts fall into two major categories. First, and most common, are efforts to decrease people's vulnerability to specific stresses; second, considerably less common, are efforts to reduce these stresses at their source.

The *prevalence* (number of cases at a specified moment in time) of any disease is a function of two independent variables—*incidence* and *duration*. Incidence is the number of new cases produced during a specified time period, and duration is the time between the initial diagnosis and the termination of the disease, by either recovery or death. The greater the incidence *or* the greater the duration, the higher the prevalence. To put it another way, two diseases may have the same prevalence, but one (such as the common cold) may have a very high incidence and low duration, while the other (such as diabetes) may have a low incidence but a high duration. Primary prevention programs serve to reduce prevalence by reducing incidence, while secondary prevention programs serve to reduce prevalence by reducing duration.

There is a final set of terms which has been found useful in viewing the spectrum of preventive services, specifically for identifying the recipients of the program. One approach has been to aim preventive programs at the *total population* in a defined geographic area. Programs of water purification and sewage disposal are community-wide in their impact. In the mental health area, efforts at mental health education through the mass media are aimed at the total community. A second approach is what might be called the *milestone program.* A preventive service is provided to the members of a community when they reach a predefined point in their life histories, a point sometimes thought to constitute a turning point or normative crisis. A transition in public school can be viewed as a developmental crisis. The major intervention program at the Woodlawn Mental Health Center in Chicago, for example, involved all first grade children in the area this center serves (see Kellam, Branch, Agrawal, and Ensminger, 1975). Anticipatory guidance services could be made available to workers getting ready to retire, or to housewives whose youngest child is within a few months of graduating from high school and leaving the parental home.

A third approach, somewhat different from the second, has been to identify groups of persons at *high risk* of developing the set of behaviors the program is designed to prevent. Because industrial health studies have shown harmful respiratory effects of certain forms of mining, or the dangers to the eye when using a grindstone, certain preventive measures (facemasks or goggles) are usually required. Similarly, crisis intervention services could be instituted for all school-age children facing such hazards as the death of a parent or sibling. Consultation could be provided to attorneys with clients petitioning for divorce, on the basis of evidence linking marital disruption with subsequent psychiatric disability.

While the identification of normative crises can proceed by informal observation, or by deductions from the analysis of changing role performance requirements in the developing individual, the identification of high risk groups most often proceeds from epidemiological investigations that seek to discover personal characteristics significantly associated with the development of psychiatric disorders. Until quite recently, people who have studied the factors associated with mental or emotional disorders have tended to concentrate their efforts on what are termed *predisposing* factors, such as parent loss or other specific traumas in childhood. But the long intervals between such events and their presumed consequences decades later have made it virtually impossible to identify any such factors with certainty.

The past decade or two has witnessed a movement away from considerations of predisposing factors in mental illnesses toward concern with *precipitating* and *perpetuating* factors. The growing concern with current reality, with those factors that precipitate significant psychopathology, is an act of great affirmation. It recognizes what John F. Kennedy called the "harsh environmental conditions" which often are associated with mental illness. It legitimizes the search for effective primary preventions and sets the tone for much that is innovative in the community mental health movement. The literature on precipitating proximal factors in the occurrence of mental disorders was reviewed by Reid in 1959 (see Reid, 1961) and has been most recently reviewed by B. S. Dohrenwend and B. P. Dohrenwend (1974).

Of all the "harsh environmental conditions," none has been more intensively and extensively studied than poverty, or what has come to be called low social class or low socioeconomic status. Research findings are persuasive in their consistency. The most recent review of studies linking social class to psychopathology (Dohrenwend and Dohrenwend, 1974) shows that out of 13 studies conducted in rural areas, nine found that the rates of all psychopathology are highest in the lowest social class, while of 18 urban-area studies, 17 showed that the rates are highest in the lowest social class. And the two studies conducted in areas neither predominantly rural nor urban give the same results.

Even so, the actual rate differences are not great, averaging around 3 to 1 (see Dohrenwend and Dohrenwend, 1969, Tables 2–13, 2–14, and 2–15, pages 28–30). This difference probably does not warrant establishing a preventive intervention program, particularly since there is so little understanding about how poverty is linked to psychopathology. The question then arises whether we have found *any* social variables associated powerfully enough with some measure of psychopathology to justify establishing such a program: that is, has any unequivocally high risk group been identified? A review of the literature suggests that one large high risk group may exist, namely people undergoing marital disruption.

In 1975 more than three million persons were directly involved in a legally defined marital disruption in the United States. There were over one million divorces during this time period, and in each divorce an average of 1.22 children. Thus, two million adults and over one million children were affected by divorce in a single year, representing 1½ percent of the total United States population (Glick, 1975; U.S. Bureau of the Census, 1974; and U.S. Department of Health, Education, and Welfare, 1976).

These figures might have little interest to any group other than demographers were it not for the growing body of evidence that

marital disruption often constitutes a severe stress, the consequences of which can be seen in a surprisingly wide variety of
physical and emotional disorders. Persons undergoing marital
disruption have been shown to be at excess risk for psychiatric
disorders, suicide, homocide, motor vehicle accidents, and a
variety of forms of disease morbidity and disease mortality (see
Bachrach, 1975; Bloom, Asher, and White, Note 1).

In 1975 there were 2,126,000 marriages and 1,026,000 divorces
in the United States—nearly one divorce for every two marriages.
As is generally known, while the number of divorces has been
increasing dramatically, the marriage rate has stabilized and
actually begun to decrease. In 1968 the number of marriages
increased 7 percent over the preceding year; between 1968 and
1972, only 2 percent. Since 1972 the rate has been dropping—
over 4 percent between 1974 and 1975 (U.S. Department of
Health, Education, and Welfare, 1976). In contrast, the nationwide increase in divorce rate is continuing. From 1963 to 1968
the average annual increase was 5 percent, and since that time it
has averaged about 8 percent. In 1970, 6.9 percent of ever-married
persons between 25 and 54 years of age were currently divorced
or separated and by 1975 that figure had increased to 10.1 percent
(U.S. Bureau of the Census, 1975).

Nationwide, about 8 percent of unmarried persons age 15 and
above get married every year, and slightly over 2 percent of married persons get divorced every year. The age at first marriage has
increased by about six months in the past decade—from 22.8 to
23.1 years in the case of males and from 20.6 to 21.1 years for
females. In 1967 (the last year for which this information was reported), the median duration of marriages that ended in divorce
was seven years. Fifteen percent of divorces were obtained by persons married less than two years and 16 percent by persons married between two and four years. At the other extreme, 12 percent
of divorces were obtained by persons married 20 years or more
(National Center for Health Statistics, 1973a).

It is impossible to know at what level marriage and divorce
rates will stabilize. Laws regarding divorce are going through a
significant liberalization, and large numbers of monogamous
unions (especially but not exclusively among the young) exist
without a legal, and thus reportable, marriage having taken place.
If a larger proportion of legal marriages takes place after success-

ful periods of "trial marriage," one might anticipate leveling off followed by a reducation in divorce rate and a lengthening of time between marriage and divorce.

With regard to remarriage, a number of facts are worth noting. Remarriage rates appear to be keeping up with the rising divorce rate, and Glick (1975) has estimated that about four out of every five persons who get a divorce will eventually remarry. Among the divorced and widowed far more men (about 13 percent) remarry each year than women (only 4 percent). Remarriage rates are highest in the youngest age groups and decline steadily with increasing age. The peak age of remarriage for women is 20 to 24; for men, 25 to 29. Persons under 30 make up more than half of all remarriages.

Divorced persons remarry far more commonly than do widowed persons, a difference partly attributable to age differences, but whether divorced or widowed, the remarriage rate is far higher for men than for women. When remarriages are contrasted with first marriages, age differences between bride and groom increase significantly. In first marriages, for example, less than 2 percent of the brides are 10 or more years younger than grooms, but in remarriages the figure rises to 27 percent. Finally, most persons marry those of like marital status. Single men and women marry each other; widowers marry widows; and more than half of divorced persons marry other divorced persons. This latter finding is unusually significant because in the age group below 30, where most remarriages take place, there are far more eligible single people than divorced people (National Center for Health Statistics, 1973b).

Thus, in any community, one might anticipate special needs for older (above 30) persons with disrupted marriages, different and perhaps more complex problems among women than men, and special needs for the widowed. In addition, there appears to be a special affinity among divorced persons that serves to support a group or population orientation to human service programs for those who are undergoing marital disruption.

In considering the research studies linking marital disruption to physical and emotional disorders, it would be useful to keep in mind four general hypotheses that have been invoked to account for the obtained relationships. First, if physically or emotionally handicapped persons marry, their preexisting handicaps may reduce the likelihood that they will remain married. Second, physical or emotional disorders arising after marriage in either spouse may significantly reduce the likelihood that the marriage will continue. Third, the status of being married and living with one's spouse may reduce vulnerability to a wide variety of diseases or emotional disorders. Fourth, marital disruption may be a life stressor which can precipitate physical or emotional disorders in married people presumably already vulnerable to them but not yet affected. Since these hypotheses are not mutually exclusive, and in fact may all be true to some extent, it has been understandably difficult to develop research designs whose conclusions could support them differentially.

Of all the social variables whose relationships with the distribution of psychopathology in the population have been studied, none has been more consistently and powerfully associated with this distribution than marital status. Persons who are divorced or separated have been repeatedly found to be overrepresented among psychiatric patients, while married persons living with their spouses are underrepresented. In a recent review of eleven studies of marital status and the incidence of mental disorder reported during the past 35 years, Crago (1972) did not find a single exception to the following summary statement: admission rates into psychiatric facilities are lowest among the married, intermediate among widowed and never-married adults, and highest among the divorced and separated. The differential appears to be stable across different age groups (Adler, 1953), reasonably stable for each sex separately considered (Thomas and Locke, 1963; Malzberg, 1964), and as true for blacks as for whites (Malzberg, 1956).

Not only are highest admission rates reported for persons with disrupted marriages, but the differential between these rates and similarly calculated rates among the married is very substantial. In the most recent data available on a national level (for the year 1970), Redick and Johnson (1974) have shown that the ratio of admission rates for divorced and separated persons to those for married persons is around 18 to 1 for males and about 7 to 1 for females. In the case of admissions into public section outpatient clinics, admission rates are also substantially higher for persons with disrupted marraiges than for married persons—nearly 7 to 1 for males and 5 to 1 for females.

Another view of the magnitude of these differences can be seen from data we collected between 1969 and 1971 in the city of

Pueblo, Colorado (Bloom, 1975). Data from public and private inpatient facilities were combined but analyzed separately by sex and by whether the patient was admitted for the first time or had a prior history of inpatient psychiatrric care. In all cases, admission rates are substantially higher for patients with disrupted marriages (divorced and separated patients combined) than for patients married and living with their spouses. Specifically, with first admissions, rates for males with disrupted marriages are nine times higher than for males with nondisrupted marriages; among the females, the difference is around three to one. Among patients with histories of prior psychiatric care the differentials by marital status are greater for both sexes: 16 to 1 for males and 6 to 1 for females.

Another way of viewing the Pueblo data is to note that while divorced and separated males constitute only 6.5 percent of ever-married males age 14 and above, they constitute 46 percent of evermarried patients of both sexes in the same age span. Similarly, divorced and separated females constitute 8 percent of ever-married females age 14 and above but 32 percent of all ever-married patients in this age span. More than 7 percent of males with disrupted marriages are hospitalized annually because of a psychiatric condition—indeed, a quiet epidemic.

Two important sources of data serve to link marital disruption and suicidal behavior. First, Schneidman and Farberow (1961) have compared some personal characteristics of attempted and committed suicides from the year 1957 in Los Angeles County.* Thirteen percent of committed suicides were divorced and 8 percent were separated. Both of these figures are more than double what would have been expected from the proportion of divorced and separated persons in the general population of Los Angeles County. Furthermore, while about the same proportion of attempted and committed suicides are married and while about twice as large a proportion of single persons attempt as commit suicide, the divorced, separated, and widowed are significantly over-represented among those who commit suicide and significantly underrepresented among those who attempt it. Schneidman and

---

*Data regarding committed suicides were obtained from the Los Angeles coroner's office, and for attempted suicides from Los Angeles physicians, records of the Los Angeles County General Hospital, and records from the sixteen Los Angeles municipal emergency hospitals.

Farberow suggest that "it seems probable that the losses and disturbances in dyadic relationships occurring among the older groups, where more divorced, separated, and widowed appear, are also more likely to result in more lethal suicidal behavior" (p. 30). In a related study, Litman and Farberow (1961), proposing a strategy for undertaking emergency evaluations of self-destructive potentiality, note that "many suicide attempts, especially in young persons, occur after the separation from a spouse or loved one. . . . When there has been a definite loss of a loved person, such as a spouse, parent, child, lover, or mistress, within the previous year (by death, divorce, or separation), the potentiality for self-destruction is increased" (p. 51).

The second source of data linking suicide with marital status comes from the continuing reports of the National Center for Health Statistics. The most recent report (National Center for Health Statistics, 1970) covers the period 1959–61 and is based on an analysis of total U.S. mortality data. With particular reference to deaths from suicide, among white females the rate is higher among the divorced than any other marital status category and is more than three times the rate found in the married, while for white men it is also highest among the divorced and is more than four times as high as for married persons. For nonwhite females, the suicide rate is highest in the widowed and second highest in the divorced, where it is twice that of the married; and finally, among nonwhite males, it is highest in the divorced and is nearly two and one-half times as great as among the married.

The figures for deaths from homicide are even more striking. In both sexes and among both whites and nonwhites, risk of death by homicide is far higher for the divorced than for any other marital status group. With white women the risk is more than four times higher among the divorced than the married and with white men, more than seven times higher. Among nonwhites, the risk is twice as high among women and three times as high among men.

Two studies demonstrate excess vulnerability to motor vehicle accidents among the divorced. The analysis of total U.S. mortality data published by the National Center for Health Statistics (1970) shows that in both sexes and for whites and nonwhites alike, automobile fatality rates are higher among the divorced than among any other marital status group, averaging about three times as high as among the married. Second, a study by McMurray (1970) demonstrated that the accident rate of persons undergoing divorce doubled during the period between the six months before and the six months after the divorce date.

A variety of studies have attempted to link stress experiences to disease morbidity. Indeed, such linkages form the empirical basis of psychophysiological disease hypotheses. Holmes and Rahe (1967; also Rahe, McKean, and Arthur, 1967; Rahe, 1968; and Theorell and Rahe, 1970) have developed a measure of stressful life events based on the amount of readjustment required by each such event and have shown that this measure (in which marital disruption figures heavily) distinguishes persons likely to become ill from those not likely to become ill (see also Cline and Chesy, 1972).

Two recent studies suggest that alcoholism (both acute and chronic) is more prevalent among the divorced than among the married, a finding that corroborates much earlier literature. Wechsler, Thum, Demone, and Dwinnel (1972), studying the blood alcohol level of over 6,000 eligible consecutive admissions to the emergency service of Massachusetts General Hospital, found that "in both sexes, the divorced or separated had the highest proportion with positive Breathalyzer readings. . . . Divorced or separated men included 42 percent with positive alcohol readings" (p. 138). Widowers had the lowest proportion with positive readings (10 percent), and single (24 percent) and married (19 percent) men were intermediate. Rosenblatt, Gross, Malenowski, Broman, and Lewis (1971) contrasted first admissions with readmissions for alcoholism and concluded that their results "reveal a significant relationship between disrupted marriage and multiple hospitalizations for the acute alcoholic psychoses at ages below 45" (p. 1094); also see Woodruff, Guze, and Clayton, 1972).

Both the widowed and the divorced have higher age-adjusted death rates for all causes combined than do married persons of equivalent age, sex, and race. With respect to specific diseases, death rates from tuberculosis and cirrhosis of the liver are consistently higher among the divorced. Among white men and nonwhites of both sexes, death rate is higher among the divorced than among the married from malignant neoplasm of the respiratory system, and among nonwhite males it is higher among the divorced for diabetes mellitus and arteriosclerotic heart disease.

Finally, an extensive literature testifies to the generally negative consequences of marital disruption for the children in the disrupted family. While empirical studies are not numerous, there is some equivocal support for this general assertion, although few studies report data from control children in nondisrupted families, and many are based on a very limited number of cases.

There is no shortage of nonempirical literature on the subject of marital disruption and its consequences. Such publications range from autobiographical accounts (see, for example, Bageudor, 1972) to clinical reports of persons seen in psychotherapy whose problems were judged to be precipitated by, exacerbated by, or associated with marital disruption (see, for example, Stewart, 1963). Given the high frequency of marital disruption and its apparent role as a stressor, it is suprising and disappointing that so little is known in any systematic sense about the problems faced by persons undergoing marital disruption, although most research, including our own, suggests that the greatest stress is around the time of separation.

Relatively little is known about epidemiological aspects of marital separation. A review of marriage and divorce statistics collected in the 100 years ending in 1967 (National Center for Health Statistics, 1973a) reported that the most recent national statistics on length of separation were collected in 1907! Little is known about the current incidence of separation, or its resolution. Even less is known about how these factors are associated with age, sex, or subsequent marital histories. Part of the difficulty results from the fact that separation is not a legally reportable event.

Because there is so little information at the national level, we have recently completed a study designed to learn more about separation on the local level. In a telephone survey of a 4 percent sample of households conducted in the winter of 1975-76 in Boulder County, Colorado (Bloom, Hodges, Caldwell, Systra, and Cedrone, Note 1), it was found that one out of every 22 married couples separated during the previous year, that the average duration of all identified separations was 13 months, and that in more than 75 percent of the cases separations terminated in divorce. Furthermore, our study suggests that between 10 and 11 percent of randomly selected children under age 14 currently live in a home where their parents are either separated or divorced.

A review of the American literature suggests six specific stresses associated with marital separation. First, the psychological and emotional problems associated with a marriage breakup appear to be intense. The termination of a marriage is the death of a relationship, requiring constructive mourning and a coming to grips with the resulting sense of failure, shame, and low self-worth. Second, particularly among women, there often are stresses associated with the need to think about employment, career planning, or additional education preparatory to establishing an independent economic existence. Third, legal and financial problems often occur, creating additional stress. Separated women often find it impossible to get loans or establish charge accounts. Parental rights are often poorly understood. Fourth, with the change from a two-parent to a one-parent family setting, child-rearing problems frequently emerge. Fifth, particularly among men, problems regarding housing and homemaking appear. And sixth, for both men and women—particularly if they are beyond the early adult years—there are often serious difficulties in finding adequate social groups and experiences.

In spite of the fact that there is a large body of research and opinion regarding the stressful character of marital disruption, a careful search of the published literature of the past fifteen years has failed to uncover a single controlled study designed to reduce those stresses.

It is important to acknowledge at the outset that the concept of a "good divorce," that is, the idea of divorce counseling in contrast to marriage counseling, remains controversial in the literature. In fact, the existence of the controversy may help explain the lack of evaluated intervention programs for persons undergoing marital disruption. Basic to the anti-divorce counseling position is the fact that reconciliation is often seen as a far more desirable outcome to marital conflict than divorce. Rutledge (1963), for example, argues that "seldom does a divorce solve the fundamental personality problems resident in a marital situation" (p. 320), and Bodenheimer (1970) suggests that with the liberalization of divorce laws many couples turn to divorce rather than trying to rebuild their marriages. She urges that "care should be taken to avoid a complete swing of the pendulum from yesterday's marriage breakdown without recourse to divorce, to today's divorce without breakdown" (p. 219).

We would be remiss if we failed to mention what appears to us the most common (also completely unevaluated) effort at intervention in the case of marital disruption, namely the preparation and sale of books written specifically for persons undergoing marital disruption or for their children (see, for example, Gardner, 1970; Hunt, 1966; Krantzler, 1973; Lantz and Snyder, 1969; Mindey, 1969; Rohner, 1967; Weiss, 1975). In fact, Hunt suggests that "as fast as the divorce rate in America is rising, the output of books on divorce seems to be rising even faster" (1975, p. 4).

It would now be appropriate to examine more closely the four hypotheses that have been advanced to account for the associations found between marital disruption on the one hand and various physical and emotional disorders on the other. First, it has been asserted that persons with physical or emotional disorders who marry will be less likely to maintain a successful marriage than persons without preexisting disabilities. Our review of the literature indicates that data have not been collected in such a way that the validity of this hypothesis can be distinguished from that of the second hypothesis, which proposes that marital disruption may be significantly increased as a consequence of disabilities arising after marriage. These hypotheses suggest that psychopathology is the cause and marital disruption the consequence.

Turner describes the hypothesized relationship linking emotional disorder with subsequent marital disruption in terms of the incipient character of psychopathology that "makes marriage less likely and, given marriage, is likely to speed divorce or separation" (1972, p. 365). Srole and his colleagues make a similar point when they indicate that "elements of mental health may be crucially involved in determining whether or not individuals choose to marry; if they do so choose, whether or not they are successful in finding a spouse; and, if they are successful in this respect, whether or not the marriage is subsequently broken by divorce" (1962, p. 175). Briscoe and his colleagues, interpreting findings in their research, suggest that "one of the implications of finding such a significant amount of psychiatric illness in a divorced population is that psychiatric illness is probably a significant cause of martial breakdown" (Briscoe et al., 1973, p. 125).

Crago, in her review of research studies linking marital disruption and psychopathology, raises the same possibility, stating: "Studies of hospitalization rates and marital status are sometimes criticized because the differences in rates may be due to effects of mental disorders on the marital status of individuals before they are admitted to a mental hospital. For example, if mental disorders tend to lead to divorce, this would boost the rate of mental disorders among the divorced and at the same time decrease the rate for married persons" (1972, p. 115).

These two hypotheses can be tested through a single prospective research design that would assess physical and psychological functioning in individuals as well as couples at the time of marriage. The first hypothesis could be evaluated by following such a cohort over a number of years, by means of an annual physical and psychological evaluation determining the relationship between preexisting disability and marital adjustment and success. In addition, by identifying couples with postmarital onset of emotional or physical disability in a group judged healthy at the time of marriage, the second hypothesis could be evaluated. In this case one would need to examine the temporal relationships between disability onset after marriage and marital dissatisfaction or disruption. Undoubtedly, the cost and personal commitment required to complete a longitudinal study lasting perhaps a decade or longer have been a major reason why such studies have not been undertaken. Yet without them, it is possible neither to evaluate the hypotheses individually nor to differentiate between them.

The third hypothesis is that the status of being married reduces vulnerability to a wide variety of illnesses. Turner, for example, suggests that different marital statuses may place an individual in diffrent social systems which may vary in their supportive character, and thus that the "marriage state . . . is seen as protective against hospitalization" (1972, p. 365). In an interesting report by Dupont, Ryder, and Grunebaum (1971) regarding their study of 44 married couples in which one spouse had been diagnosed as psychotic and hospitalized, a surprisingly large number of couples reported that the problems associated with coping with the psychosis strengthened their marriages.

Syme has recently reviewed the statistics linking disease mortality and marital status and has concluded:

It may be instructive to recall the very wide range of conditions for which married people have lower mortality rates. The list of such conditions includes lower death rates for

respiratory tuberculosis, stroke, influenza, pneumonia, and can-
cer of almost all sites including cancer of the buccal cavity and
pharynx, the digestive organs, the respiratory system, the breast,
and the urinary system. While the possibility cannot be ruled
out, it is difficult to see how people who die of a stroke when
they are 70 or 80 years old were less likely to have gotten
married 50 years earlier. Further, if the marital state provides
an environment which reduces the risk of death from this
long list of conditions, it must be that a very profound and
important influence is at work which is certainly worthy of
prompt and careful study. By such detailed study of marital
status and its varied disease consequences, we may be able to
develop a whole set of insights about social processes and health
status. (1974, p. 1045)

The notion of the special protective power of being married
suggests that never-married persons and divorced and separated
persons matched for age and sex might have similar disease morbidity and mortality experiences. But the data clearly indicate that
never-married persons are at lower risk for most disorders than
persons undergoing marital disruption. Another hypothesis suggested by this explanatory concept is that in people equated for
age, length of marriage might be inversely related to a variety of
morbidity or mortality risks. To our knowledge, this hypothesis
has not been definitely examined.

Research intended to examine the hypothesis that marriage is a
special protective environment could be accomplished retrospec-
tively and has in fact been done with respect to certain disorders.
The Pueblo study (Bloom, 1975), for example, linked psychiatric
admissions rates to marital history. What is significant about this
research is that marital history data and not merely marital status
data were collected at the time of admission, thus allowing analysis not only of the relationship of current marital status to a specific disorder (the approach taken in most of the available literature)
but also of the effect of patterns of marital history on the evolution of a specific disorder. We found that six patterns were sufficient to identify the marital histories of 93 percent of ever-married
psychiatric inpatients (1975, p. 223) and that first inpatient
admissions and patients with prior histories of psychiatric inpatient
care differed significantly in the distribution of these martial his-

tory patterns. Through an analysis of marital history it is possible to address the questions of whether the benefits of the protective power of being married are outweighed by the relative stress of separation and divorce and whether total length of marriages, or time since separation and divorce, are related to subsequent vulnerability to physical and emotional disorder.

The fourth hypothesis is that the marital disruption constitutes a significant stressor. This hypothesis can be viewed within the rubric of crisis theory (see Caplan, 1964; Parad, 1965) and, of course, it is this hypothesis that has the greatest implication for primary prevention. The national psychiatric admission rate statistics already cited, which show a substantially higher admission rate for separated persons than for divorced persons, support this hypothesis.

Perhaps, more generally, contemporary role theorists would look for stress associated with particular status assignments and would see being separated or divorced as having particularly stressful role attributes. In 1960, for example, national mental health service statistics indicated that married women had mental illness rates twice as high as those of married men. In contrast, there were no appreciable sex differences between the admission rates of divorced or separated men and women. Gove (1972) used these figures to postulate a special vulnerability associated with the role of married women in western society. More recent statistics suggest that his hypothesis may no longer be tenable. In admission rates reported since 1970, sex differences for married patients have disappeared and sex differences for separated and divorced persons have emerged, with the male admission rate far higher than the female. What has remained stable over this time period, however, is the excessive admission rate, in both sexes, of the separated and divorced when contrasted with admission rates among the married.

But the situation is far from simple. The stressor hypothesis is not consistently supported in the literature. In a recent report by Aponte and Miller (1972), for example, the presence of stressful events in a sample of fifty state mental hospital patients was found to be more closely related to prior psychiatric hospital history than to variables associated with the current hospitalization. Morrison, Hudgens, and Brachha (1968), contrasting 100 psychiatric patients with a like number of general hospital patients, were not able to show greater life stresses in either the recent or remote past in the psychiatric patient population. There is substantial likelihood that serious methodological problems may exist in this type of research, and considerable work is presently under way to clarify the issues (see Brown, Sklair, Harris, and Birley, 1973; and Hudgens, Robins, and Delong, 1970, for example).

One example of a methodological problem is the question of how one identifies a stressful event—specifically, whether to call any life change stressful or whether to restrict the term to undesirable changes. B. S. Dohrenwend's research (1973a) suggests some support for using life change rather than undesirability as the defining characteristic, but Vinokur and Selzer (1973) found that "important correlates and possible contributors to human stress and emotional disturbances include undesirable life events but not desirable ones" (p. 330). Fortunately, in the case of marital disruption the issue may be relatively unambiguous, since most people appear to see it as undesirable (see Klassen, Roth, and Hornstra, 1974; Cochrane and Robertson, 1973). Other empirical issues and methodological problems include the selection of appropriate control groups, the question of whether stressful life events occur with differing frequency in certain specifiable demographic groups (see B. S. Dohrenwend, 1973b), and the validity of self-reports of stress (see Hudgens et al., 1970).

Research in the area of marital disruption as a life stress has been further complicated by the fact that the data support the notion that marital disruption and physical and emotional disorders are clearly interactive, in the sense that each has the potential to influence the other. These interactions have yet to be explored empirically, not only because of the methodological difficulties but also, in part, because of the complexity of the task (see B. P. Dohrenwend, 1975). One needs to identify and follow a cohort of married persons who differ in marital satisfaction but not in psychological well-being to determine if differential rates of psychopathology are subsequently generated. In a companion research program one needs to identify and follow married psychiatric patients to determine how their psychopathology has a subsequent effect on marital adjustment and disruption. Improved measures of marital adjustment, marital satisfaction, and mental health need to be developed before these programs can be successfully mounted.

Perhaps the most appropriate interpretation of the research that has been reviewed is that an unequivocal association between marital disruption and physical and emotional disorder has been demonstrated and that this association probably includes at least two interdependent components: first, illness (physical or emotional) can precede and can help precipitate marital disruption; and second, marital disruption can serve to precipitate physical and psychiatric difficulties in some persons who might otherwise not have developed such problems. Conversations with newly separated persons leave no doubt that separation is an important stressor.

There are a number of provocative issues requiring additional empirical study and conceptualization. First, while this review has not examined the literature related to the assessment of marital satisfaction and marital adjustment, it seems clear that the time is ripe for new attempts in this direction. General measures of marital satisfaction have been severely criticized of late (see Spanier, 1972, for example) and yet there is no clear direction in which research aimed at doing more than developing general measures must proceed. One approach which might be unusually fruitful would be to identify the spectrum of maritally related roles (both sex-specific and sex-independent) and to develop scales for assessing the degree to which these roles are satisfactorily carried out (see, for example, Weissman, 1975). The last decade has witnessed a sharp expansion in sex-independent marital roles and this trend seems likely to continue. With such a set of role specifications it would be possible to relate marital satisfaction to specific judged role performance, to contrast judgments of own and spouse role performance, and to relate the incidence of marital disruption to the failure of particular marital role performance.

Second, marital disruption and psychopathology are, as has been indicated, clearly interactive. Given that so little is known about these interactions, it would be perhaps timely to conduct exploratory interviews with samples of married, separated, and divorced psychiatric patients (and their spouses or ex-spouses) and ask them to serve as experts regarding the complex relationships between marital disruption or the potential for marital disruption on the one hand and psychological well-being on the other hand.

Third, the "sexual revolution" has brought with it the very

rapid development of life styles involving heterosexual fidelity without marriage. There is no persuasive reason to believe that disruption of these interpersonal bonds is any less stressful than of those between married partners. No systematic investigation of this form of marital disruption appears to have been reported thus far, although Rubin and Mitchell (1976) have recently reported on their studies designed to clarify the processes important in the establishment, maintenance, and dissolution of the relationships between dating couples. It is not difficult to develop the impression that there would be no shortage of persons who would willingly serve as participants in such a research program.

Fourth, it seems evident from the research literature that persons undergoing marital disruption are differentially vulnerable to its associated stresses. Research should be undertaken to identify those personal characteristics that make an individual undergoing marital disruption unusually prone to subsequent maladjustment—perhaps by intensively following a group of newly separated persons through the period of crisis, certainly not much longer than one year, and then by annual follow-up assessments for an additional year or two. It seems clear that for some people, marital separation is a stressor of the first magnitude, while for others it serves as the stimulus for releasing all that is their very best. The latter seem to thrive after separation, and it is easy to be optimistic that major differences between persons with these two reaction patterns can be found.

Fifth, the research findings to date spell out the justification and details of a limited intervention program which could be undertaken for a randomly selected group of persons undergoing marital disruption. We are currently seeking support for just such a program. The program need not be more than six months in length and should start as soon as possible after the physical separation of the couple. While it would be beyond the scope of this review paper to outline the characteristics of such an intervention program, it seems appropriate that it should include both counseling and educational competence-building components. One final thought regarding such an intervention program should be shared. Marital disruption, as a crisis, has two attributes which taken together make it unique. First, as has been suggested, it is exceedingly and increasingly common; and second, there are no crisis intervention procedures in effect within the society, as there are for example in the case of a death. These two attributes make marital disruption an irresistible candidate for preventive intervention programs which are well thought out, economically feasible, and subject to careful evaluation.

Sixth, it is appropriate to add a special disclaimer to this literature review, namely that it is limited to research published in the English language. It is true that the divorce rate is higher in the United States than in most other countries, but the problem of divorce and separation is not unique to the United States, and there appears to be a large non-English literature on the subject. The necessity for cross-national research in the case of marital disruption is not suggested pro forma, however, but rather because there is some evidence that substantially different types of problems may exist in different parts of the world. Our assertion, for example, that the stresses associated with marital disruption are particularly severe at the time of separation is true where there is no significant housing shortage. In Czechoslovakia where housing is in short supply, it is not uncommon for divorce to occur without the possibility of separation (Prokopec, Dytrych, and Schuller, Note 5). Under these circumstances it should not be surprising that a special set of problems occurs as a divorced couple (often with children) has no alternative but to continue to share essentially indivisible and often very limited living space. This final issue is, then, a recognition of the significant contribution which cross-national research in marital disruption can make to our increasing understanding of its causes and consequences.

When the history of twentieth-century efforts to control mental disorders is written, the great contribution of the last third of the century may well turn out to be the movement away from considering predisposing factors in mental illnesses toward concern with precipitating factors. This movement, away from a concern with the past and toward a concern with the present, has come about in part from a sense of frustration with our efforts at remediation. But in addition, a growing accumulation of empirical evidence has turned our attention away from the past. Kohlberg, LaCrosse, and Ricks (1972, p. 1233), for example, reviewing the literature linking childhood behavior and adult mental health, comment:

To conscious experience, moods change, anxieties disappear, loves and hates fade, the emotion of yesterday is weak, and the emotion of today does not clearly build on the emotion of yesterday. The trauma theory of neurosis is dead; the evidence for irreversible effects of early-childhood trauma is extremely slight. Early-childhood maternal deprivation, parental mistreatment, separation, incest—all seem to have much slighter effects upon adult adjustment (unless supported by continuing deprivation and trauma throughout childhood) than anyone seemed to anticipate.

In our concern with the development of effective preventive intervention programs, we find ourselves inexorably drawn to the simple dictum of Barrington Moore (1970, p. 5): "Human society ought to be organized in such a way as to eliminate useless suffering."

REFERENCES

Adler, L. M. The relationship of marital status to incidence of and recovery from mental illness. *Social Forces*, 1953, *32*, 185–194.

Aponte, J. F., and Miller, F. T. Stress-related social events and psychological impairment. *Journal of Clinical Psychology*, 1972, *28*, 455–458.

Bachrach, L. L. Marital status and mental disorder: An analytical review. DHFW Publication No. (ADM) 75–217. Washington, D.C.: U.S. Government Printing Office, 1975.

Baguador, E. *Separation: Journal of a marriage*. New York: Simon and Schuster, 1972.

Bloom, B. L. The medical model, miasma theory, and community mental health. *Community Mental Health Journal*, 1965, *1*, 333–338.

Bloom, B. L. *Changing patterns of psychiatric care*. New York: Behavioral Publications, 1975.

Bloom, B. L., Asher, S. J., and White, S. W. Marital disruption as a stressor: A review and analysis. *Psychological Bulletin* (in press).

Bloom, B. L., Hodges, W. F., Caldwell, R. A., Systra, L., and Cedrone, A. R. Marital Separation: A Community Survey. *Journal of Divorce*, 1977, *1*, 7–19.

Bodenheimer, B. M. New approaches of psychiatry: Implications for divorce reform. *Utah Law Review*, 1970, 191–220.

Briscoe, C. W., Smith, J. B., Robins, E., Marton, S., and Gaskin, F. Divorce and psychiatric disease. *Archives of General Psychiatry*, 1973, *29*, 119–125.

Brown, G. W., Sklair, F., Harris, T. O., and Birley, J. L. T. Life events and psychiatric disorders: 1. Some methodological issues. *Psychological Medicine*, 1973, *3*, 159–176.

Caplan, G. *Principles of preventive psychiatry*. New York: Basic Books, 1964.

Cline, D. W., and Chesy, J. J. A perspective study of life changes and subsequent health changes. *Archives of General Psychiatry*, 1972, *27*, 51–53.

Cochrane, R., and Robertson, A. The life events inventory: A measure of the relative severity of psycho-social stressors. *Journal of Psychosomatic Research*, 1973, *17*, 135–139.

Crago, M. A. Psychopathology in married couples. *Psychological Bulletin*, 1972, *77*, 114–128.

Dohrenwend, B. P. Sociocultural and social-psychological factors in the genesis of mental disorders. *Journal of Health and Social Behavior*, 1975, *16*, 365–392.

Dohrenwend, B. P., and Dohrenwend, B. S. *Social status and psychological disorder: A causal inquiry*. New York: Wiley-Interscience, 1969.

Dohrenwend, B. P., and Dohrenwend, B. S. Social and cultural influences on psychopathology. *Annual Review of Psychology*, 1974, *25*, 417–452.

Dohrenwend, B. S. Life events as stressors: A methodological inquiry. *Journal of Health and Social Behavior*, 1973, *14*, 167–175. (a)

Dohrenwend, B. S. Social status and stressful life events. *Journal of Personality and Social Psychology*, 1973, *28*, 225–235. (b)

Dohrenwend, B. S., and Dohrenwend, B. P. *Stressful life events: Their nature and effects.* New York: Wiley and Sons, 1974.

Dupont, R. L., Ryder, R. G., and Grunebaum, H. U. An unexpected result of psychosis in marriage. *American Journal of Psychiatry*, 1971, *128*, 735–739.

Gardner, R. A. *The boys and girls book about divorce.* New York: Science House, Inc., 1970.

Glick, P. C. *Some recent changes in American families.* (Current Population Reports, Series P-23, No. 52. Bureau of the Census.) Washington, D.C.: U.S. Government Printing Office, 1975.

Gove, W. R. The relationship between sex roles, marital status, and mental illness. *Social Forces*, 1972, *51*, 34–44.

Holmes, T. H., and Rahe, R. H. The social readjustment rating scale. *Journal of Psychosomatic Research*, 1967, *11*, 213–218.

Hudgens, R. W., Robins, E., and Delong, W. B. The reporting of recent stress in the lives of psychiatric patients. *British Journal of Psychiatry*, 1970, *117*, 635–643.

Hunt, M. M. *The world of the formerly married.* New York: McGraw-Hill, 1966.

Hunt, M. M. Review of *Marital separation*, by R. S. Weiss. *New York Times Book Review*, Nov. 30, 1975, p. 4.

Kellam, S. G., Branch, J. D., Agrawal, K. C., and Ensminger, M. E. *Mental health and going to school: The Woodlawn program of assessment, early intervention, and evaluation.* Chicago: University of Chicago Press, 1975.

Klassen, D., Roth, A., and Hornstra, K. Perception of life events as gains or losses in a community survey. *Journal of Community Psychology*, 1974, *2*, 330–336.

Kohlberg, L., LaCrosse, J., and Ricks, D. The predictability of adult mental health from childhood behavior. In B. Wolman (Ed.), *Manual of child psychopathology.* New York: McGraw-Hill, 1972.

Krantzler, M. *Creative divorce: A new opportunity for personal growth.* New York: M. Evans and Co., 1973.

Lantz, H. R., and Snyder, E. C. *Marriage: An examination of the man-woman relationship* (2nd ed.). New York: Wiley and Sons, 1969.

Litman, R. E., and Farberow, N. L. Emergency evaluation of self destructive potentiality. In N. L. Farberow and E. S. Schneidman (Eds.), *The cry for help.* New York: McGraw-Hill, 1961.

Malzberg, B. Marital status and mental disease among Negroes in New York State. *Journal of Nervous and Mental Disease*, 1956, *123*, 457–465.

Malzberg, B. Marital status and the incidence of mental disease. *International Journal of Social Psychiatry*, 1964, *10*, 19–26.

McMurray, L. Emotional stress and driving performance: The effect of divorce. *Behavioral Research in Highway Safety*, 1970, *1*, 100–114.

Mindey, C. *The divorced mother: A guide to readjustment.* New York: McGraw-Hill, 1969.

Moore, B., Jr. *Reflections on the causes of human misery and upon certain proposals to eliminate them*. Boston: Beacon Press, 1970.

Morrison, J. R., Hudgens, R. W., and Brachha, R. G. Life events and psychiatric illness. *British Journal of Psychiatry*, 1968, *114*, 423–432.

National Center for Health Statistics. *Mortality from selected causes by marital status*. (Series 20, No. 8A and B. U.S. Department of Health, Education, and Welfare.) Washington, D.C.: U.S. Government Printing Office, 1970.

National Center for Health Statistics. *100 years of marriage and divorce statistics: United States, 1867–1967*. (Vital and Health Statistics, Series 21, No. 24. Washington, D.C.: U.S. Government Printing Office, 1973. (a)

National Center for Health Statistics. *Remarriages: United States*. (Vital and Health Statistics, Series 21, No. 25.) Washington, D.C.: U.S. Government Printing Office, 1973. (b)

Parad, H. J. (Ed.). *Crisis intervention: Selected readings*. New York: Family Service Association of America, 1965.

Prokopec, J., Dytrych, Z., and Schuller, V. Rozvodova chovani a manzelsky nesoulad (Divorce and marital discord). *Vyzkumny Ustav Psychiatricky Zpravy*, No. 31, 1973.

Rahe, R. H. Life-change measurement as a predictor of illness. *Proceedings of the Royal Society of Medicine*, 1968, *61*, 44–46.

Rahe, R. H., McKean, J. E., Jr., and Arthur, R. J. A longitudinal study of life-change and illness patterns. *Journal of Psychosomatic Research*, 1967, *10*, 355–366.

Redick, R. W., and Johnson, C. *Marital status, living arrangements and family characteristics of admissions to state and county mental hospitals and outpatients psychiatric clinics, United States 1970*. (Statistical Note 100, National Institute of Mental Health.) Washington, D.C.: U.S. Government Printing Office, 1974.

Reid, D. D. Precipitating proximal factors in the occurrence of mental disorders: Epidemiological evidence. In E. M. Gruenberg and M. Huxley (Eds.), *Causes of mental disorders: A review of epidemiological knowledge, 1959*. New York: Milbank Memorial Fund, 1961.

Rohner, L. *The divorcee's handbook*. Garden City: Doubleday, 1969.

Rosenblatt, S. M., Gross, M. M., Malenowski, B., Broman, M., and Lewis, E. Marital status and multiple psychiatric admissions for alcoholism: A cross-validation. *Quarterly Journal of Studies on Alcohol*, 1971, *32*, 1092–1096.

Rubin, Z., and Mitchell, C. Couples research as couples counseling: Some unintended effects of studying close relationships. *American Psychologist*, 1976, *31*, 17–25.

Rutledge, A. L. Should the marriage counselor ever recommend divorce? *Marriage and Family Living*, 1963, *25*, 319–325.

Schneidman, E. S., and Farberow, N. L. Statistical comparisons between attempted and committed suicides. In N. L. Farberow and E. S. Schneidman (Eds.), *The cry for help*. New York: McGraw-Hill, 1961.

Spanier, G. B. Further evidence on methodological weaknesses in the Locke-Wallace Marital Adjustment Scale and other measures of adjustment. *Journal of Marriage and the Family*, 1972, *34*, 403–404.

Srole, L., Langnor, T. S., Michael, S. T., Opler, M. K., and Rennie, T. A. C. Mental health in the metropolis: The midtown Manhattan study. New York: McGraw-Hill, 1962.

Stewart, C. W. Counseling the divorcee. *Pastoral Psychology*, 1963, *14*, 10–16.

Syme, S. L. Behavioral factors associated with the etiology of physical disease: A social epidemiological approach. *American Journal of Public Health*, 1974, *64*, 1043–1045.

Theorell, T., and Rahe, R. H. Life changes in relation to the onset of myocardial infarction. In T. Theorell (Ed.), *Psychosocial factors in relation to the onset of myocardial infarction and to some metabolic variables—a pilot study*. Stockholm, Sweden: Department of Medicine, Seraphimer Hospital, Karolinska Institutet, 1970.

Thomas, D. S., and Locke, B. Z. Marital status, education and occupational differentials in mental disease. *Milbank Memorial Fund Quarterly*, 1963, *41*, 145–160.

Turner, R. J. The epidemiological study of schizophrenia: A current appraisal. *Journal of Health and Social Behavior*, 1972, *13*, 360–369.

U.S. Bureau of the Census. *Current population reports,* Series P-20, No. 271. *Marital status and living arrangements: March, 1974*. Washington, D.C.: U.S. Government Printing Office, 1974.

U.S. Bureau of the Census. *Current population reports*. Series P-20, No. 287. *Marital status and living arrangements: March, 1975*. Washington, D.C.: U.S. Government Printing Office, 1975.

U.S. Department of Health, Education, and Welfare. Births, marriages, divorces, and deaths for 1975. *Monthly Vital Statistics Report*, 1976, *24*, (12), 1–8.

Vinokur, A., and Selzer, M. L. Life events, stress, and mental disorders. *Proceedings, 81st Annual Convention, American Psychological Association*, 1973, 329–330.

Wechsler, H., Thum, D., Demone, H. W., Jr., and Dwinnel, J. Social characteristics and blood alcohol level. *Quarterly Journal for the Study of Alcoholism*, 1972, *33*, 132–147.

Weiss, R. S. *Marital separation*. New York: Basic Books, 1975.

Weissman, M. M. The assessment of social adjustment. *Archives of General Psychiatry*, 1975, *32*, 357–365.

Woodruff, R. A., Jr., Guze, S. B., and Clayton, P. J. Divorce among psychiatric out-patients. *British Journal of Psychiatry*, 1972, *121*, 289–292.

DISCUSSION BY STEPHEN E. GOLDSTON

Dr. Bloom has identified an important public mental health problem. Such a problem, by definition, requires systematized social or community action for resolution, affects large aggregates of population, has high incidence or prevalence rates, and calls for identifying and enumerating populations at risk.

The convincing biometric data on the relation of marital disruption to psychiatric hospitalization rates, accident rates, incidence of disease occurrence, and other indices cited by Dr. Bloom raise some perplexing questions. These data have been known for years, yet no significant efforts have been made on a major scale to do research or to program interventions on behalf of the populations at risk. Why? Several hypotheses come to mind: (a) researchers may be unaware that public health concepts are relevant and can be applied, and, particularly, they may be unfamiliar with epidemiological approaches; (b) researchers may have sensed an impending disapproval by application grants review committees about research projects on such multifaceted social problems as marital disruption; and (c) there may not be enough applied behavioral scientists who can both amass and analyze large data banks and then proceed to apply relevant intervention strategies and techniques.

My point clearly reflects two biases. First, public health concepts and values are directly relevant to mental health work. Second, researchers have a social responsibility (what Dr. Ansbacher termed a maturity on the part of the researcher) to apply knowledge on behalf of populations at risk. Emory Cowen's paper* addresses a point that is equally germane: the need for

*See above, pp. 7-24.

clarity about what mental health workers can and cannot do. If mental health workers are not now capable of doing research, providing services, and developing interventions for large-scale problem areas like marital disruption, such competencies should begin to be developed immediately.

Dr. Bloom's action research proposal contains elements common to other stress or crisis situations viewed from a public health perspective. Much of my work during the past two years has been focused on the mental health aspects of the Sudden Infant Death Syndrome (SIDS), especially the needs of surviving parents and siblings. I see many similarities between the interventions proposed by Bloom for the area of marital disruption and my SIDS activities. Eight elements appear to characterize such interventions. First, by definition, the issue is a public health problem. Second, physical as well as mental health factors are involved. Third, entire families, rather than just individuals, are implicated. Fourth, loss and separation (i.e., attachment-detachment-reattachment) are major considerations. Fifth, numerous community agencies and resources participate in interventions. Sixth, although mental health workers may not be the sole or even the key group of helpers, they must provide active outreach, rather than waiting passively for the psychiatric casualties to appear at the doors of mental health facilities. Seventh, mutual-help support systems are vital to the success of any community intervention program. And eighth, such interventions deal with "transition states" among persons in crisis, a concept that Tyhurst (1957) first identified twenty years ago but which until recently was not widely known among mental health workers.

A model based on these elements is evolving for primary preventive interventions in crisis situations. As a result, we have an opportunity for incorporating public health approaches into community mental health practice, thereby demonstrating that primary prevention approaches are feasible and productive. To the extent that the mental health field can respond to these opportunities, we may find that such pioneering work points the way to more effective mental health services directed at early intervention and education, with the consequence being a decrease not only in psychiatric morbidity but in the misery and anguish associated with maladjustment and failure to cope adequately.

Bloom's paper reminds us that there are other areas beyond

marital disruption that hold similar promise for meaningful interventions. Though the data are not as convincing as those which
Bloom presented in his review of the literature on marital disruption, biometric data do exist for other large populations at risk for
mental illness or needless psychopathology: I refer to the aged
living alone, elderly bereaved surviving spouses, young children
who have lost a parent through death, and pregnant women with a
past history of mental illness. Additionally, in the absence of
massive supporting biometric data, there are presumptive evidence,
anecdotal material, and accumulated clinical impressions to suggest other groups at high risk, such as parents who lose a child
from the Sudden Infant Death Syndrome, children of divorce, and
the offspring of alcoholics.

Need for planned interventions exists at two points: before the
onset of a normative developmental crisis, using anticipatory
guidance approaches, and immediately after the traumatic event.
Opportunities also exist for preventing "learned helplessness"—a
concept which will prove to be of increasing applicability in the
years ahead.

One might ask whether such endeavors, working with groups at
high risk, are appropriate concerns for mental health workers. In
response, I quote the recent report of the American Psychological
Association Task Force on Health Research (1976): "The assessment of life styles and life crises as they affect near-future illness . . . is certainly a proper study for psychology"—to which I
would add, "if not for all people in the mental health field."
Yet a review of NIMH research grants indicates that little work is
being done on life styles and life crises.

A computer printout I requested from the NIMH data bank on
all research grants and contracts from 1965 to the present listed 47
projects on the subjects of marital separation, marital stress, and
divorce. Twenty-six of these, however, actually had nothing to do
with the subjects: 15 related to the treatment of marital pairs; six
dealt with difficulties and adjustment in marriage; four focused on
communications in marriage; and one fit most appropriately into an
"other" category. On the subjects of divorce and marital separation,
there were three projects each. From my perspective, all the projects fell short of center target; they were tangential in terms of
their salience to major issues requiring investigation. In brief, much
research in the area of marital disruption remains to be done.

Similarly, research on other life crises areas is not being carried out, at least with NIMH grant support, at this time. Indeed, the ongoing NIMH inventory of research grants on primary prevention reveals few projects focused on any crisis area. There are no research projects about coping mechanisms in crises, on techniques of crisis intervention or counseling, or on specific subpopulations at risk. Are the writers and reviewers of research grant applications perceiving life crises as taboo subjects—best left unexplored, like the prevailing popular view about the crisis of death? These critically important areas *must* be investigated.

DISCUSSION BY IRWIN ALTMAN

Participants at many conferences argue about the importance of distinguishing between applied and basic research, between academic and real-world orientations, between the laboratory and the field settings, between analysis and synthesis. Bloom's paper suggests that instead of being sidetracked by these pseudo issues, we must focus on key philosophical issues.

Psychology is said to be the study of behavior. I suggest it should be defined as the study of behavior in naturally occurring intact social units: families, couples, teams, and communities. The traditional approach has been to study such individual, fragmented, separate behavior as aggression or love. Some of the papers at this conference have spoken about the individuals as the object of study. Bloom, on the other hand, talked about marital units and disrupted couples. One of the differences between so-called "academic oriented" approaches and "relevant applied oriented" approaches has to do with what is described as the unit to be studied. Bloom clearly focused on a unit of behavior that was naturally occurring; a great deal of our research does not. A few years ago, Ivan Steiner wrote an article entitled, "Whatever happened to the group?"—an excellent example of the issue I am raising. The critical point is not basic versus applied study or real-world versus hypothetical irrelevant study, but what kinds of social units to study.

Bloom's paper raises important theoretical issues, and although he does not present us with a theory, he does lay down some important dimensions. The first (which he suggested but did not articulate) is this very need to ask ourselves what units of behavior we should be studying. A second is that we must begin to think more about concepts of causation. We tend to accept a linear model of causation—that A leads to B, to C, and to D. The fact is, as Bloom and others have commented, that the world does not work this way. We live in a multicausal linear world, and Bloom's analysis of disrupted couples (social units that are no longer intact) reflects a multicausal approach. In our research we try to discover a particular link between phenomena, but that does not mean that at a conceptual level the link really works this way; in fact, according to Bloom's review, it may be almost irrelevant to ask what causes what at some levels of understanding a phenomenon. In a complex system there are many relationships, and when you begin to integrate them, you are at a particular level of understanding and theorizing—a level usually considered higher, but not necessarily reflecting any better real-world relationships.

Finally, there is no single way to intervene in a malfunctioning system. A single intervention will reverberate elsewhere. Because of the mechanics of the setting, most of us who do "basic" research have accepted the linear mode of thinking, and we have forgotten that there is a difference between how you conceptualize research and how you actually do it.

SELECTED DISCUSSION

Dr. Bloom was asked several questions about the philosophy of helping: should the effort be concentrated toward ameliorating serious mental disorder or toward alleviating general unhappiness and maladjustment?

Dr. Bloom: We must view communities as collections of interdependent people, not as the advantaged and disadvantaged. The world is not divided up that way. We are all disadvantaged in some ways and advantaged in others. In an ideal community—which we are trying to establish in a trailer park in Boulder—I wish to set things up so that we can identify the strengths of everyone in the community. The objectives are Utopian in response to the conviction that what is missing in our communities and in our lifestyle is the concept of social supports. Psychologists develop poor social support systems, and social workers do no better. A profession should not be designed to be the social support of the community; rather, people support each other. The ideal community-wide prevention service is the deliberate development of comprehensive social support systems. My present concern is marital disruption. A person in need of help—for this problem or any other—ought to be able to find it, because there are other persons trying to be helpful. A social support system is far more useful for creating a growth-inducing community than training and employing more caretakers.

III
Theoretical Approaches to Mental Health

7

Strange Bedfellows:
The Yogi and the Commissar

ROBERT SOMMER

Robert Sommer received his Ph.D. in Psychology in 1956 from the University of Kansas. Since that time he has served as a Research Psychologist at the Saskatchewan Hospital in Canada, as Assistant Professor of Psychology and Director of the Psychological Clinic at the University of Alberta, as Associate Director of Research at the Alcoholism Foundation of Alberta, as an Assessment Officer in the Peace Corps, and as a Psychologist at the Mendocino State Hospital. He has also been a Visiting Professor in the Department of Architecture at the University of California (Berkeley) and the University of Washington. He is presently Professor of Psychology and Environmental Studies at the University of California (Davis), where he has been since 1964.

His six books include Personal Space *(1969)*, Design Awareness *(1972)*, Tight Spaces *(1974)*, Street Art *(1975)*, and The End of Imprisonment *(1976)*. He has been a consultant to various state and federal agencies and has worked on many design projects: bicycle paths, college dormitories, geriatric housing, airports, and offices.*

In his influential essay, *The Yogi and the Commissar*, Arthur Koestler contrasts two styles of social change (Koestler, 1942). The yogi tries to change the world from the inside out, the commissar from the outside in. This is the romantic versus the rational —the yoga night and its dreams opposed to the commissar's day and conscious plans. Because the essay was written in the heat of World War II, it is easy to understand why Koestler was primarily concerned with political beliefs; but his typology is equally applicable to psychology. Prototypic examples of the yoga approach in psychology are biofeedback training and meditation, techniques designed to give people control over their inner processes. Prototypic examples of the commissar approach are the token economy and environmental psychology. Like Koestler, I am using the anthropologist's method of ideal types rather than describing the myriad hybrids, mutations, and mixtures of these styles that actually exist. The yogi and the commissar are exemplars rather than typical patterns. It is unlikely we could find a pure commissar in the Soviet Union or in *Walden Two* or a pure yogi in India or Esalen. By a pure commissar I mean someone who has no interest in trying to change individuals through education or training, and by a pure yogi I mean a person who has no interest in changing institutions or environmental conditions.

For the yogi, the personal is more important than the political—you have to change your own head before you can do anything else. Working politically therefore means changing one's own consciousness and that of other people. This can be done through some combination of education, exhortation, psychotherapy, meditation, biofeedback, body work, and natural foods. The current interest in transcendental meditation (TM) illustrates the continuing popularity of the yoga approach. The mayor of my city recently launched a seven-week campaign to bring TM to Davis, California, and make this an ideal city. If more people meditated, he asserted, crime would be reduced, tension would disappear, job efficiency would increase, student grades would rise, and personal relationships would improve. Unlike most practitioners of other therapy techniques on today's market, advocates of TM are quick to cite research studies supporting their views: they claim that the number of crimes and accidents begins to decrease when one percent of the community practices it. Apparently five percent is needed for substantial change:

> *Just as it takes only one light bulb to light a whole room, with five percent of our city practicing the TM technique, the orderly and positive influence of meditators will be so intense, that problems and suffering will begin to fade away in all areas of our community.* (California Aggie, *1976)*

Jerry Rubin, the social activist of the sixties transformed into the psychological explorer of the seventies, announced that the revolution of today is taking place inside people's heads (Rubin, 1976). Rubin foresees social change through the determined efforts of an elite that is "together" in mind and body who will conduct workshops, set up encounter groups, establish natural food stores, and conduct alpha rhythm training in the hinterland. When they have created a significant level of awareness in the general population, the existing social order will topple and be replaced by a more humane one. This is somewhat different from the TM people, who, like the advocates of the psychedelic movement a few years ago, use an additive model of social change, with room for dynamic increments when a critical mass is reached. Both approaches rely upon the principle that you can change society by changing individuals. Most education and psychotherapy in America follow the yoga model. Teaching Johnny to read, or giving him some insight into his behavior, will improve the world to some degree. If there are enough increments of improvement, we will have an educated, rational, aware citizenry that will evolve methods for handling crime, poverty, racism, and other serious social problems.

The commissar advocates a different solution to society's ills. He believes that to change people is difficult at best and inadequate in any case as a long-range solution. Individuals are formed by the environment, and the only way to change them is to change the environment. Also been described as the environmental or materialistic position, this is exemplified by the design theory of Buckminster Fuller (Fuller, 1972). "Reshape the environment," Fuller declares, "don't try to reshape people." When the environment is properly designed, people will behave properly. Adherents of this approach would include behavior mod practitioners, environmental psychologists, and Marxist psychologists, who feel that without changes in the larger social system, individual change is of little value and will not in any event make a dent in the enormous amount of individual and social pathology. The commissar follows Lenin's theory that the contents of consciousness are an intensive reflection of the material conditions of society (Koran, 1972). Koestler defines the commissar as the human type who has completely severed his relations with his subconscious.

Just as there are different schools of yoga, there are different types of commissars. When a Skinnerian and a Sierra Club member describe themselves as environmentalists, they mean different things. Skinnerians identify the environment with reinforcement contingencies, Marxists with social institutions and ownership of the means of production, Sierra Club members with the natural world, and environmental psychologists with the experienced environment. Skinner and his associates have not been particularly interested in wildlife preservation, Sierra Clubbers have tended to neglect the built environment and concentrate their efforts on wildlife and wilderness areas, Marxists have not been particularly strong supporters of the ecology movement in this country or anywhere else, and environmental psychologists are not closely identified with either behavior modification or Marxism and they have not been noteworthy as environmental activists.

Koestler maintained that the yogi and the commissar differ primarily along the means-end dimension. The commissar believes that the ends justify any means; the yogi regards the means as everything, since the ends are unpredictable. For reasons that I do not fully understand, this analysis seems more appropriate for understanding political than psychological ideologies. The yogi and the commissar of psychology share the same long-range dream of a world without poverty, unemployment, crime, and mental illness. The difference between them centers on the means by which this is to be reached. It is expressed in conflicts about whether money and programs should go toward attempts to change institutions or should go directly to people. For example, is it more important to renovate a school building or to use the money to hire more teachers? Is it better to build new public housing for people or to provide more mental hygiene clinics, social workers, and other people services? The question I have been asked numerous times as an environmental psychologist is which is the cart and which is the horse.

When my associates and I attempted to improve mental hospital environments, we were told that this was a trivial task. "Brains, not bricks" was the main need, asserted Karl Menninger. Psychotherapy could be done in a ramshackle building provided one had a dedicated staff and the right sorts of patients. It would be nice to brighten up the walls, install better plumbing, and improve the lighting, but if resources are limited, and they always are, the highest priority should go to hiring more staff. The same argument appeared when I became involved with prison architecture. The yogi position was succinctly stated by Austin McCormack when he declared that with the right staff, he could rehabilitate criminals in an old red barn (Sommer, 1976); the highest priority should therefore go to hiring more correctional staff, increasing the number of therapy programs, improving vocational education and basic skills, and so on. Yes, it would be nice if each inmate had a single cell, with decent lighting and plumbing and if the institution were painted in brighter colors, but the highest priority should go toward obtaining more and better staff. The same argument appeared when we attempted to change school environments. The real problem, we were told, was not the desks bolted to the floor, the drab institutional environment, the forbidding wire mesh fence around the building, but the relationship between teacher and students. Rather than putting money into new buildings, it would be preferable to hire more teachers and guidance counselors and arrange more in-service training workshops.

Even though I am a member of the Sierra Club and I like trees, wildlife, and marshlands, I have never considered myself anti-people. I have the greatest respect and sympathy for the teacher attempting to work with 30 pupils or the mental hospital so badly staffed it cannot afford therapy programs. I will also admit that artists have painted masterpieces in basements and many of the most effective drug rehabilitation programs have taken place in ramshackle old houses that didn't meet local fire and safety codes. Heroes can triumph in spite of poor environmental conditions. But heroes can usually look after themselves quite well; in most cases they triumph *in spite of* oppressive environmental conditions. It is the worst sort of paleologic to believe that drab, overcrowded, and inflexible buildings improve programs.

On the road to utopia there is not one horse and one cart but many. The horse that stands in front of one cart stands behind another. Arguments about which comes first imply a limited view of the road. When it comes to social change, we have to reform institutions and improve environmental conditions *and* change people's attitudes. Within the same long-range strategy there are innumerable combinations and sequences of tactical moves that will generate public awareness and create a proper climate for meaningful reform. Biofeedback is being used to make people more sensitive to environmental cues. A business executive may be taught to monitor her stomach muscles to detect incipient anxiety and thus head off an ulcer attack. Operant conditioning is preceded today with a verbal contract between client and therapist, in which the details and goals of the procedure are discussed and the reward system is negotiated. City planning is becoming increasingly involved with citizen participation in all stages of the design process.

My title describes the yogi and the commissar as strange bedfellows. "Fellow" in its Icelandic origins means a lying together.
When it comes to accomplishing anything significant, the yogi and
the commissar cannot occupy twin beds; they have to know one
another in the biblical sense and be of different sexes to produce
offspring who are equipped both to change people's heads and to
change environments. Anyone who has been involved in social
change knows that the movements, like lovemaking, are nonlinear:
for every motion forward there are many to the sides and always
some backward motion. Such encounters are as spatial as sequen-
tial. The great push of the 1950's to reform mental hospitals
meant undertaking campaigns on several fronts simultaneously:
investing money to improve old buildings and building new ones
to relieve overcrowding; hiring new staff and training existing staff
through in-service programs; developing new treatment methods
and delivering them as needed; and educating the public to the
value of all these programs and the desirability of community
treatment. If any step had been omitted, the entire effort would
have succeeded less well. There is little point in preparing chronic
patients for discharge if there are no places outside for them to go.
This remains a source of frustration in many institutions for the
retarded. Training programs have brought severely retarded individuals to the point where they no longer need 24-hour institutional
care, but there are not enough foster homes. This is another way
of saying that the state will not pay foster families enough money.
If the State of California, for example, were willing to pay foster
families the $45 a day that it costs to keep a severely retarded
child in a state hospital, an ample supply of foster homes would
appear. That money alone is not the root of the problem became
apparent in the numerous hospitals that were able to improve
ward conditions, discharge rates, and community acceptance with a
very nominal increase in budget. Some of the most productive
programs in state hospitals during the 1950's, such as the tremen-
dous increase in use of volunteers, cost little extra money (Mering
and King, 1957). Charismatic leadership and commitment to
reform were more important than the staff-patient ratio and an
increased budget. The reform movement was aided tremendously
by the new somatic therapies and the introduction of new staff
from a variety of professional backgrounds. Almost every combination of the yogi and the commissar approach was used. Sometimes

therapy was successful in an old red barn. Sometimes the reforms were successful as long as a charismatic figure was still there, but once she left and the outside funds dried up, the reforms, lacking a structural base in the community or the institution itself, were quickly eroded. It was necessary to change staff attitudes and community attitudes and to change environmental conditions and role relationships and treatment methods at the same time.

ENVIRONMENTAL PSYCHOLOGY

We may now ask how the emerging field of environmental psychology fits into all this. Environmental psychologists think more like commissars than yogis, though not exclusively, since their subject matter is the interrelationship between people and their surroundings. Important topics in this emerging field are such subjective phenomena as mental maps, landscape preferences, crowding, density, and other spatial behaviors. We do not study buildings as pure form or great hollow sculpture but rather as residences, workshops, or symbolic places. A major problem is conceptualizing levels of environment. A school building is not a single setting but many related spaces. A single classroom contains numerous micro-environments: the front of the room has a different significance, to the teacher as well as the students, than the middle or the rear; the area next to the window has more natural light, is often colder, and may be more distracting. The child's location in the room, the teacher's location, the arrangement of chairs, tables, and desks, the heating and light levels, all affect what goes on there. The class routine will also be affected by noise from the corridor, school policies on recesses and discipline, the style of teaching, the ratio of students to teacher, and so on. The schools' policies themselves are affected by the character of the surrounding neighborhood, attitudes of the school board, budgetary vicissitudes, and Supreme Court decisions. To paraphrase John Donne, no behavior setting is an island.

Much remains to be done in educating both our clients and our colleagues about the interdependency of physical and social systems. There has been a tendency to consider institutions as roles and rules without physical attributes, so that improvements in the physical plant of the prison, say, are perceived as "not really" changing the prison, Institutions, however, also include buildings, open spaces, and various other structures, all interdependent. A change in one part of the system will produce reverberations elsewhere. Changing the people in the way that a yogi might advocate, through either education or meditation, will be likely to change their use of a building and their interpretation of the rules; changing the rules will change the use patterns and the behavior of the occupants; altering the building will change both behavior and work patterns. Such changes are not always reflected in short-term productivity measures. This is also true of psychotherapy and of such techniques as meditation and body work. Using production records, there is no evidence that any of these techniques improves performance in factory, classroom, or office. The investigator who introduces environmental changes may have to settle for proximate criteria of success, such as improved morale based on self-report and supervisors' ratings. A government office, even one involving 200 employees, is still a case study with an N of 1. It is very difficult to prove causality in a single case unless one has the capability of the Skinner box to systematically alter contingencies over a long period of time.

Any program of social change will affect the physical environment, and any program to alter the physical environment will affect people. Revisions in Medicare payments will affect hospital utilization rates and, ultimately, hospital construction and the layout of facilities. Giving students more voice in school policies will affect their use of corridors and yard spaces and perhaps the layout and decoration of classroom spaces, and in the long run is likely to affect school design. Unwillingness to recognize the interdependency between social and physical systems, and between people and the environment, has resulted in the failure of many worthwhile programs. In explaining the problems encountered by compensatory education programs, sociologist Amitai Etzioni declared:

> It seems to me that the key reason for the failure of compensatory education lies in the fact that the disadvantaged children are locked into total environments, which include home, neighborhood, parental poverty, discrimination, and inhibiting models of behavior. We cannot hope to change one without changing the other. (Etzioni, 1972)

John Hill of Cornell agrees. "Headstart and similar programs," he states, "do not seem to be innoculations of social and cognitive vaccines that give everlasting benefits regardless of the environment in which they occur" (Hill, 1971). Since social programs cannot be expected to have environment-free effects, we must develop neighborhood supports for new social programs. This requires a radical departure from the experimental model introduced into the social sciences from physics and chemistry. Rather than altering one variable at a time, we must *deliberately* change many things at once. Changing one aspect of a complex situation and trying to hold everything else constant is a prescription for ineffectiveness. It is not enough to provide open-plan schools; one must also train teachers how to use them, provide the educational hardware to make them work, and develop new teaching-learning roles appropriate to the setting. The independent variable is not the building itself but a whole constellation of changes. Philip Zimbardo, on a tape of his experiences with simulated prison, justifiably expressed displeasure with his colleague who inquired what the independent variable was (Haney, Banks, and Zimbardo, 1973). The independent variable was the entire prison situation, which included the basement of the Stanford Psychology building, the rules and policies set by the experimenters, the guards' uniforms and the degrading clothing worn by inmates, and everything else that impinged upon the participants. In a study attempting to change a single aspect of the environment, such as lighting or plumbing, a critical variable will be to involve the occupants in the planning process. I cannot conceive of a study of a school, office, or factory in which it would be accurate to say that "only" lighting was changed. When one alters the lighting, one changes the people—even in the fact that one hasn't consulted them.

Environmental psychologists have coped with the interdependence of causal conditions in a number of ways. Urban-area studies that try to isolate out causes of stress and mental illness statistically usually come out with inconsistent results. The main reason, of course, is that poor environmental conditions are causally related to low income, lack of education, bad housing, and poor medical care, and in cases where these relationships do not hold—such as poor people who have the same amount of space as middle-income people—unusual circumstances are operating.

Some researchers have attempted to deal with interdependence by creating stress artificially in the laboratory. Ethical considerations severely limit the degree to which this can be done with humans. Generally speaking, the laboratory approach has not been very successful in yielding positive results. Jonathan Freedman has shown that the short-term crowding of college students does not have much short-term or long-term effect (Freedman, 1975). Studies of confined astronauts and aquanauts and people who have lived for weeks in simulated civil defense shelters have also producted negative results.

Some environmental psychologists feel that the strongest support for the environmental approach comes not from correlational studies of cities or from laboratory studies with college sophomores, but from studies of animal populations. In the early days of environmental psychology, there was a love affair between us and such animal biologists as Hediger, Lorenz, Kummer, and Wynne-Edwards, who had been investigating the spatial needs of animals. Whatever passion originally fed the romance seems to have dissipated. There was also Daniel Calhoun's classic study of his mouse utopia (Calhoun, 1973). His best known experiment began in June 1968, when four male and four female mice were placed in a 10-x-10-x-10-foot air-conditioned enclosure and given all the food and water they needed and total protection from predators. When the population reached 150 and all the desirable physical spaces and meaningful social roles were occupied, things went downhill. Breeding ceased completely when the population reached 2,200 and extinction of the colony became inevitable; the last mouse died in 1973.

Calhoun's experiment provides strong support for an environmental approach to stress. I have some misgivings, however, about following the examples of the learning researchers who renounced the study of natural situations in favor of the animal laboratory where total control was possible. Animal learning became a subject in its own right and lost all connection with schools, teachers, and pupils. Recent attempts to apply operant conditioning and other learning principles in the schools are independent of the earlier animal research. The investigators have had to develop new techniques suitable to the school situation and to the ethical demands of society, and they have drawn very little (except perhaps inspiration) from the animal studies. Montrose

Wolfe a pioneer in applying behavioral modification in the schools, declared:

I thought that we would have to do a lot of precise animal research before we would be ready to work with people. I was wrong. Almost none of the animal research has been used in the behavior modification field. . . . If we had never done any animal work that went beyond the research in Skinner's first book, we would be doing essentially the same thing we're doing now. (Goodall, 1973)

EVALUATION MODEL

The lack of success in laboratory studies with humans and the difficulties in generalizing from laboratory studies with animals have led some researchers, including myself, to advocate the use of an evaluational model. Evaluation is the study of programs that are in operation to determine their effectiveness in relation to cost and conditions. It operates under different constraints and time-tables than experimental research even when it involves a before-and-after assessment. Evaluation has generally been neglected in graduate training, and as a result psychologists often attempt to apply the experimental model in situations where an evaluation model would be more appropriate. Evaluation attempts to determine whether an overall package of environmental changes has any effect along a good-bad dimension (comfort-discomfort, sickness-health, satisfaction-dissatisfaction, attractiveness-ugliness) without spending too much time trying to untie the package and find specific causal relationships. The main concern is on major before-and-after changes rather than multiple and partial correlations using demographic variables. A third-order interaction between age, religion, social status, and stress is probably a statistical artifact. Even if it does happen to check out in a replication study, chances are it is of little practical importance.

Frances Carp studied a relocation project in San Antonio in which ambulant elderly people moved from tacky boarding houses and tenements into a new apartment complex for the elderly (Carp, 1966). In the new environment, social life blossomed and most everyone felt better off. Using an evaluational approach, Carp attempted to see which elements of the new situation were more satisfying than others. She asked people about the availability of public transit, adequacy of medical facilities, and satisfaction with the new neighborhood, as well as questioning them about more specific items—the new stoves, washers and dryers, lighting, and elevators. The move was seen as a constellation of related factors which could be asked about separately and which were conceptually related. Such research works best when it is done in conjunction with the agency that has responsibility over the setting, as the San Antonio Public Housing Corporation had in Carp's study, so that there can be feedforward to future projects.

The evaluational model requires a different timetable from a research model. An eighteen-month delay between writing a report and seeing it in print is inappropriate for disseminating information on a new government program. We must overcome our professional reputations as pathologists of dead programs. A study of relocated institutionalized elderly patients which showed a significant increase in death rate right after the move achieved its impact upon legislators, regulatory agencies, and in court decisions *before* the results ever appeared in a journal (Bourestom and Tars, 1974). Timing is crucial in evaluational studies. Quick-and-dirty methods that produce results in six months' time are likely to have more impact on legislative action than a more comprehensive and expensive study that appears two years after the program has ended. Evaluational research should not be a single major study but a linked series of ongoing studies, each feeding information to policymakers in order to influence the course of the program. This kind of involvement on the part of the researcher is, I realize, anathema to the laboratory investigator. I would not advocate a 100-percent shift from long-run to short-run studies, since this is not an either-or matter. We need both, and we have to understand the tradeoffs involved. We also have to train students to work to the erratic and arbitrary timetables of architectural practice, health care, and city planning agencies. Students should know how to work in the field as well as in the laboratory, to speak to public housing tenants and government officials as well as to their colleagues, to devise short-run as well as long-run studies, and to convey their findings in colloquial English as well as in professional jargon.

CONCLUSION

I began this essay with a description of two models of social change and came quickly to the conclusion that each had something to offer environmental psychologists. We cannot ignore people's surroundings any more than we can ignore what is inside their heads. Decisions about sequences and timetables must be judged tactically within an overall strategy of reform. I do not consider environmental psychology a detached value-free discipline. We must be objective in gathering and interpreting our data, but the problems themselves should be dictated by the needs of society, long-range as well as short-range, and we should have the same commitment to environmental quality that physicians have to health, engineers to efficiency, and teachers to learning. This does not mean that we know in advance the conditions for an optimal environment for any group of people, much less for all of humanity. Ideally we should be able to generate as much information as we can regarding tradeoffs and present this to people who can then plan, build, and renovate their homes, work places, and communities. Without a commitment to environmental quality we are not likely to get the support from society that we need for either basic or applied research. In considering the transactions between people and the physical environment, we have a broader view of motivation and behavior than most other fields. It would be unfortunate if that vision were not to be shared with our colleagues as well as with policymakers and community groups. What frightens me most at this stage in the development of environmental psychology is the possibility that we will become neither yogis nor commissars—both of whom are committed to perfecting society—but rather that we will follow the path of academic social psychology, learning theory, or perception psychology into irrelevance and become a coterie of like-minded individuals capable of discoursing only among ourselves without regard for the larger concerns of society.

128   Robert Sommer

REFERENCES

Bourestom, N., and Tars, S. Alterations in life patterns following nursing home relocation. *The Gerontologist,* 1974, *14,* 506–509.

Calhoun, J. B. Death squared: The explosive growth and demise of a mouse population. *Proceedings of the Royal Society of Medicine,* 1973, *66,* 80–89.

"TM Campaigns for 'Ideal' Davis," *California Aggie,* May 3, 1976, p. 1.

Carp, Frances M. *A future for the aged.* Austin: University of Texas Press, 1966.

Etzioni, A. Human beings are not very easy to change after all. *Saturday Review,* June 3, 1972, p. 47.

Freedman, J. L. *Crowding and behavior.* San Francisco: Freeman, 1975.

Fuller, R. B. New forms versus reforms. *World,* September 12, 1972, p. 31.

Goodall, K. A conversation about behavior modification with Montrose N. Wolf. *Psychology Today,* June 1973, p. 65.

Haney, C., Banks, C., and Zimbardo, P. Interpersonal dynamics in a simulated prison. *International Journal of Criminology and Penology,* 1973, *1,* 69–97.

Hill, J. P. We seem to be conditioned by the belief that environments only affect us in extreme cases and only in a negative way. *Human Ecology Forum,* 1971, *2,* p. 3.

Koestler, A. *The Yogi and the Commissar.* London: Horizon, 1942.

Koran, L. M. Psychiatry in Mainland China. *American Journal of Psychiatry,* 1972, *128,* 89.

Mering, O. von, and King, S. H. *Remotivating the mental patient.* New York: Russell Sage Foundation, 1957.

Rubin, J. *Growing up at 37.* New York: Evans, 1976.

Sommer, R. *The end of imprisonment.* New York: Oxford University Press, 1976.

SELECTED DISCUSSION:

Dr. Sommer commented on his own work as follows: The evaluation model I described can be used to determine what needs to be changed in a man-environment system. At the same time, necessary solutions require a model which ties researcher to policy change. Knowing the problem does not automatically point out the solution. One can try a number of things, but Kurt Lewin's notion of action research tied to policy change is probably the best model, where research is an adjunct to social change and the researchers conduct studies and feed information back to the policy people as they proceed.

I am not opposed to either basic or long-term research; they are needed, as are short-term and applied research. Heber's research is extremely important in answering the surmise of Jensen and Shockley and others that nothing can be done to prevent poor cognitive development in certain groups. On the other hand, it is probably too late to help Head Start. When such social programs are started, research must accompany them to guide the program, and the researcher must have direct access to program managers so that the latter do not get entrenched in policies based on bias or supposition.

So, both the evaluational research model and long-term basic research aid the applied researcher; he does not simply guess at problem solutions. When I am asked to consult on the problems of people who are underground, I do not guess at what is wrong; rather, I use the methods of the social sciences to try to find out. This involves not only asking questions of those underground but observing them to see if, for example, they put up Sierra Club posters and bring in plants.

The ensuing discussion was concerned largely with strategies in man-environment studies and manipulations, applied research strategies to produce quick results, and the role of theory in such studies.

Dr. Sommer: The important consideration is where you start. Many things that need to be done in applied projects are not financially impossible. For example, a dormitory-improving policy on our campus is to let students repaint their own rooms at the beginning of every year. The Housing Office provides the paint and the brushes, and the scheme is cheaper than letting Physical Plant decorate. Other possibilities are to let students have gardens on campus to grow their own fresh vegetables.

Dr. Schoggen: I am concerned that Sommer advocates quick-and-and dirty research to give policy makers good information quickly. A little bit of scientifically based truth is a very difficult thing to come by. We all use quick-and-dirty methods at an early stage in a piece of work, but we know that results obtained in this way are no basis for advising government officials on public policy; rather, they provide a way of getting better relevant hunches. There is danger in accepting the recommendation that we rush into the real world and cope with complicated problems using our best quick-and-dirty techniques. In doing so we risk jeopardizing whatever minimal public credibility we may still have left as scientists.

Dr. Sommer: The researcher's job is not to come up with guesses but rather to decide the best steps to take—a consultative matter for the people involved. The researcher then guides the changes through a series of evaluations. I am not proposing a single quick-and-dirty study but rather continuous involvement in the policy decisions. We should not act as designers or city planners. The role I see for the environmental psychologist is to help evaluate social changes and to guide them on a dialectical basis.

Dr. Altman: Much that has been discussed here does not involve any theoretical notions; that worries me. It also worries me that theory does not emerge from the real-world problem-solving approach. Ultimately, contributions we will make toward solving practical social issues will be based on theories, implicit or explicit, and we ought to be working toward "relevant" theoretical notions.

Dr. Sommer: I think very highly of Kurt Lewin, who was not only a theorist but developed the whole notion of action research. By working on actual social problems, one can develop much larger ideas, for example, about participation or about interdependency. An ecological model is a wider theoretical structure.

Some of the most significant notions in environmental psychology are now coming from what is called third-force or humanistic psychology. This is the theoretical orientation many of us evidence by emphasizing participation and the value of environments that help people grow and develop. The self-actualization theory is implicit in much of our discussion.

Dr. Freedman: We don't know enough in the environmental field to have theories. What passes for theory there is actually an attempt to explain a small set of data; it should be called, at most, a theory of the middle range. Sometimes it is nothing more than a summary or generalization. Very broad theories, like humanistic theory or learning theory, are available, but when we face actual problems, our approach is largely atheoretical. This is the way it should be. Without a good deal of knowledge, one should be careful about theory development. It will be a waste of time for us to try to make policy decisions or even to build experiments on theoretical bases.

Dr. Heber: In the center where I work in Wisconsin, there are extensive teams in virology, neurophysiology, reproductive physiology, neuroendocrinology, and biochemistry—the most sophisticated sciences that relate to the nervous system. One never hears these scientists utter the word "theory." But in the psychiatry unit, the specialists talk obsessively of theory.

The remaining questions and comments, excerpted below, concerned research strategies to be used specifically in primary prevention research.

Dr. Forgays: The methodology one chooses in man-environment studies depends on the questions you are asking. These differ at different stages of research development. For example, the broad sweep that Heber has described, with many variables operating interactively and inseparably, can still answer the heritability issue well.

In psychology, for many years, we have used an additive approach in information building and research. We manipulate minor variables, study the effects on consequent behaviors, and attempt to piece these bits of information together into a meaningful whole. Perhaps we ought to replace this approach with a subtractive model in which we start with a broad demonstration, like Heber's successful attempt to show that heritability is not the cause of all retardation. The original study can be of either the yogi or the commissar type. Further study can begin to examine the effect of removing variables, not one by one, but probably six by six, based on a logical priority system. This approach gives us the advantage of answering some questions—whether inspired sociopolitically or psychologically—fairly rapidly (the heritability issue, for example). Then as research time becomes available, we can do the more precise studies. There is a danger here if one uses the correlational approach in the early studies: one can point out interesting relationships but cannot extricate them, since all sorts of other variables are interacting in an unspecified manner. Obviously, then, one has to do follow-up experiments. It is important not to consider the correlations as demonstrating causal relationships before the experiments with more specific variables are begun. Perhaps the compromise model, then, is to collect data for immediate answers, and then proceed to more careful research—but as a single design.

Dr. Sommer: In the phrase "quick and dirty," only the word "quick" is appropriate. Even in quick research I recommend using a control group and have always used one myself (although I use the word "baseline" rather than control group). For example, San Quentin had 84 stabbings in 1974. Using these as a baseline or control observation, I can try to reduce the number through environmental manipulation. I can also use Folsom Prison as my "control group" by matching the two prisons in certain ways.

Dr. Heber: There is a practicality issue in prevention research which ought to be mentioned. If the cost of retardation intervention is $5,000 per child per year from birth to six years of age, you will have invested $30,000 in the single individual. If, in fact, you do prevent him from becoming mentally retarded and compare your investment with the cost of special education placement in the schools, vocational rehabilitation, or institutionalization, surely there is a substantial saving. In addition, the prevention study may help find ways to effect prevention on a really practical and less costly basis.

8

Privacy and Mental Health

IRWIN ALTMAN

Irwin Altman received the Ph.D. degree in Psychology from the University of Maryland in 1957. He taught for a year at American University before spending two years as Research Scientist and Vice President of Human Sciences Research, Inc., in Arlington, Virginia. After spending two years at American University as Senior Research Scientist and Associate Research Professor, he served for seven years as Research Psychologist at the Naval Medical Research Institute at Bethesda. Since 1969 he has been Professor and Chairman of the Department of Psychology, University of Utah.

His writings include over thirty-five articles, four books, and chapters in fifteen other books. His well known book, Environment and Social Behavior: Privacy, Personal Space, Territory, and Crowding, *published in 1975, is directly related to his paper included in this volume. Over the years he has studied small-group behavior, dealing especially with the influence of social isolation, while his recent research has focused on human ecology and environmental psychology.*

Altman has been a consultant to national, state, and local agencies, including the Veterans Administration and the NICHD. He has served on the editorial boards of seven journals and as a reviewer for six journals, and acts as consulting editor to two publishing companies. Through his chairmanship of the Task Force on Environment and Behavior of the American Psychological Association, he is contributing importantly to the development of environmental psychology.

This chapter presents a conceptual analysis of privacy as a self-other boundary control process and includes discussion of such privacy mechanisms and dynamics as verbal and paraverbal behavior,

*Portions of the material in this chapter are adapted from my recent book, *Environment and Social Behavior: Privacy, Personal Space, Territory, and Crowding*, Monterey, Calif.: Brooks Cole, 1975.

personal space, territorial behavior, and cultural practices. Several functions of privacy are also proposed: regulation of interpersonal interaction, self-other relationships, and self-definition. Finally, the chapter considers privacy in relation to mental health issues.

There has been little empirical research on, and only some theorizing and discursive analysis of, privacy in the social and behavioral sciences. Privacy has been traditionally the domain of political scientists, lawyers, and philosophers, and only recently have sociologists and others begun to treat it. Much of the concern with it, moreover, has been in the context of legal matters—case law, legal theory, legislation on issues of wiretapping and interrogation, and personality and ability testing. A central theme of this chapter is that privacy is a key construct and that it has potentially important implications for the mental health area.

As a first issue, consider the meaning of the term. One group of definitions emphasizes seclusion and avoidance of interaction, with a person or group seeking to remove itself from contact with others. A second type of definition stresses concepts of control, opening and closing of the self to others, freedom of choice, and options regarding accessibility to others. The latter approach broadens the concept and, as demonstrated below, is compatible with my theoretical framework (Altman, 1975). For present purposes privacy will be defined as *the selective control of access to the self or to one's group.*

A conceptual analysis of privacy.

Given the preceding definition, this analysis will treat the following features of privacy: units of analysis which vary from individuals to groups, the dialectic nature of privacy, the optimization nature of privacy, privacy as a boundary regulation process, and privacy as a bidirectional process.

(1) Units of privacy analysis. As an inherently interpersonal event, privacy involves different combinations of persons. For example, one person may seek privacy from another person or group, or two or more persons may seek or avoid interaction with a particular other person or group. One aspect of Westin's (1970) analysis of privacy is related to social units: *solitude* involves one

person seeking privacy from others; *intimacy* involves a group of people separating themselves from others; *anonymity* is one person avoiding many others; *reserve* is psychological separation of one person from one or more other persons. Thus, an important area of analysis deals with privacy in different social units.

(2) The dialectic nature of privacy. It is postulated here that social interaction is a continuing interplay of people coming together and moving apart. People are neither solely social beings nor solely asocial beings. There are times when we want to be alone and there are times when we seek out others. Privacy, therefore, will be treated here as a changing process which reflects a momentary desired amount of social contact, which can be high or low.

Privacy as a dialectic process is implicit in other conceptual approaches. Proshansky, Ittelson, and Rivlin (1970), for example, viewed privacy as involving freedom of choice or options to use the environment to regulate interaction; Simmel (1950) wrote of a dialectic between self-revelation and self-reserve, even in very intimate relationships, which involves a balance between mutual knowing and mutual separateness.

(3) The optimization nature of privacy. Another feature of my approach to privacy is that either too much or too little interaction at a given time is unsatisfactory, and that people seek an optimal level of social contact. Most privacy literature addresses only one type of imbalance: when people attempt to avoid interacting and are unable to do so, they refer to intrusion or "crowding." According to my approach, another imbalance exists when more seclusion and withdrawal occurs than desired, representing a condition of social isolation.

Others have proposed similar ideas. For example, Proshansky et al. (1970) cited people's need to maximize freedom of choice and control over environmental options: Schwartz (1968), Rapoport (1972), Westin (1970), and others pointed to the need to maintain some balance between seclusion and interaction, under- and overstimulation, or social isolation and stimulus overload.

(4) Privacy as a boundary regulation process. Privacy regulation is also hypothesized to operate in a dynamic sense, much

like a cell membrane, whose boundary properties change in relation to the state of the external and internal environment. As circumstances change, the membrane is differentially permeable, and shifts its boundary properties so as to achieve a viable state. It is proposed here that privacy is an analogous boundary process, such that the openness-closedness of a person or group alters with different personal and social circumstances.

The idea of boundaries is not new to the environment and behavior field. For example, territory implies an area which a person or group sometimes defends and preserves. Similarly, personal space involves an invisible boundary around the self, intrusion into which can result in tension or discomfort. An important goal of the present framework, however, is to expand the concept of privacy boundaries to include both a "keep out," exclusion component and an "open up," intake component.

(5) Desired and achieved privacy. Privacy can be viewed from two perspectives: (1) desired privacy, or a momentary ideal state regarding social interaction; (2) achieved privacy, or the outcome of social interaction, which may or may not match what was desired. Thus, a person may have hoped for very little contact with others, but found himself in a room full of people. Or, conversely, a person may have desired maximum social contact but ended up alone.

Regulation of social inputs and outputs involves relationships between desired and achieved privacy. When achieved privacy equals desired privacy, optimum control exists. When achieved privacy is less than desired privacy, we commonly refer to a condition of intrusion or invasion of privacy. On the other hand, when achieved privacy is greater than desired privacy, we speak of loneliness or social isolation.

(6) Input and output processes. The present framework hypothesizes a two-way privacy process involving inputs and outputs. Thus, one can deal with *inputs* from other persons, or with *outputs* from the self to others. As examples of outputs, a person may wish to include others in an activity or may wish to have them listen to his problems.

Privacy mechanisms

People attempt to realize privacy regulation by means of verbal and paraverbal behavior, nonverbal use of the body, environmental behaviors, and culturally defined norms and customs. Privacy regulation is thus a "whole-person" process involving a variety of behaviors. Furthermore, these mechanisms operate as an integrated system; verbal and nonverbal behaviors, for example, sometimes substitute for one another, sometimes amplify one another, sometimes conflict and thereby convey ambivalence or nongenuineness.

These mechanisms are also dynamic and responsive to circumstances. A person who cannot achieve a desired level of privacy may marshall additional mechanisms. If a closed door is ignored, an intruder might be verbally told to leave, might be given nonverbal cues of disapproval, or might even be tossed out bodily. Privacy regulation involves an array of mechanisms which can be mobilized to achieve a match between desires and outcomes.

Verbal privacy mechanisms

A primary mode of social interaction is verbal behavior. Speech, which conveys all manner of emotional and cognitive states and desires, can be considered from the perspective of its content and structure. Verbal content refers to the substance of a communication or *what* is said. Obvious content in regard to privacy includes "Keep out," "Come in," "I'd like to be alone." People can also use verbal content to convey discrepancies between desired and achieved privacy: "Don't you know what a closed door means?" "I called you and you didn't come when I needed you."

Structural aspects of verbal behavior refer to *how* a statement is made, or such paraverbal characteristics as language styles, pronunciation and dialect, voice dynamics, speech rates, and intensity.

Nonverbal privacy mechnisms

Nonverbal behavior involves use of the body—the head and face, limbs, trunk. Patterson, Mullens, and Romano (1971) found that the closer an invasion the greater the incidence of glaring, leaning away, blocking (placement of a hand or elbow between the self and the invader), and shifting of the body away from the intruder. Felipe and Sommer (1966) reported that the closer an intrusion, the greater the probability of flight and nonverbal behaviors designed to ward off the intruder—turning away, pulling in elbows, and the like. In these examples, adjustments of nonverbal behavior reflect attempts to establish acceptable boundaries between the self and others. The examples also suggest the linkage between nonverbal behavior and personal space, the latter a use of the environment to achieve desired contact.

There is some cultural material on nonverbal communication as a privacy mechanism. Westin (1970) stated that many cultures do not have extensive environmental privacy mechanisms, but do have some form of privacy regulation, often nonverbal. Covering the face, avoiding eye contact, and speaking softly often occur in place of environmental barriers. Murphy (1964) described the Tuareg male's use of the veil around the face as a privacy mechanism; Rapoport (1967) reported that among the Yagua (an Amazon society) people signify being absent by turning toward the dwelling unit wall.

Environmental privacy mechanisms

Environmental analysis has been the traditional route to understanding privacy—how people use doors, windows, furniture arrangements, apartment and home designs, and neighborhood and community plans, to regulate inputs from others. Two basic aspects of the environment in relation to privacy are *personal space* and *territorial behavior*.

Personal space refers to the invisible boundary surrounding the self (Hall, 1966; Sommer, 1969). Hall (1966) proposed four distance zones linked to interpersonal intimacy: (1) an *intimate distance*, ranging from actual body contact to about 18 inches is usually appropriate to intimate relationships in private situations, and permits extensive communication involving heat, sound, smell, and close physical contact; (2) *personal distance*, which spans the area from 1.5 to 4 feet and also permits considerable exchange of cues; (3) *social distance*, 4 to 12 feet, occurring in impersonal, work, or casual relationships; and (4) *public distance*, beyond 12 feet, appropriate to formal meetings and interactions with higher status persons.

Violations of appropriate distance zones against the desires of a person may result in confict, tension, or discomfort. McBride, King, and James (1965) demonstrated differential physiological arousal as people were approached at varying distances and from several angles (front, side, and rear). Hall also provides anecdotal examples of this process: persons from Middle Eastern and Mediterranean cultures, for example, are accustomed to very close distances, often to the dismay of North Americans and Englishmen.

Territories represent another level of environmental privacy regulation. Lewis (1959, 1961) illustrated how physical environments are used to regulate desired levels of privacy among poor families in Mexico. In one family, where the parents and many children lived in a single room, the adults located their bed behind a wall fashioned out of empty crates. In another family living in a tenement, privacy from neighbors was achieved by a practice of not visiting and always keeping outside doors closed.

Other studies of families also demonstrated how the physical environment is used to manage social interaction. Bossard and Boll (1950) identified family rituals, including bathroom policies, by which privacy was regulated; Jourard (1966) stressed the value of people in families having rooms of their own, where they could be alone and away from others; Schwartz (1968) described how doors, fences, signs, and so on, can be used to prevent unwanted intrusions; Chermayeff and Alexander (1963) proposed that homes have a firm boundary from the public environment, and that interior designs provide balanced contact with the outside world and with family interaction on the inside.

The universality of culturally based privacy mechanisms

Cultural groups have norms and customs which facilitate management of interpersonal boundaries. For example, Schwartz (1968), Kira (1966), Bossard and Boll (1950) and Altman, Nelson, and Lett (1972) noted the sacred role of the bathroom in our culture, as a place where people can be assured of privacy when the door is closed. An important feature of privacy management is that different societies have evolved alternative mechanisms and behaviors. Thus, some cultures do not rely as heavily on environmental mechanisms as other cultures, but may use nonverbal,

verbal, or other means. I agree with Westin's (1970) point that all societies probably have some mechanisms to regulate privacy, although not always in the form of physical environmental control. Geertz, for example, (cited in Westin, 1970), reported few physical symbols of privacy in Javanese society, but he described other techniques for maintaining boundaries between people: social relationships are restrained, people avoid expressing feelings, etiquette and politeness are very important values, and people speak softly.   The English do not often have private offices or exclusive ownership of places (Hall, 1966), but they obtain privacy through interpersonal reserve; they speak less loudly than Americans, direct their voices and remarks carefully, and employ nonverbal and verbal mechanisms, not just environmental ones, to regulate their contacts with others. Naturally, many societies use environmental mechanisms to achieve privacy. In Bali, for example, Geertz (cited in Westin, 1970) noted the presence of walls around homes, and the fact that people only infrequently entered other people's homes. Or, as Canter and Canter (1971) observed, Japanese homes are carefully designed and located to maximize privacy. High walls and lot and site locations prevent visual access, and inside the home miniaturization of detail and flexible room and wall arrangements permit control over privacy. Thus, if one examines cultures carefully, he will probably uncover a variety of verbal, nonverbal, or environmental mechanisms to regulate interaction. One might even say that such mechanisms are universal. While some cultures may appear to have little privacy, this is probably due to the observer's traditional view of privacy as strictly a physical and environmental process, not as a complex system involving several levels of behavior.

There are numerous examples of privacy regulation mechanisms in different cultures (Altman, 1977), but two are particularly striking. The first, a culture in central Brazil called the Mehinacu, has been described by the anthropologists Roberts and Gregor (1971). The Mehinacu are a small tribal group who live in isolated communities. To an outside observer, they appear to have no privacy whatsoever. There is considerable visual and auditory access of people to one another. The village is arranged around an open plaza; the huts are very close together and several families live in the same dwelling. Everyone can hear and see almost every part of the village. Agricultural fields are also adjacent to one another, and the paths leading out of the village are perfectly straight, so that people can be seen coming and going at long distances; in fact, Roberts and Gregor report that villagers recognize one another's footprints in the sand, and thereby know who has been where and when.

Is this a society without privacy? Observing only the physical features of Mehinacu life makes it appear so. Upon closer examination, however, Roberts and Gregor found a variety of mechanisms used by the people to regulate contact. Even though several families live in the same dwelling, they avoid intruding on one another's spaces. The men have a small building from which women are barred, and outside the village beyond the straight paths, there is a maze of paths and secret clearings where people go when they want to be alone. The child-rearing process also includes privacy management. Boys between the ages of 9 and 12 spend most of their time inside, alone; they learn to speak quietly and to control their emotions, and have little contact with other people. There is a cultural practice not to probe or question one another, nor to intrude socially.

Thus, while there is an apparent lack of privacy in this society, a series of mechanisms permit people to regulate and control interaction. Privacy and the lack of it occur simultaneously, as a dialectic process. The culture illustrates how privacy regulation not only involves the physical environment, but can also include cultural norms and nonverbal behavior.

Another example from a different part of the world (Murphy, 1964) is the Tuareg, a pastoral, nomadic people who live in groups of 50 to 200 in southern Algeria, northern Mali, and Niger and whose main activity is tending camels, sheep, and goats. Their dress consists of a long flowing robe, a turban, and a veil wrapped around the head covering the face and leaving only a narrow slit to reveal the eyes. The men wear the veil constantly, even when they sleep and eat. The Tuareg believe that covering the mouth prevents a person from being vulnerable to others. In one sense the veil is a symbol of almost total privacy, but in another sense it is not. It is important in communication and is used flexibly: for example, when a high-status person deals with a low-status person, he lowers his veil, which thus serves as a changeable boundary between people. The Tuareg also use nonverbal communication, including shifting body positions and eye movements, in social interaction. Like the Mehinacu, then, the Tuareg have a complex but different set of mechanisms to regulate and control privacy.

Functions of privacy regulation

What needs does privacy regulation serve? What are its functions? It is proposed here that privacy is concerned with (1) relationships between a person or group and others, (2) the interface of the self and others, and (3) self-definition and self-identity.

1. Interpersonal functions of privacy. One function of privacy is to regulate interaction with others. An example is limited and protected communication (Westin, 1970). This involves pacing one's interaction with others, to adjust boundaries between the self and others and to achieve a balance between revealing and withholding information about the self.

Regulation of self-other boundaries plays an important role in self-definition. It is a source of self-knowledge based directly on overt, ongoing interaction with others. In one sense, the ability to control boundaries (and the failure or extreme cost in so doing) provides key information about the self: it tells a person what the social world thinks as reflected in behavior toward him. If I discover that I cannot regulate interaction successfully, I am thereby provided with important information about the social environment and my ability to manage it. If it happens with many people and in many situations, such information will contribute to how I ultimately define myself as a person.

2. The interface of the self and the world. Westin (1970) postulated that self-evaluation is a privacy goal. When out of the presence of others, the individual can integrate social experiences, process information received from interactions, and formulate alternative plans of future behavior. As Westin stated, self-evaluation often occurs in religious retreats and in the self-exile of religious and political leaders. Such separations provide the opportunity to assimilate and integrate experiences, and to examine the form of future relationships with others.

3. Self-definition. This function builds upon and integrates the preceding purposes, and is the ultimate goal of privacy regulation.

For purposes of this discussion, self-definition is a person's cognitive, psychological, and emotional understanding of himself. It includes knowing where he begins and ends in relation to others, and which aspects of the physical and social environment are parts of the self and which aspects are parts of others. It includes some appreciation of one's abilities and disabilities, emotions and cognitions, and beliefs and disbeliefs.

Privacy in relation to self-definition appears in the writings of many people. Westin (1970), for example, referred to personal autonomy, i.e. a person's sense of integrity, independence, and ability to avoid being manipulated by others, as a major function of privacy. As such, it is "basically an instrument for achieving individual goals of self-realization" (p. 39). Pennock and Chapman (1971), Beardsley (1971), and Gross (1971) wrote of invasions of privacy as particularly harmful because they interfere with an individual's autonomy, self-respect, and dignity and because they remove control of a person's life and self from him. In the context of mental institutions Goffman (1961) and Jourard (1966) pointed to the critical role of privacy for a patient's self-identity. Goffman (1961) noted how the violation of patients' physical selves may retard rehabilitation, since it contributes to the degradation of the self and to the loss and confusion of self-identity, self-esteem, and self-worth.

The notion of self-definition is a central construct associated with privacy regulation. For a person to function effectively in relating to others requires some understanding of the self, where it ends and begins, when self-interest and self-expression can be exhibited. If one's self-definition is that none of the world belongs to the self, if the self has no boundaries or controllable boundaries, then the person is literally *nothing* as an intact social unit. Or, if everything is viewed as a part of the self and controlled by the self—for example, the young child who does not separate the world from the self—then there is also no sense of self-definition, for the self is *everything* and there is no uniqueness or separation from others. Privacy mechanisms thus help define the limits and boundaries of the self. Being able to change the permeability of the boundaries around the self fosters a sense of individuality. But it is not the inclusion or exclusion process which is central; it is the ability to apply it which fosters healthy self-definition. If I can control what is me and not me, if I can know the limits and scope of my control, then I have taken major steps toward defining what I am. All the mechanisms of privacy described thus far—verbal, nonverbal, environmental, and cultural—serve to help me define me.

Implications for Mental Health

The present analysis centered around privacy as a whole-person or whole-group concept—that is, as a feature of intact social units such as individual people, couples, families, and other groups. Several general implications of this thesis follow.

1. To understand a person or group from a social-unit perspective requires tapping into several levels of behavior—verbal, nonverbal, environmental, and cultural practices. Because different cultures, individuals, and groups may employ different mixes of behavioral mechanisms, it is essential that one be sensitive to the variety of behavioral processes which play a role in such a process as privacy regulation in order to avoid forming a distorted picture of privacy regulation in other cultures.

2. A social-unit orientation suggests that one should deal with patterns or profiles of behavior, not separate and isolated behaviors. Not only must the multiple levels of behavior which occur in privacy regulation be heeded, but it should be recognized that these behaviors operate in patterns and as a coherent system. Different profiles of verbal, nonverbal, environmental, and cultural styles of functioning can occur at different times, or specific individuals may have developed unique styles of interaction control. A social-unit orientation thus calls for an appreciation of cultural, group, and individual differences and for attention to the people's patterns of behavioral mechanisms. Put in another way, a social-unit orientation elevates the appropriate unit of study from isolated, single behaviors to patterns or profiles of behavior.

3. A social-unit orientation also emphasizes dynamic and interdependent aspects of social behavior. Privacy regulation systems change from circumstance to circumstance and from time to time, depending upon a person's or a group's definition of situations along with a host of other factors. To conceive of privacy regulation as a static, fixed, unchanging system is erroneous and is likely to result in an incomplete analysis of a situation. Further-

more, privacy regulation systems involve interdependent components, and a change in one part of the system is likely to affect other parts in a reverberatory fashion. Thus, for example, if one cannot use an environmental mechanism to achieve a desired level of privacy, alternative mechanisms may be mobilized. Finally, as another systems principle, a maximum level of privacy for an extended period of time is likely to generate forces to achieve a greater amount of contact at a later time, and vice versa, according to the dialectic property of privacy described earlier. In short, not only is privacy regulation a dynamic process, but it reflects a social system of interdependent parts.

These general ideas can be applied to mental health issues, especially primary prevention, where we are dealing with people who function in a relatively healthy fashion or with people who are potentially high risk groups. Because privacy regulation is a central facet of individual and group functioning, I will examine its relationship to mental health and primary prevention in assessment and intervention contexts.

An Assessment Context

In diagnosing the effectiveness of the social interaction of an individual or group, the framework of this chapter suggests a number of issues to be addressed. At a descriptive level, given a social unit orientation and the features of privacy regulation proposed here, an assessment process should be holistic, with an attempt to understand how a particular person, class of persons, or group functions in the regulation of social interaction. Questions such as the following can be posed: How does individual X or members of group Y regulate privacy? What repertoire of verbal, nonverbal, environmental, and cultural mechanisms are used to manage social interaction? As discussed previously, answers to these questions require an analysis of different levels of behavior, and an appreciation of how these behaviors fit together in coherent profiles. Furthermore, the assessment process should be circumstance- and time-contingent; that is, if privacy mechanisms vary across settings and times, an assessment strategy should attempt to obtain a representative sampling of coping mechanisms used in different circumstances. Assessment should thus deal with persons and groups in a broad range of settings. Just as the anthropologist taps many aspects of a culture, so should an analysis of privacy regulation probe many aspects of a person's or group's life.

For assessment purposes I suggest that privacy processes be viewed as involving (1) dialectic, dynamic, changing features, and, (2) a social unit orientation which emphasizes patterns of behavior which operate in a system-like fashion. By explicitly adopting such a theoretical perspective we can insure attention to significant features of privacy management.

Beyond the question of description is the matter of assessing system effectiveness. We can ask, how well does a privacy regulation system evolve? To what extent does a person or group succeed in regulating interaction with others? Are there some privacy mechanisms which seem to work and others which do not? Are some people more able or less able to regulate their interaction with others? If so, what features of their systems are associated with effective control? Not only must we be able to describe privacy management systems; we should also deal with their effectiveness.

Another assessment issue concerns the relative efficiency or "costs" of a privacy regulation system. It may be that a person or group successfully uses a pattern of mechanisms to achieve desired contact or noncontact with others but their system may be quite expensive in terms of physical, physiological, or psychological costs and may require considerable energy to sustain its successes. For example, if avoiding other members of my family always requires intense activity, such as yelling, slamming doors, or leaving the house, then I have evolved a privacy system which works but it also might be psychologically costly to maintain.

Another facet of assessment which derives from the framework of this chapter concerns the inherent social or interpersonal character of privacy regulation. Not only must we understand the mechanisms by which a person or group regulates openness-closedness of others, but it is important to consider the social milieu and the reactions and counterregulatory processes of others. The compatibility or incompatibility of privacy needs and regulatory processes among family members, among members of a couple, among people at work and in other settings must be examined in order to deal with such questions as, how do others react to a particular style of privacy regulation exhibited by a person? What mix of mechanisms seems to work best in a family context to enhance regulation of privacy among parents and children, among siblings, and so on?

In summary, the framework of this chapter suggests an assessment strategy which is holistic, is social-unit oriented, and emphasizes regulation of social interaction as a dynamic process that changes over time and with circumstances. The framework also highlights the need to examine privacy as an interpersonal process and in terms of the costs and effectiveness of regulatory systems. While these assessment guides are stated abstractly, and in some sense may already be practiced, they are useful because they derive explicitly from a conceptual system and because they are applicable to the everyday social behavior of such intact, naturally occurring social unit as individuals, couples, and families.

An Intervention Context

There are several ways in which the approach taken here can be applied to intervention facets of primary prevention. These center around the qualities of a well functioning privacy regulation system and the nature of education and training to use privacy systems.

One issue concerns the features of an "ideal" privacy regulation system. Keeping in mind the assessment process described above and on an understanding of the environmental and social milieu within which a person or group functions, one can ask: What privacy regulation mechanisms are available and usable by a person or group? This question deals with the realistically available resources which people can use to manage social relationships. Just as other cultures have evolved mechanisms that rely heavily on elements of a behavioral repertoire that were available in the social and physical environment, so should an intervention strategy maximize use of such mechanisms. If families necessarily live in conditions of high population concentration, then rather than seeking to use traditional environmental mechanisms (such as separate rooms) for escape, one may have to focus on development of noverbal, verbal, or other mechanisms; conversely, for people who have access to a wide variety of environmental mechanisms (spacious homes, separate rooms), use of elaborate verbal and nonverbal avoidance mechanisms may not be crucial. Privacy management involves a blend of mechanisms, not a fixed set. An intervention strategy should be designed to function within a particular social and environmental setting, and the resources of the setting must be considered in developing a behavioral change strategy.

Another intervention issue concerns the degree of flexibility required in a well functioning privacy system. The present conceptual framework emphasizes the dynamic and dialectic quality of privacy regulation and the need for a system which permits people and groups to be more or less voluntarily accessible to others. It is essential, therefore, that an intervention strategy should facilitate both openness *and* closedness, and it should avoid overshooting the mark in either direction. There is a particular danger, especially in such environmental intervention strategies as the design of hospitals, homes, or offices, of maximizing either access *or* nonaccess to others in a rigid and fixed way. To use an oversimplified analogy, the optimum intervention strategy has a kind of "venetian blind" capability, at all levels of behavior, whereby people can open or close themselves off from others in a readily manageable fashion.

A related matter deals with the degree to which a privacy regulation system operates over a broad versus a narrow range of situations. To the extent that a person or group is involved in many-versus-a-few role relationships, it is likely that a greater repertoire of mechanisms will be necessary. A young child, for example, probably requires a less complex and varied system of privacy management than does a teenager or young adult. An intervention system should be designed to prepare people to cope with the variety of interaction contexts within which they function.

Another intervention issue concerns the need for education and training in regard to privacy regulation. The last two decades have seen the growth of human relations training, encounter and sensitivity groups, and the like, which sensitize people to others and to themselves as social beings in terms of verbal and nonverbal facets of their behavior. Intervention strategies should attune people to how the physical environment affects their contacts with others and can be actively used to regulate them. Perhaps more important, education and training should emphasize the systemlike quality of privacy regulation and the interplay of all levels of behavior. People should be educated about how to select privacy strategies for different circumstances and settings, the dynamic quality of privacy regulations, the variety of methods which can be used to vary openness-closedness to others, and so on. In the last decade, our culture has emphasized openness, honesty, and self-disclosure; at other times in history, privacy and minding one's own business have been central values. We need, according to the logic of this chapter, to create primary prevention strategies which permit people to move in either direction, to learn how various techniques involving verbal, nonverbal, and other behaviors can be used to achieve whatever level of interaction is appropriate and desired at a given time.

This chapter has viewed privacy, a concept that traditionally has been environmentally oriented, as involving far more than the physical environment alone. Specifically, privacy has been treated as a *social systems* concept. Rather than focusing on privacy as being attached to the environment or to any other level of behavior alone, I have emphasized its central role as a dynamic, multilevel, systems-oriented concept. Ultimately, I have described privacy as a holistic, social unit concept. It is hoped that the process of translation to the area of mental health and primary prevention can be more easily accomplished now that these ideas about privacy have been explicitly stated.

150   Irwin Altman

REFERENCES

Altman, I. *Environment and social behavior: Privacy, personal space, territory and crowding.* Monterey, California: Brooks Cole, 1975.

Altman, I., Nelson, P., and Lett, E. E. The ecology of home environments. *Catalog of Selected Documents in Psychology,* Journal Supplement Abstract Service, 1972, *2,* 65.

Beardsley, E. L. Privacy: Autonomy and selective disclosure. In J. R. Pennock and J. W. Chapman (Eds.), *Privacy.* New York: Atherton Press, 1971, pp. 56–71.

Bossard, J. H. S., and Boll, E. S. *Ritual in family living.* Philadelphia: University of Pennsylvania Press, 1950.

Canter D., and Canter, S. Close together in Tokyo. *Design and Environment,* Summer 1971, *2,* 60–63.

Chermayeff, S., and Alexander, N. Y. *Community and privacy: Toward a new architecture of humanism.* New York: Doubleday, 1963.

Felipe, N., and Sommer, R. Invasions of personal space. *Social Problems,* 1966, *14,* 206–214.

Goffman, E. *Asylums,* New York: Doubleday, 1961.

Gross, H. Privacy and autonomy. In J. R. Pennock and J. W. Chapman (Eds.), *Privacy.* New York: Atherton Press, 1971, pp. 169–182.

Hall, E. T. *The hidden dimension.* Garden City, N. Y.: Doubleday, 1966.

Jourard, S. M. Some psychological aspects of privacy. *Law and Contemporary Problems,* 1966, *31,* 307–318.

Kira, A. *The bathroom.* Ithaca, N. Y.: Cornell University Center for Housing and Environmental Studies, 1966.

Lewis, O. *Five families.* New York: Mentor, 1959.

Lewis, O. *The children of Sanchez.* New York: Random House, 1961.

McBride, G., King, M. G., and James, J. W. Social proximity effects on galvanic skin responses in adult humans. *Journal of Psychology,* 1965, *61,* 153–157.

Murphy, R. F. Social distance and the veil. *American Anthropologist,* 1964, *66,* 1257–1274.

Patterson, M. L., Mullens, S., and Romano, J. Compensatory reactions to spatial intrusion. *Sociometry,* 1971, *34,* 114–121.

Pennock, J. R., and Chapman, J. W. (Eds.) *Privacy.* New York: Atherton Press, 1971.

Proshansky, H., Ittelson, W. H., and Rivlin, L. G. (Eds.) *Environmental psychology.* New York: Holt, Rinehart and Winston, 1970.

Rapoport, A. Yagua-Amazon dwelling. *Landscape,* 1967, *16* (3), 27–30.

Rapoport, A. Some perspectives on human use and organization of space. Paper presented at Australian Association of Social Anthropologists, Melbourne, Australia, May 1972.

Roberts, J. M., and Gregor, T. Privacy: A cultural view. In J. R. Pennock and J. W. Chapman (Eds.), *Privacy.* New York: Atherton Press, 1971, pp. 189–225.

Schwartz, B. The social psychology of privacy. *American Journal of Sociology,* 1968, *73,* 741–752.

Simmel, G. *The sociology of Georg Simmel.* (Trans. by K. H. Wolff). New York: The Free Press of Glencoe, 1950.

Sommer, R. *Personal space.* Englewood Cliffs, N. J.: Prentice-Hall, 1969.

Westin, A. *Privacy and freedom.* New York: Atheneum Press, 1970.

DISCUSSION BY BERNARD L. BLOOM

Trying to deal with intact social units, as Altman is doing, is one of the struggles in social psychology. It is not the same as the struggle between applied and laboratory research, another area of considerable debate.

Intact social units can be dealt with in the laboratory setting. Two examples occur to me. One is the idea of an annual family check-up. As part of the normal service of a health maintenance organization, you could bring in an entire family—the intact social unit—and, using modern computer technology, assess how they function interdependently. Just as the Kaiser plan gives you a print-out of your biology and physiology, this check-up would result in a print-out of your family's sociology. Within the concept of family medicine, family check-ups are an entirely legitimate part of the medical care concept, broadened substantially in terms of what it means.

Another area of the field-setting study of intact social units is illustrated by Gerald Bauman's work, reported some years ago, in which he calculated what he called a couple's IQ. He gave the Weschler Adult Intelligence Scale to a husband and wife individually and figured their separate IQ's. He then asked them to agree on answers to the same test; from this he calculated the couple's IQ, and he could contrast this figure with the IQ that would have resulted had they agreed on the worst answer either gave individually. He was thus able to assess the couple as a functioning unit, at least in terms of a limited domain of their work. These two examples combine the best of the controlled laboratory study with the study of existing intact social units.

Altman is at the point of theory development where he has to begin looking for propositions that derive from the abstract ideas, and also for what scientists call "refutable propositions". The notion of privacy regulations are enormously appealing, but Altman has to get to the point where he begins to test the hypotheses.

It is important to remind ourselves of the great Lewinian equation that behavior is a function of the person and the environment. We tend to act as if behavior is a function of the person, and much psychological research attempts to develop a better understanding of how personal characteristics are related to behavior. A review of the literature indicates that you cannot get correlations much higher than 0.40 between any measure of personality and a measure of behavior, no matter how many personality and other tests you add. But when you introduce measures of the environment into the equations, the correlations increase dramatically. People are different in different settings. Barker was probably correct when he said that "the environment coerces people," and we must learn more about how this comes about.

Finally, I want to say something about causation. Altman reminded us how complicated it is to make assertions about what causes what. I want to share with you something I learned from Public Health training. When epidemiologists are asked to find out what causes an ailment, they apply three tests, and if they identify something that meets all three criteria, they call it cause, even though they don't know why the causation occurs. The three criteria are these. First, if you think that A causes B, you must show that A occurs before B. Second, you must show that if A is present, there is a strong likelihood that B will occur, and that if A is absent, there is a strong likelihood that B will not occur; you don't have to assert that if A is present B will always occur or that if A is absent B will never occur. Third, if A causes B, you must show that when you reduce A, you find a subsequent reduction in B.

If you can do these three things, you have identified a cause from the point of view of the epidemiologist. He recognizes the importance of the question "How does cigarette smoking cause lung cancer?" and is aware that it has not been answered. But he has a practical concrete tool by which to reduce the incidence of lung cancer—*stop smoking.* From the standpoint of primary prevention, the epidemiologist takes a reasonably useful approach to the concept of cause.

SELECTED DISCUSSION:

Dr. Altman was asked for a definition of environmental stimuli and specifically whether his definition refers only to physical stimuli or includes social stimuli also.

Dr. Altman: People have used the term environment to mean both the physical and the social environment. For example, when Rudy Moos talks about the environment, he means the social climate, including role relationships. Lewin viewed the psychological environment as being extremely crucial since it consists of those aspects of the physical and the social environment that have psychological significance for a person. Other aspects of the physical environment, which he called the foreign hull, move in and out of the psychological environment, but if they don't have psychological significance they are irrelevant. The problem of defining the environment is enormously complex and is not independent of psychological processes.

Dr. Altman was asked if one could study Moos's multidimensional variables in meaningful social units. What is the appropriate level of analysis?

Dr. Altman: Kurt Lewin instructed us to pick the level of analysis appropriate to the phenomenon, and he warned us not to be reductionistic. The past 40 years of social psychological research have focused on the individual, not on social units such as groups or families. For the most part, social psychology centered around attitudes and attitude theory, and the functioning of individual attitude processing. We did not attend consciously to the appropriate level of social functioning. Some others, however, including Schoggen and Barker, decided there was another level of social functioning to study, called the behavior setting, which involves complexes of people in interaction with the environment. One must be very sensitive to the level he deals with for the phenomenon he is interested in. Regarding privacy, my artistic judgment is that we should not look at it solely in terms of environmental processes but should mesh together different levels of behavior in the context of intact social units, for example the family. In a sense, there is no right level of analysis; all levels are right depending upon what it is you want to know.

Question: What advice would you give researchers like Heber and Bloom on analyzing the social units in their studies?

Dr. Altman: A married couple in disruption reflects their disturbance in many different levels and areas of their lives. Bloom should make the best guesses he can about the greatest range of processes going on between members of a married couple, not tapping in at only one level, such as their economic or sexual or child-rearing functioning, but making judgments about a disparate, multilevel series of behavior that characterizes the particular social unit. The second thing that must be done is to identify patterns of those behaviors and adopt a multivariate statistical strategy to analyze the data. In this way it is possible to generate profiles, patterns, stereotypes, and typologies of the social units in a finite set of behaviors.

Question: How does the privacy notion relate to psychopathology?

Dr. Altman: Malfunctioning of privacy regulation systems between people of the type that I describe are primary sources of variance. My theory has cause-and-effect elements. Start looking at the privacy regulation system, for example, in disrupted couples or disrupted families: you may find that a lot of the variance associated with the disruption centers around privacy regulation.

IV
Environmental Psychology and Prevention

9

Research Strategies in
Environmental Psychology

JONATHAN L. FREEDMAN

Jonathan L. Freedman did his undergraduate work at Harvard and received his Ph.D. degree in Psychology at Yale in 1961. He taught at Stanford University for eight years before going in 1969 to Columbia University, where he is presently Professor of Psychology.

His major research interests are in the area of Environmental Psychology, with special attention to the effects of crowding, personal space, architectural design, and urban living. His research also includes studies of attitude change, the relationships between attitudes and behavior, long-term memory, and problem solving.

He has written over thirty articles and four books. Crowding and Behavior *(Viking Press, 1975), his most recent book, summarizes much of his research of the prior several years.*

Environmental effects are complex. You can't evaluate the effect of an environmental factor without considering everything that could conceivably be part of the context—noise, size of corridors, open or closed offices, the color of the walls, how much light there is, and so on. Almost any effect depends on what other factors are present. In my work on crowding (Freedman, 1975), for example, we found that it was almost meaningless to ask, "Is crowding bad or good?" In study after study the answer turned out to be, "Sometimes it has negative effects, sometimes positive; much of the time it has no effect at all." For one thing, the makeup of the population is crucial. Sometimes crowding is positive for females and negative for males, sometimes the reverse. It is not just a sex-by-density interaction, but a sex-by-density-by-conditions interaction—a triple interaction, which even replicates. When you are dealing with environmental factors, there are likely to be four-, five-, and even six-way interactions. Probably we will never find most of them; if we did, we could never understand them, though we might be able to describe them.

We psychologists have been tied too much to the laboratory and basic research and have shied away from applied research. In American psychology applied research has had an unsavory reputation, particularly in the universities, and our graduate students have been trained to avoid it as not being worthwhile.

The traditional approach to research in psychology, particularly environmental psychology, is frustrating. We don't know much now, and our progress is so sluggish that it is sometimes difficult to perceive. The old notion that science is a staircase and we are constantly moving upward is clearly unrealistic. It is much more like a very wide spiral staircase: as you walk very gradually around, perhaps the general trend is upward, and at the turns you can see that you are a level above where you were, though on any given rotation you may dip below a previous level. We deal with such complicated problems that it is not surprising to find progress is slow, in spite of the millions of dollars spent in behavioral science research; but it is frustrating. As psychologists, we want to have an impact. We would like to be able to tell the world something that will help in solving certain problems.

What do we do about this state of affairs? Sommer* suggests changing as many factors in an environment as we want to, and evaluating the results. But I am not sure the multiple-change approach is likely to succeed. How do we know what to change? If we knew, we would have the answers already. Many psychologists can make good guesses, but in the complicated situations we deal with, good guesses may be canceled out by bad ones. It is even conceivable that of two good guesses, either would work alone but together they cancel each other out. One of the things we have learned from the little environmental psychology we have done is that we make bad guesses about environmental factors. Everyone knew, for example, that high-density living was bad (e.g. Calhoun, 1962); everyone knows intuitively that living in New York City, or in a crowded apartment, is bad for you. Well, it isn't true: dozens of studies have shown this. Sometimes it is good, sometimes bad (Freedman, 1975). The more complicated the situation, the worse human beings are at guessing how it affects them.

*See above, pp. 115 ff.

If you know what needs to be changed, you don't need the research. If you don't, it's up to the psychologists to find out. One of our problems is that we cannot try out changes of factors for a few days to see if they work. We deal with long-term operations. If you change a mental hospital or a school system, you're stuck with it; and in any case, you won't even be able to evaluate the changes for several years.

The second question, a basic methodological one, is: how can you tell that something worked? Supposing you have built, or renovated, a mental hospital or a school with some new principle incorporated: if there are changes, are they *real* changes? We are all familiar with the Hawthorne effect, which is that any time you change anything, people like it, at least for a while; you've given them attention. Even with Heber's study, taking a group of candidates for mental retardation at birth and providing massive intervention,* it is conceivable that a substantial part of the effect he achieved resulted from the enormous effort and attention given to the children rather than from the specific treatments.

Next is the question of trying to isolate the factor that worked. It is not always successful to ask the people involved which factor they are responding positively to: if they could tell you that in the first place, you would already have the answers. If they say, "What I really like about the new hospital is that I'm allowed to wear my own clothes," that may indeed be the crucial factor; much more likely, though, it is an interactive effect. What may be important really is that the lighting is better, or that staff morale is higher because something new is happening. In the history of psychotherapy, every new technique works—at least for awhile— unless it doesn't. You may move poor people from tenements to modern housing and find that they hate it because it is new: they were comfortable in the old place.

Another question is how to separate the unique features of your situation from the more general situation. You cannot know that the effect you have produced with one hospital, one schoolroom, one small population of black children, will generalize to anything else. When dealing with such complicated interactive features, it is very hard to generalize. If you have a control group, you can make comparisons; without it, you can only say that there was a

*See above, pp. 39 ff.

change. If the changes was positive, so much the better. But a group of factors that produces a positive effect in one situation may produce a disastrously negative effect in another. In our crowding research, for example, we found that a high-density stiuation with all-female groups under certain conditions produced a strong positive effect, whereas the same situation with all-male groups brought about negative results.

We must do systematic research. If we change a number of factors, we must have control groups; then when we get an effect, we can try to isolate the important factors. It may turn out that we should have done a less complicated (but still systematic) study in the first place.

Systematic research on these factors should be done not in the laboratory but in the real world, where the factors we wish to study are varied. For example, if we are studying the effects of different kinds of housing on health, satisfaction, morale, crime, and so on, it is not necessary to build a number of different kinds of housing: the cities have built them for us. We can then observe a number of already built housing units and try to figure out how they differ. We might hypothesize that high density is not an important single variable but that high density combined with high rise housing is bad. Correlational research of this kind is not clean or neat, but it can produce scientific results and hard data. We might be able to conclude, for example, that high-rise housing is not as healthful as low-rise housing, or that high-rise housing is healthful for the rich but not the poor. Similar studies could be done in mental hospitals, schools, or virtually any other environment. The great advantage of correlational studies is that they are efficient—you get a lot of data very quickly. The resulting studies do not supply definitive answers, but they give us a start.

Putting aside extreme physical environmental factors that clearly interfere with behavior, such elements as noise, lighting, and space are in my opinion not as important as some believe. All of the research that has been done on them indicates they are not crucial variables and that the amount of variance they explain is very small because people are so adaptable. Interactions among people are much more important than the size of the rooms, the color of the walls, or the width of the corridors.

Systematic research into these problems—however slow and tedious—is our only route to finding reliable answers to important questions.

REFERENCES

Calhoun, J. B. Population density and social pathology. *Scientific American,* 1962, *206,* 139–148.

Freedman, J. L. *Crowding and Behavior.* San Francisco: W. H. Freeman and Co., 1975.

10

Utility of the Behavioral Settings Approach

PHIL SCHOGGEN

Phil Schoggen received the Ph.D. degree in Psychology from the University of Kansas in 1954. From 1955 to 1957 he was Assistant Director of the Midwest Psychological Field Station of the University of Kansas and Lecturer in Psychology, University of Kansas Medical School. He spent the years from 1957 to 1966 at the University of Oregon, where he was Assistant Professor of Psychology and Director, Graduate Training Program in Rehabilitation Counseling (1957-1962), Associate Professor of Psychology (1962-1966), and Assistant Dean, College of Liberal Arts and Director of Academic Advising (1965-1966). From 1966 to 1975 he was Professor and Chairperson, Department of Psychology, George Peabody College for Teachers. For the last year of that period he was also Associate Director of the John F. Kennedy Center for Research on Education and Human Development. From 1975 to 1977 he was Professor of Psychology at York University, and since 1977 he has been Professor and Chairperson of the Department of Human Development and Family Studies at Cornell University. For several years he was a member of the Committee on Ethical Standards in Psychological Research (1966-1973) and the Committee on Teaching Awards (1970-1971) of the American Psychological Association.

Schoggen has written over a dozen articles and reviews, is co-author of two books, and has contributed ten chapters to eight other books. Virtually all of this work is in the area of psychological ecology, with special emphasis on the influence of environmental forces on the lives of young children.

Others at this conference have commented that the field of environment and behavior suffers from a serious lack of proper theory; this evaluation is conspicuously true. Altman's use of the concept of privacy at least starts toward integrating a number of central phenomena in the field, including crowding, personal space, and territoriality. It is an important contribution and the field needs badly such contributions. If the case he has made for privacy as a pancultural universal is not altogether convincing, it is still enticing. Altman would be the first to recognize the need to document the process with much more systematic empirical evidence.

Altman's notions of environmental privacy mechanisms—how a person implements or achieves privacy—are of particular importance. These ideas show the greatest congruence with those of the behavior setting I will be describing.

The concept of the behavior setting can be seen as another environmental mechanism which, in Altman's terms, serves the goals of privacy. It is a part of the field that has come to be called ecological psychology. Work started in the fall of 1947, when Roger Barker and Herbert Wright of the University of Kansas set up the Midwest Psychological Field Station in Oskaloosa, Kansas. They considered themselves naturalists of child behavior (Barker and Wright, 1951; 1955). Deploring child psychologists' preoccupation with the laboratory, the clinic, and surveys, they felt it was important to get out into the real world and watch children going about their ordinary, everyday lives. My wife and I joined them in January 1948 and have been in this line of work ever since (Schoggen, P., 1963, 1975; Schoggen, M., and Schoggen, P., 1976).

Ecological psychology is the study of organism environment relations under natural conditions (Barker, 1968). We contrast "natural" with other research settings—the laboratory, the clinic, or the field survey—where investigator control is the essential feature. The value of ecological studies has long been recognized in many other sciences. Perhaps the psychologist should more closely emulate the natural scientist by merely observing and recording data, rather than try to manipulate and control events. Barker calls ecological psychology a transducer science in which the psychologist functions only as a docile receiver, coder, and transmitter of psychological phenomena.

Phenomena are what we are really interested in—what happens out there without benefit of input from the investigator. That is a key feature of the psychologist as transducer: the investigator supplies no input to the data-generating system. His intent is not to change, not to manage, not to control, but simply to record what is there whether or not he is studying it. The goal of the psychologist as transducer is to get data about a world he did not make—data on naturally occurring behavior in its true, real-life, natural context.

This contrasts with the more usual role of the research psychologist, called by Barker the psychologist as operator, who manages and controls the data-generating system by means of inputs he carefully selects in line with his special interests, and quite properly so. For example, in the experimental trial, it is always the *experimenter's* trial. The questions in an interview or on a questionnaire are always the *investigator's* questions, problems, or tasks. The ecologist, though, wants to look at what is going on the rest of the time when social scientists are not out manipulating and controlling and managing the behavior stream of the persons. That is what we mean by a somewhat special approach.

Another important difference between the transducer and the operator is that the transducer seeks to discover naturally occurring units—units of behavior and situation which have self-generated —rather than investigator-imposed boundaries. But the operator is committed to a different policy, namely inventing or creating his own units for his own special purposes. I am not saying that is wrong or bad science, only that the operator and transducer roles are different and that psychology needs them both.

The ecological psychologists assert the importance of a naturalistic, descriptive approach to answer basic questions about the distribution of psychological phenomena in the real world, a task for which transducer methods are required. This poses a serious methodological problem, however, because psychology early adopted the experimental model in an effort to be scientific, hard-nosed, and tough-minded, and with a few notable exceptions that has been the dominant point of view in psychology.* As a result, the standard tools of psychological research are for the most part not suitable for a transducer science. Experiments, tests, and interviews destroy the very object of our interest in ecological psychology: naturally occurring behavior in its full, rich, real-world context. Much work over the last 20 years has had

---

*I once heard Michael Scriven give a talk making a strong case that Newtonian physics, which psychology early adopted, is the worst possible model for psychology. Geography, he argued, would have been a much better model—a very interesting idea indeed.

to be dedicated simply to developing research methods—special, tender-minded, phenomena-preserving, transducer methods.

The first of these was very simple. We set out to watch children. We followed them around with notebooks, took notes, and came back to the office to dictate what we call specimen records (Barker, 1963b). We got long samples of what ordinary life was like for children in this small town for long periods of time, some of them even up to a full day. In the process, we got on to the notion of behavior settings.

We observed that behavior in a small town like Oskaloosa is not randomly distributed over the whole town but occurs in standing patterns or charactistic waves in different places at certain times. If you go to the Post Office at nine o'clock on a weekday morning, you see a certain pattern in the behavior of those present. At the counter of the drugstore at ten o'clock, you see a different but equally stable pattern. You don't need to sample randomly over the whole town. If you want to see basketball playing, you go to a basketball game: what you need to do is identify these clusters of time-thing-place constellations where standing patterns of behavior occur.

In the study of behavior settings, the focus is upon particular situations or concrete contexts of molar behavior. The ecological psychologist studies consistencies in behavior which are associated with specific place-thing-time constellations regardless of which persons are involved. Just as the student of personality seeks to identify regularities or consistencies in behavior of single individuals over time related to such personal characteristics as genes, prenatal conditions, early experience, and child-training practices, the student of behavior settings seeks to identify regularities or consistencies in behavior across individuals over time related to the particular concrete situations in which the behavior occurs. The concepts, theories, and research methods of personality psychology may be required to understand why a particular 13-year-old boy is fascinated with fire and loves to light matches, but they are neither needed nor appropriate to understand why lighting matches and making fires among 13-year-old boys in general occur more often on Boy Scout cook-outs than in Sunday School classes: the cook-out setting requires match-lighting and fire-making but the Sunday School class setting resists them, requiring instead such behavior from 13-year-old boys as Bible reading, discussions between teacher and class members, and praying, regardless of the identities or individual personality characteristics of the people involved. The pressures and constraints of settings are so clear and strong that occupants of the settings must conform or face vigorous sanctions, as a boy who lights matches in Sunday School or reads the Bible on cook-outs will certainly find out. The behavior setting survey is essentially a method for studying, systematically and quantitatively, the environments that place situational coercions on people's molar behavior. The study of settings is the study of the concrete environmental situations with respect to which people direct their molar behavior—having lunch in the Pearl Cafe, buying groceries at Reid's Grocery Store, worshiping at the Methodist Church Worship Service, working on academic activities in the fifth grade, rooting for the home team at the high school basketball game. The behavior patterns in these examples represent the behavior of people in general in the settings. Having lunch, buying groceries, worshiping, and so on are stable, extraindividual patterns which regularly and consistently occur in the settings specified and are independent of the behavior of any particular person.

The behavior setting method, therefore, is a peculiar approach to psychology, an approach that focuses not on individual behavior or even on social interaction, but rather on the behavior of persons en masse associated with particular environmental settings. Deliberate exclusion of the individual personality is the basis for the not completely tongue-in-cheek reference to the method as "the psychology of the absent organism."

The concept of the behavior setting has been carefuly defined and precise operations for behavior setting identification and description have been published (Barker, 1968; Barker and Schoggen, 1973). For the present purpose, it will suffice to define a behavior setting as a cluster of *standing patterns of behavior* of people en masse occurring within a *particular part of the milieu* (a specific place-thing-time constellation)—where there is a *synomorphic relation* between the behavior patterns and the milieu. That is, the behavior and the milieu part fit together; there is a similarity of shape between the behavior and the environment.

As an example, consider the Methodist Church worship service which occurs every Sunday morning at eleven o'clock in a certain small Midwestern town. The cluster of *standing patterns of behavior* includes sedate entering of the sanctuary, worshipers sitting quietly in their pews, the playing of appropriate organ music, the rising and singing of hymns on signal from the minister, the collection of the offering, giving and listening to the sermon, and so on. The *particular milieu part* is the main sanctuary of the Methodist Church in the town of Midwest, Kansas, U.S.A., together with its component parts and objects: pews, chancel, choir loft, organ, pulpit holding the big Bible, hymn books, attendance register, and so on. The *synomorphic relation* between the milieu parts and the behavior patterns is seen, for example, in the fact that the pews face the chancel and are the proper size and height to support sitting and listening; the pulpit has a surface which slants away from the pews to support the Bible and the minister's notes as he speaks facing the congregation.

The ecologists did not invent or create the behavior settings, they merely discovered them, gave them a name, and studied them systematically. Settings are objective, hard, empirical realities, with a prior and continuing existence independent of the scientists' interest in studying them. The settings of Midwest—the Rotary Club meeting, the high school basketball game, Mrs. Trackett's first grade academic class, and several hundred more—are well known to the residents, for whom the settings are as visible and objective as rivers, trees, and tornadoes. Settings are natural units in the sense that their boundaries are self-generated as opposed to investigator-imposed. A related and important characteristic of behavior settings as ecological units is that each has a particular, denotable locale in space and time. Thus, unlike the processes designated by some abstract concepts in social science, behavior settings are easily locatable, observable, enterable, and, therefore, studiable occurrences.

A behavior setting survey is a comprehensive inventory and description of all the behavior settings occurring within a particular community or institution during a stated period of time, usually a calendar year. Settings are identified in terms of their intrinsic structural and dynamic properties. Equivalence across units is obtained by procedures which recognize as settings only those which display a given degree of internal interdependence of interior parts and independence from external events (see Barker, 1968, chapters 3 and 4, for details).

The data for a behavior setting survey are obtained by a variety of methods, including extensive direct observation by trained field workers who spend many hours in settings as participant observers; reference to public records (newspapers, directories, school schedules, organization programs and bulletins, membership rosters); and consultation with informants selected for their knowledge of particular areas of community life. These sources provide data sufficient to enable independent analysts to identify and describe behavior settings and many of their characteristics with an acceptable level of agreement.

In most applications to date, the studies have arbitrarily limited themselves to behavior settings which occur in the public areas of a town or an institution; homes and other areas for private or personal use have been omitted. Except for this limitation, a behavior setting survey of a town or institution includes all the behavior that occurs there during the survey year, because behavior settings are ubiquitous. All behavior occurs in one or another behavior setting—there are no gaps or interstices between settings, and the people are always in one or another of the behavior settings.

Once all the public settings in a town or institution have been identified, the final step in making the survey is to describe them in terms of whichever of their many attributes and characteristics may be of interest. In studies reported so far, these have included such dimensions as the characteristics of the setting inhabitants in terms of age, sex, social class; how much time inhabitants spend in the setting; which inhabitants exercise control over the operation of the setting; which population subgroups the setting is intended to serve primarily; and a variety of other habitat qualities.

Studies have been completed in small Midwestern towns (Barker and Wright, 1955; Barker, 1968), in an English village (Barker and Schoggen, 1973), in high schools of varying size (Barker and Gump, 1964), in an institution for handicapped children (Newton, 1953), in churches varying in size (Wicker, 1969), and in preschool programs (Schoggen, M., 1973). The most recent and extensive of these reports (Barker and Schoggen, 1973) describes a study of two small towns, Midwest, Kansas, U.S.A., and Yoredale, in Yorkshire, England, on two different occasions separated by a decade, 1954–55 and 1963–64. Midwest was selected originally for its manageable size, cultural vitality, and geographic location— proximity to the University of Kansas and independence from larger metropolitan centers. Yoredale was chosen for its similarity to Midwest on dimensions of obvious importance. Both towns are seats of local government and centers for trade and educational, recreational, and cultural activities for the surrounding rural areas.

From the great wealth of findings about Midwest and Yoredale as environments for molar behavior, reported in this study, the one with the greatest significance for the present purpose is summarized here, in truncated and simplified form.

Although the towns were quite similar in overall habitat extent and many other respects, there was one apparently important difference: the number of *habitat-claims*. A habitat claim is a certain locus (slot, position) that must be filled by a human being. An example is the instructor's position in Yoredale's Evening Institute German Class. The position requires a human component with the necessary knowledge and skills to become operational. Habitat-claims are stable, structural, and dynamic features of a town's habitat. Their number is the number of positions of responsibility that must be filled for the normal occurrence of the setting. Presbyterian Church worship service in Midwest, for example, requires twenty operatives (one minister, one organist, twelve choir members, two ushers, two candle lighters, two greeters); thus there are twenty habitat-claims in this setting. The towns' habitats are highly dependent upon human components for their operation and maintenance.

In 1963–64, the 884 behavior settings of Midwest had a total of 10,220 habitat-claims for operatives, many more than the 7,764 found in Yoredale's 758 behavior settings (Barker and Schoggen, 1973, chapter 3). Thus there were in Midwest many more positions of responsiblity (chairmen, hostesses, entertainers, cooks, speakers, and so on) to be filled than there were in Yoredale—132 percent as many altogether. Midwest's habitat called for more proprietorships, captaincies, chairmanships, and presidencies; its behavior settings had more places for secretaries, choir members, janitors, team members, bandsmen, waitresses, speakers, entertainers, umpires, salesmen, librarians, and so on. Midwest's habitat had more positions that are important and difficult than Yoredale's habitat.

The impact of this very substantial difference is compounded by the fact that Midwest had fewer town residents available to fill the greater number of habitat-claims—a total of 830 human components available to staff its 10,220 habitat-claims, as contrasted with Yoredale's 1,310 human components to fill its 7,764 habitat-claims. Thus Midwest had 2,456 more habitat-claims to be filled by 480 fewer town inhabitants, an average of 12.3 habitat-claims per resident in Midwest compared to 5.9 per Dalesman. In 1963–64, therefore, the average Midwesterner was about twice as likely as the average Dalesman to be called upon to accept responsibility for operating the town's public settings. Relative to Yoredale, the behavior settings of Midwest were undermanned. Additional data documenting this difference are also reported (Barker and Schoggen, 1973, chapter 8).

These and similar data obtained in several of the ecological studies over the years (Barker and Wright, 1955; Barker, 1960; Barker and Barker, 1961; Barker and Gump, 1964; Barker and Schoggen, 1973) led Barker to develop behavior setting theory with special reference to the consequences of undermanning on inhabitants' behavior. The main point of the theory, presented in detail elsewhere (Barker, 1968), is that undermanned settings—settings with unfilled habitat-claims—exert more pressure on potential participants to enter and take part in the operation and maintenance of the setting than adequately manned or overmanned settings. If the junior class play has parts for 12 actors and there are only 15 members of the class, no member is likely to be exempt from pressure to take a part, or at least to help backstage; but if there are 50 juniors, only the more talented or highly motivated are likely to become involved. Concretely, the theory predicts that Midwest's habitat, with its relatively undermanned settings will generate the following differences in the behavior output of Midwesterners as compared with Dalesmen: Midwesterners, on the average, will (a) spend more time per person in the public settings of the town; (b) more frequently assume positions of responsibility in operating the town's behavior settings; and (c) carry out many more actions of highest leadership responsibility.

The findings of the study (Barker and Schoggen, 1973, chapter 8) strongly support all three of these predictions: (a) the average Midwesterner spent 125 percent as many hours per year in the public behavior settings of the town (Midwest, 1,356 person-hours per year per person, Yoredale, 1,089); (b) the average Midwesterner occupied positions of responsibility 250 percent as frequently as Dalesmen (Midwest, 8.0 positions per year per person, Yoredale

3.2); (c) the average Midwesterner carried out 257 percent as many actions of highest leadership responsibility (Midwest, 1.8 leader acts per year per person, Yoredale 0.7).

The theory of undermanning has also been tested in studies of high schools differing in size (Barker and Gump, 1964). One of these studies (Gump and Friesen, 1964) compared a large high school (2,287 students) with four small ones (83–151 students) in Eastern Kansas in terms of student participation in voluntary non-class behavior settings. They found that, as expected, the settings of the small schools were in fact undermanned by comparison with those of the large school (mean number of persons per behavior setting: 12 in small schools, 36 in the large school).

The results showed that students in the small schools participated in just as many extracurricular settings as large school students despite the fact that the large school had more such settings available. Also consistent with theoretical expectations was the finding that on the average small school juniors occupied positions of responsibility in twice as many behavior settings as did large school juniors (small school, 8.6; large school, 3.5 positions per student):

	Large	Small*
Total Number of Juniors	794	23
Total Number of Settings	189	48
Mean Positions per Junior	3.5	8.6

*Average data from four small schools.

Thus, while the large school provided a richer habitat in terms of total number of settings available, the small schools much more often co-opted students into positions of responsibility in operating their settings.

In a follow-up study, Willems (1964) attempted to assess the psychological effect on the students of the differences in behavioral participation. Juniors were interviewed, using both open-ended and card-sorting techniques for identifying psychologically experienced forces toward participation in the nonschool settings. The data are reported in terms of own forces (attractions) and induced or external forces (pressures) reported by the students as reasons for participating in the voluntary activities. Results are given for both *regular* (ordinary, average) students and for students designated *marginal* (at high risk for dropping out because of low academic aptitude and other background factors).

Both the card-sort and the open-ended data showed that small school regular students reported significantly more forces, both own and foreign, toward participation in settings than did large school students. Regular students and marginal students in the small schools did not differ appreciably in either the number of pressures or the number of attractions reported. In the large school, on the other hand, marginal students reported both fewer attractions and fewer pressures, though only the latter difference was statistically significant. Willems comments on these findings as follows:

> The data on forces and responsibilities are relevant to the question of the comparative efficacy of personal variables and ecological variables in influencing behavior. The absence of differences between regular and marginal students in the small schools and the presence of such differences in the large school indicates that school size, as well as the kind of person, is a determinant of forces toward participation. The fact that marginal students of the small schools reported more forces than did the regular students of the large school is relevant too. In the large school, the academically marginal student appeared to be truly an outsider, while in the small schools being marginal made no apparent difference on the experience of pressures, attractions, and responsibilities. (Willems, 1964)

In an altogether independent investigation, Baird (1969) subjected the central hypothesis of the *Big School, Small School* report to critical examination and obtained relevant new data from a very large national sample of 21,371 students drawn randomly from the 712,000 who took the ACT (American College Test) and Student Profile for college admission. High school size was studied in relation to number of high school achievements and activities. Baird reports that, consistent with behavior setting theory, students in small schools participated to a greater extent in a variety of areas than did students in large schools.

Wicker and his students have addressed the theory of undermanned behavior settings in a series of studies of churches varying in size (Wicker, 1969; Wicker and Mehler, 1971) and report findings that are generally consistent with the theory.

Beyond the derivations from behavior setting theory reported and documented above, a number of probable psychological consequences of undermanned behavior settings have been suggested (Barker, 1968; Barker and Gump, 1964; Barker and Schoggen, 1973). While not derived from the theory of undermanning in any strict sense, these are psychological consequences on inhabitants of undermanned ecological environments which it seems reasonable to expect on the basis of common observation and some empirical evidence.

(a) Persons in undermanned habitats have *less sensitivity to and are less evaluative of individual differences*; they are more tolerant of their associates. When the supply is short and the demand is high, those who are available to do the job must be accepted even if their skills and experience are limited. In Midwest, with its severe manpower shortage relative to Yoredale, less experienced and less able persons (children, adolescents, and old people) are accepted into settings and given leadership responsibilities more commonly than their English counterparts. Discrimination on the basis of appearances and superficial traits is less likely in undermanned settings. When there is a manpower surplus, on the other hand, competition among many possible contenders for the limited number of available opportunities to participate sometimes becomes so keen that many persons with appropriate experience and excellent functional skills are excluded, sometimes on the basis of superficial personality traits or other largely irrelevant considerations.

(b) Persons in undermanned habitats *see themselves as having greater functional importance*. The relative scarcity of setting inhabitants makes them more important people and they experience this directly without needing to be told. It is obvious to all that a setting, to operate, must have a minimum number of participants, and each person's contribution therefore is seen as more valuable. In a small church choir with only two tenors, both feel a strong obligation to attend rehearsals and performances because they understand the serious consequences for the tenor section and the threat to the choir as a whole of their absence. Small school students expressed similar feelings about being needed to help make the setting go.

(c) Persons in undermanned habitats have *more responsiblity*. Responsibility is experienced by a person when a behavior setting and the gain it provides to others depend upon his actions. A setting that is optimally populated does not burden itself with indispensable personnel; the people are too unreliable, so substitutes, vice presidents, a second team are regular features of optimally manned or overmanned settings.

(d) Persons in undermanned habitats have *greater functional identity*: they are seen in terms of what they can do in the setting. A person with an essential function is seen as more than a person— as a person-in-context. The concern is with getting the job done, not what kind of person he is.

(e) Persons in undermanned habitats *experience greater insecurity*. Faced with the need to perform more difficult and more varied actions often without proper training or appropriate experience, a person in an underpopulated setting is in greater jeopardy of failing to carry through his tasks. The problem is exacerbated by the lack of reserves to turn to for help. This amounts to increased dependence upon every other person to carry through on their responsiblities. But the risk of failure also implies the opportunity for success, and this gives meaning and personal significance to the activity.

The implications of the theory of undermanning for the primary prevention of psychopathology should now be apparent. The evidence sketched above from studies of small towns and institutions suggests that ecological environments with surplus manpower exert stultifying and debilitating pressures on their human inhabitants, while undermanned ecologies tend to enhance growth and development by providing opportunities and challenges for meaningful participation in important activities. High schools, churches, towns, and other ecological environments with manpower surpluses appear to be ruthless in excluding, or limiting primarily to spectator positions, all but the most able of the available inhabitants. But undermanned settings reach out to almost any potential participant with encouragement to enter and take an active part in operating the setting, even though his skills may be limited.

In more general terms, it would appear that the analysis of ecological environments in terms of behavior settings is a promising method of increasing our understanding of how environmental factors relate to psychological processes. Only through such improved understanding will it ever be possible to design, construct, and maintain environments that minimize psychopathology through providing environmental properties that are conducive to optimal mental health.

REFERENCES

Altman, Irwin. *The environment and social behavior.* Monterey: Brooks/Cole, 1975.

Baird, L. L. Big school, small school: A critical examination of the hypothesis. *Journal of Educational Psychology,* 1969, *60,* 253–260.

Barker, R. G. Ecology and motivation. In M. R. Jones (Ed.,), *Nebraska Symposium on Motivation.* Lincoln: University of Nebraska Press, 1960.

Barker, R. G. On the nature of the environment. *Journal of Social Issues,* 1963, *19,* 17–38. (a)

Barker, R. G. *The stream of behavior.* New York: Appleton-Century-Crofts, 1963. (b)

Barker, R. G. *Ecological psychology: Concepts and methods for studying the environment of human behavior.* Stanford: Stanford University Press, 1968.

Barker, R. G., and Barker, L. S. Behavior units for the comparative study of cultures. In B. Kaplan (Ed.), *Studying personality cross culturally.* New York: Harper and Row, 1961.

Barker, R. G., and Gump, P. V. *Big school, small school.* Stanford: Stanford University Press, 1964.

Barker, R. G., and Schoggen, P. *Qualities of community life: Methods of measuring environment and behavior applied to an American and an English town.* San Francisco: Jossey-Bass, Inc., 1973.

Barker, R. G. and Wright, H. F. *One boy's day.* New York: Harper, 1951.

Barker, R. G., and Wright, H. F. *Midwest and its children.* New York: Harper and Row, 1955. Reprinted by Archon Books, Hamden, Connecticut, 1971.

Gump, P. V., and Friesen, W. Participation in nonclass settings. In R. G. Barker and P. V. Gump (Eds.), *Big school, small school.* Stanford: Stanford University Press, 1964.

Newton, M. R. A study in psychological ecology: The behavior settings in an institution for handicapped children. Masters Thesis, University of Kansas, 1953.

Schoggen, M. Characteristics of the environment of three classrooms: An exploratory study. Peabody College, J. F. Kennedy Center, Nashville, Tennessee, 1973 (mimeographed).

Schoggen, M., and Schoggen, P. Environmental forces in the home lives of three-year-old children in three population subgroups. *Catalog of Selected Documents in Psychology,* Journal Supplement Abstract Service, 1972, *6:* 8.

Schoggen, P. Environmental forces in the everyday lives of children. In R. G. Barker (Ed.), *The stream of behavior.* New York: Appleton-Century-Crofts, 1963.

Schoggen, P. An ecological study of children with physical disabilities in school and at home. In R. Weinberg and F. Wood (Eds.), *Observation of pupils and teachers in mainstream and special education settings: Alternative strategies.* Leadership Training Institute in Special Education, University of Minnesota, Minneapolis, 1975.

Wicker, A. W. Size of church membership and members' support of church behavior settings. *Journal of Personality and Social Psychology*, 1969, *13*, 278–288.

Wicker, A. W., and Mehler, A. Assimilation of new members in a large and a small church. *Journal of Applied Psychology*, 1971, *55*, 151–156.

Willems, E. P. Forces toward participation in behavior settings. In R. G. Barker and P. V. Gump (Eds.), *Big school, small school*. Stanford: Stanford University Press, 1964.

DISCUSSION BY F. RICK HEBER

As an activist who would like to see himself as an instrument of change in some of our institutional structures, I endorse Freedman's plea that psychology move out of the laboratory and into the real world, where research ideas can be generated from observations of human phenomena in a relevant environment. The very survival of the science of psychology may demand that much of our work relate increasingly to problems that are important to legislative bodies and to the general public.

I appreciate the concern over the fact that the role of physical environmental facilities in our social intervention programs has been neglected. Present government policies make it relatively easy to find money to hire people to perform services yet virtually impossible to procure funding to construct facilities for providing these services. And when you *can* get current funds for facility construction, federal and state building standards make it impossible to consider aesthetics and other psychological dimensions in the design. The bureaucratic criteria seem to emphasize only net usable square footage at the lowest possible cost. I am concerned with this aspect of the physical environment because in my own field of mental retardation, it is a valid concern. With the mentally and physically handicapped, the mentally ill and retarded, and handicapped adults, funds for vocational rehabilitation are virtually limitless through federal and state programs. What cannot be done is to construct physical facilities: funds for this purpose do not exist. Across the nation, with few exceptions, rehabilitation facilities for the adult handicapped are located in the most derelict, depressing facilities—storefronts, warehouses, factories that have long been abandoned by the private sector of the economy.

The last two United States presidents have directed that we empty our institutions for the mentally retarded. In response, we have begun to build group homes in the residential neighborhoods of small communities. But citizens have enacted protective zoning ordinances prohibiting construction in many places; so the programs are at a virtual standstill and in many states people are being moved back into institutions.

Sommer* suggested that enrichment programs are not productive because they don't change the institutional structures. That is a meaningful and frustrating comment. People in many communities over the country have tried in vain to change the structures of our community agencies. In Milwaukee, the greatest barrier to providing effective services to problem families is the obvious display of highly compartmentalized community agencies; efforts to coordinate these agencies have met with failure. Hardened institutionalized attitudes are inimicable to change; they reflect the attitudes of the power structure within the institution. Public schools, by and large, have remained unresponsive and unchanged over the past century.

I would ask our environmentalists if they have any strategies to facilitate the attitude changes which must occur before we can bring about what we feel are desirable changes in our institutional structures. Additionally, I would ask them to comment on the possible increased activist or interventional role for psychology in the future. Psychology has not distinguished itself in the past as an agent of social change. What is the future role of environmental psychology—or behavioral science in general—in effecting changes in public policy?

Bernard L. Bloom commented on Schoggen's paper: Schoggen's presentation of Barker's ecological psychology was provocative. I was struck by the big-school, small-school data and the terrible social cost of impersonality—the implication that there are surplus people. If I ran a mental health center, I would not have a large building; rather, I would take the cachement area and divide it up into small communities, thereby reducing the likelihood of impersonality and surplus people, and create with my staff people a true sense of an interdependent community, in the best Lewinian sense of that term. It is important to obtain some persuasive documentation of the positive impact on mental health of undermanning in a small interdependent community.

*See above, pp. 115 ff.

V
Integration

11

Conference Integration

M. BREWSTER SMITH

M. Brewster Smith received the Ph.D. degree in Psychology from Harvard University in 1947, then remained there for two years on the faculty. After that, he spent three years as Professor of Psychology and Department Chairman, Vassar College. In 1956 he became Professor and Director of Graduate Training in Psychology at New York University. Between 1959 and 1968 he was Professor of Psychology at the University of California, Berkeley; during much of that time he was also on the administrative staff of the Institute of Human Development there. From 1968 to 1970 he was Professor of Psychology and Department Chairman, University of Chicago, and ever since has been Professor of Psychology at the University of California, Santa Cruz, where he was also Vice Chancellor for Social Sciences from 1970 to 1975.

Over the years he has published extensively, particularly in the humanistically oriented aspects of social psychology. In addition to scores of articles, he has written four books, including Volume 2 of The American Soldier *series in 1949 and* Humanizing Social Psychology *in 1974. At present he is preparing a book on the psychology of self.*

He has been editor of the Journal of Social Issues *and the* Journal of Abnormal and Social Psychology, *and has also served on the editorial boards of* Health and Society, Journal of Youth and Adolescence, Ethos, *and* Human Motivation.

In addition to all his other activities, Smith has served on advisory groups to state and federal government, including various committees of the National Science Foundation and the National Institute of Mental Health. He has also been on various boards and committees of the American Psychological Association and became president of that organization in 1976.

His present scholarly activity is in personality and social psychology, with emphasis on the theory of the self.

Four subagendas are implicit in the foregoing conference papers. First is the concern over clarifying and sharpening our conceptualization of primary prevention. This is reflected particularly in Goldston's report but also in those of Cowen, Altman, and Bloom. They do not spend much time on definitional exegesis and controversy—it seldom seems profitable—but their presentations contribute some real help. Second, two solid substantive papers focus squarely on the primary prevention target: Heber's account of his Milwaukee program, aimed at preventing mental retardation (with a rich obbligato from Hunt's Iranian orphanage experience), and Bloom's scholarly paper on marital stress and its relevance to primary prevention. Third, in the area of environmental psychology, a certain amount of intramural discussion among the environmentalists sometimes gets near to making contact with primary prevention but does not always do so. One can see why, in principle, this relatively new area of psychology is extremely relevant to primary prevention. Probably its very newness has led to more time being spent on internal controversies about how it should go about its job and less on how it relates to primary prevention. Finally, led by our environmentalists but also with wider ramifications, there is a good deal of strategic methodological discussion about how we ought to go about our research, our conceptualization, and our interventions in this area. These four subagendas overlap and intersect and it makes sense to talk about them side by side.

Heber's and Bloom's presentations relate in interestingly different ways to the continuum of primary prevention—if there is one. I had heard of the Milwaukee study and I have also heard echoes of Ellis Page's critical memorandum. On the basis of Heber's presentation, his project seems like a splendid instance of primary prevention, although mental retardation, not psychopathology, is at issue. I admire the wisdom of the strategic decisions to saturate the lives of children at risk with a very strong intervention, then to carry it out for the entire preschool period and follow through for several years thereafter.

In recent years, evaluative research on compensatory education has been in an unfortunate state. It has included such misguided studies as the Westinghouse evaluation of Head Start (Westinghouse Learning Corporation, Ohio University, 1969). It seemed that everything was done wrong. Head Start itself was launched as a massive national program without proper preliminary piloting. There has been a succession of small inconsistent studies and one big uninformative study, leaving us with an embarrassment of inconclusive, but mainly negative, results.

Previous work has mostly dealt with trivial inputs (trivial when you compare the conceivable impact of the program interventions with the locked-in-ness of slum children in damaging social systems), mostly by means of short-term studies of impact. Such studies do not provide any basis for projecting what will or will not happen when stronger inputs and longer term follow-through are involved. One consequence of Heber's contrasting strategy is that he is dealing not with tiny effects but rather with findings that show startling differences between his experimental and control groups. His data are unlikely to be vulnerable to the sort of technical methodological criticism that undoubtedly will continue to be argued. Surely there will be artifactual components, impact of repeated testing, and so on, in spite of the safeguards that were taken. Differences of the order that Heber says he obtained, however, cannot be explained away artifactually.

For me, Heber has restored hope for the primary prevention of mental retardation. I do not think his findings prove that Jensen (1969) and Herrnstein (1973) are wrong about their claims for heavy genetic components, but they certainly refute the conclusions of people who, following Jensen and Herrnstein, think the strongly genetic basis of intelligence test performance implies that you can't get anywhere with intervention programs. And this is a very important thing to have established.

Where next? Once Heber's massive impacts have been replicated with similar results, we still need to know a lot more about what produces them. This was one of Ellis Page's criticisms (though it was out of order; it is crucially important to show first that an intelligent massive program using all of our current knowledge does indeed produce substantial effects). Heber should develop some quasi-clinical insights on which treatments were most essential, by looking at individual differences and process records within his experimental group, by talking with his teachers, and so on. He should milk his experience for as much as he can learn, even though the gain is in hunches rather than proof. We are already given some clues in his paper: apparently the effects followed primarily from the massive direct input to the children rather than from the mediated input through the mothers, simply because there was so little demonstrated change in the mothers other than vocational. There must be other similar clues in his data.

If major effects *can* be produced by saturation at high cost, it is time for a research and development effort to see what components of the Heber program are essential and how much effect could be produced by a scaled-down program that we could afford politically and economically. This job may be less exciting than Heber's research, but it is no less essential. Such follow-through engineering would test whether Heber's program could be adapted to school or to substitute homes. It might of course indicate that you cannot reduce the input much and still get major effects. Heber's input greatly exceeded what could be practical on a natural basis: absorbing eight hours of every day of a child's life from birth until entry in school, initially on a one-to-one basis and later at a still very high ratio of helper to child. If it should turn out that anything much short of that does not undo the damage of the slum, the news would be grim; but we would need to know it. That kind of information would provide strong grounds for a radical attack on our social system as the only way to be fair to the children being born in our country.

Bloom's paper on marital discord approaches primary prevention in the middle of life in contrast to Heber's focus on events happening at the beginning. Heber is concerned with a *developmental* input to primary prevention; Bloom is concerned with a recurring human *situation* in which one may either try to control and mitigate maladjustive responses to crisis or to use the crisis as an occasion for fostering growth. Additionally, Heber reported his findings at the end of his research program, whereas Bloom is at the beginning of his. Bloom made a compelling case for the promise of investment in studies of marital discord as a setting for preventive intervention. He is moving into new territory for psychologists, a terrain sociologists and social workers know well under the rubric of marriage and family relations. I am surprised that psychologists have left this area so much to others in their preemptive concern with general laws and processes at the expense of attention to the major contexts in which human lives occur.

The second major subagenda of this conference was concerned with issues in environmental psychology—the new field of behavior and the environment. Prevention must focus on the environment. Any intervention, apart from unforseeable genetic ones, have their impact through modifying the environment of the target people. They can be one-to-one interventions to change the interpersonal environment; they may involve changes in the larger interpersonal social systems in which a person is embedded; or they may require modifications of the physical environment. One of the reasons that the new field of environmental psychology has development problems is that, in principle, environmental psychology really ought to include virtually all of psychology—any psychology, that is, which is other than a kind of physiology. In selecting topics to go with the new heading, it is therefore hard to find boundaries that are rationally justified. The field is still searching for paradigms, and in its short lifetime it has suffered in more acute form from the kind of faddishness that has also characterized the related field of social psychology because of *its* lack of a solid paradigmatic base. Given this state of affairs, I found Altman's (1975) book, which he drew upon in his paper, informative and helpful. Jonathan Freedman's (1975) book on crowding, too, is one of the more solid experimental contributions. Still, the field is searching for identity, and we at the conference have witnessed a certain amount of identity struggle in our environmentalists' contributions.

Long before the term environmental psychology appeared and began looking for content, Roger Barker (1968) had been working in what he called "ecological psychology." As Schoggen described it, this was a fairly isolated and self-contained tradition. The group of workers was enormously patient with their long-term data gathering in rural Oskaloosa. They were regarded by others—and perhaps by themselves—as a kind of collective John-the-Baptist-crying-in-the-wilderness, calling for attention to the importance of environmental factors. Until recently they won respect but not very close attention. Now, however, the scene has changed. A field calling itself environmental psychology has independently arisen with enough potency to generate an American Psychological Association task force and to change the name of the APA division that wanted to absorb it. Schoggen and his colleagues in ecological psychology seem still to be crying in the new wilderness, wanting to be heard. They are saying: "We have a paradigm. We know what we're doing. Please, the rest of you environmental psychologists, learn about the behavior setting, learn about the setting survey, understand what we are up to, and you will be helped by it."

How might environmental psychology relate to primary prevention? The conference provided evidence of a strong, warranted consensus—at least among Schoggen, Altman, and Freedman—that physical environmental factors are unlikely to control much variance of the parameters we are interested in. For Schoggen the behavior settings are a melding of what are essentially sociocultural phenomena—the standing behavior pattern—with the associated physical milieu. He is concerned not strictly with the physical environment, but with the psychological environment, in Lewin's (1935) sense in which the sociocultural components are probably more important than the sheer physical ones. Altman's treatment of privacy brought in the cultural perspective, which has been absent in much of the recent literature. Compare life in a centuries-old Hopi pueblo or in a high-density area in Hong Kong, where there has been urban crowding for a long time, with life in Harlem. Here, the urban population was rural a generation or so ago and was uprooted and transplanted without any real chance to develop adequate cultural norms for regulating interaction in a crowded urban setting. If you ignore culture, how can you make any psychological sense of privacy and crowding? Once the importance of culture is recognized, the critical point is how people define and use the physical environment, rather than the physical features of the environment itself. Freedman comes to the same conclusion by emphasizing that we do not find strong main effects by analyzing variance of environmental influence; instead, we find complex multiple interactive effects, showing that the physical environment has impact only in conjunction with a great many other variables. Perhaps Sommer would give more weight to the physical environment, but the rest of us seem to feel that studying the direct impact of the physical environment is probably not the major contribution of the environmental psychologist.

If we ascribe a strategic role to environmental factors in primary prevention, we need not suppose that people are passively shaped by environmental manipulating. Environmental psychologists can turn to environmentalist strategies in primary prevention and still recognize people's active roles in selecting and modifying their environments. Active roles are central to my own conception of human effectiveness and positive mental health. In Altman's view of privacy, one's personal control over his own social boundaries is critical. I would not like to think that by emphasizing the environment we imply that people are passively molded by it. If we are fortunate enough to live our lives well, we gain the capacity to select and modify our environments in many respects.

The organizers of the conference were well advised to bring environmental psychology in close contact with primary prevention. In the future, the interrelationship will be important and geniune. At this relatively early stage, we should not expect to find major results, although such ideas as Barker's undermanning and overmanning hypothesis are suggestive and useful (Barker and Schoggen, 1973).

A third subagenda topic at the conference concerns methodological issues. I agree with Sommer's suggestion that we need to get the yogi and the commissar into the same bed, since they should be concerned with an interactive approach. I like Altman's nonlinear, *systems* way of thinking, not as a theory—it isn't that— but as a general framework for theorizing that explains why neither yogi nor commissar can rightfully hold the day in isolation. But I strongly disagree with Freedman's sense of strategy in using the experimental approach. My disagreement stems from some broad judgments about the role of experimentation in psychology and social science and, indeed, about the kind of science we are aiming for and what we can reasonably expect (see Smith, 1976).

Schoggen quoted Michael Scriven to the effect that psychology and the behavioral sciences have been badly set back by picking Newtonian physics for a model. I agree. Perhaps meteorology is a better model. We are all folk meteorologists. There is a phenomenology of clouds; there is an untheoretically, statistically predictive aspect of weather that is important practically; and there is a kind of microphysics of the air with processes that can be studied in wind tunnels and condensation chambers. Meteorology is a theoretical hard science. Yet one cannot leap from it to a complete accounting for the global weather. Human psychology in its social aspects may be in much the same situation. Freedman's view of the experimental strategy would have us shoot for a Newtonian science, not a meteorology. Progress is supposed to come from cumulative experimentation involving laborious parametric variation of the many variables involved. And in the very long run, Freedman hopes the endeavor will lead to a grand Newtonian scheme integrating it all.

I do not think that is the way things have gone or will go in the human sciences. Important research achievements have been demonstration studies rather than contributions to such a cumulative Newtonian system. Consider Solomon Asch's (1961) work on conformity, Mazafer Sherif's work in the same area and in intergroup conflict (Sherif, 1936; Sherif and Sherif, 1953), Lewin's work in styles of leadership (Lewin, Lippitt, and White, 1939), and Leon Festinger's (1957) earlier work introducing the concept of cognitive dissonance; in each of these cases experimentation dramatized a new way of looking at behavior determinants in the real world. Each time such a dramatic demonstration study captures our attention, a period of busywork follows that fills our journals with attempts to vary things parametrically and tease out all the implications. Usually these attempts peter out before long, a damping-off effect occurs, and attention shifts. Some cumulative information results but not as much as might be hoped, and no steady march toward a grand Newtonian scheme is seen.

Real advances have probably consisted rather in our becoming sensitized to variables, reconceptualizing problems, and encountering new situations with sharpened eyes for what may really be going on. When we assess that new sophistication by rereading the textbooks of 30 or 40 years ago, we regain a strong conviction of progress, though not the direct cumulative sort that Freedman hopes for. Also, when we deal with the kind of intrinsically human content that this conference is concerned with, we are dealing with people immersed in history and culture; they are not going to remain unchanging while we work through all the parametric variations. Social relations and people will not be the same groupings and creatures by the time we finish the extensive research program as they were when we began it.

Evaluation research was brought up by Sommer. In the area of educational research, Michael Scriven distinguished between what he calls *formative* and *summative* evaluation (Scriven, 1967). Summative evaluation is illustrated by Heber's attempt to assess the overall impact of a program. You do this kind of study to justify a yes-or-no decision on further investment of funds in a given area, and it requires rigorous experimental controls sufficient to convince a skeptic. Formative evaluation, on the other hand, is exemplified by the kind of in-house study you would do to guide program development. (Heber's study, of course, also has its formative aspect.) Quite different considerations enter into formative evaluation projects than for well-designed summative evaluation projects. The latter are not best described as "quick and dirty"; rather, their basis is a greater readiness to substitute judgment for complete proof, a higher priority set on qualitative information, and an adequate description of what is really going on as contrasted with some more distant appraisal of overall effects.

Most discussion of evaluation in the current literature focuses on the summative kind. There has been very little codification of the considerations involved in good formative evaluation. That is unfortunate, because formative evaluation is always needed in the development and guidance of programs, whereas summative evaluation is warranted only in special circumstances. Good summative evaluation makes sense when there is a massive, expensive program and where the political context allows a negative answer to be received (all too rarely). Current evaluation research typically involves amateurish, incompetent, small-scale, self-serving summative evaluation, which is basically dishonest, wasteful, and unhelpful. We have no ground rules to help us do the kind of steering, cybernetic evaluative work that might improve our programs (see Smith, 1975).

A further word about Schoggen's distinction between the transducer role and the operator role. I like the distinction, but I think it has to be understood as an ideal type, not as a classification of actual roles. I have seen primary prevention done; but I have not seen anybody play the pure transducer role. Whenever we record facts we impose on them some kind of conceptual scheme, and we impose assumptions to start with. My epistemology says there is no way to avoid that. One is safer if he knows how he is shaping the data being gathered rather than pretending he is simply discerning things as they are out there in the real world. Furthermore, in all social research we get deeply involved in Heisenberg-like effects, in which our studies impact upon the phenomena we are studying. Again, the safer road is to be aware of this, not to pretend we can avoid it.

In addition to the transducer and operator roles, there is a third kind of role—extensively promoted by Harry Stack Sullivan (1953)—that fits the traditions of sociological rather than psychological research. This is the role of the participant observer, and it may well be the most appropriate one for the practicing clinician or preventive mental health worker doing research. We know we are participating in the phenomena under study, but at the same time we are attentive to what we can learn from the participation. This fits in well with the proposal of Leona Tyler (1973) and others for psychologists to present themselves to the world not as experts, technocrats, and superiors, but as equal-status consultants to and collaborators with the people they serve.

The fourth subagenda item is conceptual, and I have already touched on some issues that are closely tied to methodological ones. Certain consequences appear to follow from Goldston's four frameworks for thinking about primary prevention. The first of these, it will be recalled, involves primary prevention of mental illnesses with known etiology—a function that tends to fall into the hands of public rather than mental health people, though there may be roles for the latter in connection with the human behavior component in these known illnesses. Second is primary prevention of mental illnesses of unknown etiology—schizophrenia, for example—where Goldston advised us to go slow, be cautious, and not make strong claims. Third is the primary prevention of emotional distress, based on gains in knowledge about causes of human misery. And fourth is the promotion of positive mental health, including competence, maturity, and effectiveness. Now, the concern of this conference is the primary prevention of *psychopathology;* and that appears to fit the first two of Goldston's frameworks better than the last two. This is surprising, as the first two are most congruent with the medical framework for dealing with pathology and illness. The last two would seem to fit better with educational, sociocultural, and other nonmedical models. It may well be that positive mental health—by any criteria—and absence of signs of pathology do not show high correlations. Possibly the relationship is quite modest and we are making assumptions about them that will not stand up.

Now let me identify some cross-cutting conference issues. One has to do with criteria. If we are concerned with promoting mental health, we must certainly come to grips with the question of what we mean by positive mental health. To give some shape to the dependent variables, we might consider Marie Jahoda's (1958) multiple criteria along with Cowen's focus on competence as a measure. It makes good pragmatic sense to frame the problem in terms that we can deal with through some distinctive competence of our own. I endorse Ansbacher's suggestions that we think in terms of maturity and that we conceive of maturity as involving a movement from an egocentric to a more socially interested relation to the world. I have read with much excitement Jane Loevinger's (1976) important new book on ego development. If she is right, we can go a good deal further than Ansbacher in elaborating a view of psychological maturity and growth that might be very relevant to the primary prevention effort. Further work to investigate the promise offered by Loevinger's stage-theory approach is decidedly worth the investment.

Another issue follows from considering Goldston's four frameworks. Should we orient ourselves mainly to psychiatric medicine, to public health in the epidemiological sense shared by Goldston and Bloom, or to our common ground with sociology, anthropology, and education? I used to be an ideologist on these matters, feeling that we risk our integrity if we let ourselves use the terminology of the medical model. Now I have ceased to be quite so concerned about terminological issues. Perhaps a real advantage of specific mental health terminology is that it allows us to relate both to health concerns and to social and educational ones. Mental health is not a clean theoretical concept, and perhaps it *should* identify an arena in which we can bring a variety of frames to bear.

What are we to say about the issue between those (like Cowen and Heber) who emphasize an early development approach and those (like the social environmentalists) who would rather emphasize the contemporary situation as a determinant of healthy behavior and as a focus for primary prevention? Like the yogi-and-commissar issue, the choice may be unnecessary, and perhaps we need both emphases. The focus on early development leads to implications that have not been discussed here. One of the better research efforts on primary prevention with children was the Bank Street study of progressive versus traditional schools, in which data collected almost two decades ago was published in a book (Minuchin et al., 1969) on the psychological impact of these schools. One of the findings was that children in the progressive school were more *childlike:* they were less controlled and more expressive; they didn't try to act grown up, they acted childish. The Bank Street investigators saw this outcome as good. Childhood, they felt, is a part of people's real lives, and it should be as good as possible while it is being lived. It is not purely preparation. One needs to be concerned with the morale, happiness, and gratification of children while they are children rather than simply with the instrumental relationship of their childhood years to some distant future. The Bank Street group made the assumption that children who were encouraged to *be* children wholeheartedly, not prematurely pseudo-adults, would be more happy, effective, and mentally healthy as adults. This is a longitudinal prediction based on sheer assumption, with no supporting data. If we are going to work on primary prevention issues in the early years of life, we incur an intellectual and even ethical obligation to invest substantially in longitudinal studies. No such investment has been made. Adequate longitudinal studies are expensive, but they must be done; there is no other way of knowing whether we are promoting or preventing qualities for good adult life in our children's programs. Of course we also need more situationally oriented work with adults, and we cannot dismiss the miseries of the aged as totally without value or consequence.

In closing, let me return to Cowen's citation of Kessler and Albee's (1975) Annual Review chapter with its tongue-in-cheek catalogue of all the things that primary prevention might be. Cowen suggested that we give up the spiritualism, get down to the nitty-gritty, and bite bullets in the areas where we have a contribution of our own to make. I agree, with one reservation based on a distinction between our role as researcher and our role in practice. If our research shows that aspects of modern life—including schools and slums and housing and the physical environment—are relevant to primary prevention, that is by no means trivial. It does not mean we have to claim that as mental health professionals we are competent to deal with crime, divorce, and all the other major social problems of our time. A new conservatism seems to be sweeping the country, in which all kinds of justifications are being sought and found for accepting a far from satisfactory status quo. In this context, firm evidence—if it can be firm—that the many factors outside the competence of mental health specialists are relevant to human effectiveness, and possibly to the avoidance of mental disorders, would be socially important. If we can develop such evidence, we should do so; but we do not have to engineer the primary prevention that such knowledge would call for. Finally, we must recognize that much of the knowledge is simply unavailable at present.

REFERENCES

Altman, I. *The environment and social behavior*. Monterey, California: Brooks/Cole, 1975.

Asch, S. E. Effects of group pressure upon the modification and distortion of judgment. In H. Guetzkow (Ed.), *Groups, leadership, and men*. Pittsburgh: The Carnegie Press, 1951, pp. 177–190.

Barker, R. G. *Ecological psychology*. Stanford: Stanford University Press, 1968.

Barker, R. G., and Schoggen, P. *Qualities of community life*. San Francisco: Jossey-Bass, 1973.

Festinger, L. *A theory of cognitive dissonance*. Evanston, Ill.: Row, Peterson, 1957.

Freedman, J. L. *Crowding and behavior*. New York: Viking, 1975.

Herrnstein, R. J. *I.Q. in the meritocracy*. Boston: Atlantic Monthly Press, 1973.

Jahoda, M. *Current conceptions of positive mental health*. New York: Basic Books, 1958.

Jensen, A. R. How much can we boost I. Q. and scholastic achievement? *Harvard Educational Review*, 1969, *39*, 1–123.

Joint Commission on Mental Illness and Health. *Action for mental health. Final report of the Joint Commission on Mental Illness and Health*. New York: Basic Books, 1961.

Kessler, M., and Albee, G. W. Primary prevention. *Annual Review of Psychology*, 1975, *26*, 557–591.

Lewin, K. *A dynamic theory of personality*. New York: McGraw-Hill, 1935.

Lewin, K., Lippitt, R., and White, R. K. Patterns of aggressive behavior in experimentally created "social climates." *Journal of Social Psychology*, 1939, *10*, 271–299.

Loevinger, J. *Ego development: Conceptions and theories*. San Francisco: Jossey-Bass, 1976.

Minuchin, P., Biber, B., Shapiro, E., and Zimilies, H. *The psychological impact of school experience*. New York: Basic Books, 1969.

Scriven, M. The methodology of evaluation. In R. W. Tyler, R. M. Gagné, and M. Scriven (Eds.), *Perspectives on curriculum evaluation*. Chicago: Rand McNally, 1967, pp. 29–83.

Smith, M. B. Beyond journalistic scouting: Evaluation for better programs. *Journal of Applied Behavioral Science*, 1975, *11*, 290–297.

Smith, M. B. Social psychology, science, and history: So what? *Personality and Social Psychology Bulletin*, 1976, *2*, 438–444.

Sullivan, H. S., in H. S. Perry and M. L. Gravel (Eds.), *The interpersonal theory of psychiatry*. New York: Norton, 1953.

Tyler, L. E. Design for a hopeful psychology. *American Psychologist*, 1973, *28*, 1021–1029.

Westinghouse Learning Corporation—Ohio University. *The impact of Headstart. An evaluation of the effects of Headstart on children's cognitive and affective development*. 2 vols. Presented to Office of Economic Opportunity, June 12, 1969.

SELECTED DISCUSSION

Dr. Sommer: I would like to speak to the issue of how environmental psychology can interface with primary prevention. In Heber's study, for example, the specific questions for the environmental psychologists become: How do we provide more stimulating environments for children? How do we generalize his findings into housing projects, day care centers, and schools? How do we coerce parents to play more with their children? How do we design our housing projects to get more mother-child and father-child interaction? We know a good deal about how physical arrangements affect behavior and we should use this information in further studies.

The same approach pertains to the elderly. Again using the concept of the high-risk group, how do we design retirement facilities and housing projects, or even transportation systems within cities, to minimize pathology and optimize the potential of the elderly? This is a design problem. Often, you can use a transportation system in lieu of designing more high-rise facilities for the elderly.

With respect to Bloom's study, it is possible to consider the environmental aspects of divorce. Among other things, divorce means, with few exceptions, that one person leaves the home territory. There are serious consequences of leaving a home and familiar objects; and attachments to places and objects need exploration. By getting these kinds of information and working within existing community forces, we can do much to forestall the development of pathology. The essence is that we intervene at an environmental as well as personal level. We can help people get the kind of physical environment that helps them attain their goals.

The principal issues that emerged from the remainder of the discussion follow.

1. The urgent need for follow-up studies to the Heber research. There are prototypes for such studies in the animal psychology literature, where intellectual enrichment research was done first as demonstration investigations and later as highly specific variable testing investigations.

2. Concern for the future adjustment of Heber's experimental

subjects. Elevating their intellectual performance but leaving them in a poor cultural setting may confront them with a very difficult adjustment situation.

3. An attempt to distinguish between the prevention of pathology and the development of competence. They are not necessarily the same thing, although in some observations, such as Heber's, they appear to be so.

4. A need to explore the complex sociopolitical problems involved in primary prevention efforts. Broad cultural changes will ultimately be involved in any successful long-term prevention programs; these will be very difficult to bring about and may take generations to effect.

5. The interesting proposal that future research be concerned with those who pass through a disadvantaged childhood and emerge well adjusted and intellectually sound. Study of these people may suggest clearly and quickly what can be done to prevent failure in others.

12

Epilogue

DONALD G. FORGAYS

A specific goal of the Second Vermont Conference on the Primary Prevention of Psychopathology was to bring experts in environmental psychology together with behavioral scientists who had been actively manipulating environmental variables as attempts to prevent or alleviate behavioral disorder. It was hoped that intensive interaction, even for only a few days, would have cross-fertilization benefits and perhaps lead to better designed future social-action intervention programs. Did the conference succeed? The answer, as one might expect, is partly "yes" and partly "no."

The papers presented by Cowen, Heber, Hunt, and Bloom— the active practitioners who were dealing with interesting and provocative variables—were well received and attracted much of the attention during discussion periods. Long before the rest of us, these scientists recognized the importance of the variables they had investigated and the need to do hands-on research on them.

On the other hand, each of them is dealing with his problem area in a limited fashion. Cowen spent years intervening in the lives of school-age children displaying problems. He correctly described his school mental health program as secondary prevention, since the children's behavioral problems had already developed. He suggests that in our primary prevention efforts we focus on analyzing and modifying social environments and that we develop programs of competence training for the young. Even though there has been pertinent research by Moos, Spivack and Shure, and others, this is still a formidable task. The variables are difficult to define explicitly and more difficult to measure in reliable and valid ways. Moreover, as Cowen points out, most mental health personnel probably lack the "wherewithal to bring off these developments." If development of such competences necessitates the marriage of clinical, social, and educational psychologists or the development of new professional training programs, it will be extraordinarily slow to appear.

Heber described a complex and expensive interventional system aimed at preventing mental retardation in high-risk black children. Clearly primary prevention, since it begins shortly after birth, it appears to be a very effective scheme. His evidence is persuasive even for those who may not have a humanistic orientation. Human potentialities are being wasted in the world today, and any program which successfully transforms a potentially retarded person into an intellectually average or above-average citizen should be warmly welcomed. On the other hand, Heber's program appears prohibitively expensive in terms of time, personnel, and money if generalized to a large sample of the population. To reduce the scope would require more specific knowledge of what variables are contributing what amounts to the ultimate effect—information that Heber clearly cannot provide. After commending Heber's outstanding contribution, Hunt wishes that the relationships between the experiences provided in the educational day care and the nature of the developmental advances were clearer and more specific.

Bloom presented a great deal of data, largely collected by others with actuarial or epidemiological interests. His marital disturbance speculations are intriguing, and the data relating such discord to physical and emotional disharmony are provocative. Bloom is well aware that correlational data, no matter how fascinating, cannot contribute to conclusions concerning cause-and-effect relationships. Thus, we will have to await the data that Bloom is just beginning to collect before we can pass judgment on the merits of his inquiry.

Hunt not only provided a superb review and evaluation of Heber's presentation, but did so in the context of his own research. His program differs from Heber's in that he varied the environmental exposure provided the various groups of high-risk children in the Tehran orphanage and also measured resultant effect by using several developmental scales measuring rather specific skills. His results substantiate Heber's findings that desirable intellectual growth was associated with extensive early stimulation and that intellectual assessment in the experimental subjects was more homogenous than the control subjects. Hunt's approach is more specific than Heber's and can be viewed as a step in the direction of defining what early experiential variables are important to what aspects of intellectual development. Those attempting to follow up Heber's demonstration project would be wise to study the Hunt findings carefully.

The reported studies are intriguing, and these researchers have responded to an important lacuna in existing information, looking at critical variables in the relationships between behavioral malfunctioning and environmental deprivation. They have not specified what changes we should make or how we can make them easily and efficiently, but they indicate that changes *can* be made and encourage us to continue investigating the variables they presume to be relevant.

Did the environmental psychologists communicate effectively with the clinicians, and did they contribute ideas that will stimulate the clinicians to a more sophisticated appreciation of environmental variables? To some extent yes, but not to the extent hoped for. One difficulty was that the environmental psychologists, in the tradition of experimentalists, differed greatly among themselves—take as example the points of view presented by Sommer and Freedman. Sommer is an action-oriented environmental psychologist who believes in hands-on studies and he has done many of them. He recommends doing many more short-term studies than have been done in the past and he suggests that researchers use an evaluation model. Freedman, however, denies that this approach is science. It is clear that we need to be admonished to be as scientific as possible in working with real issues in the real world. On the other hand, it is equally clear that we must get to the business of studying behavior related to important social problems outside of the laboratory. Both the Sommers and the Freedmans have much to offer to the researching clinician. Sommer's distinction between the two basic approaches to working on important social problems should interest any active researcher.

A specific idea contributed by the environmental psychologists, which should be of immediate use to the clinical researcher, is the Barker notion of undermanning and overmanning, presented by Schoggen. If we agree with Cowen that the development of competences is an important approach in primary prevention work, perhaps the most manageable way of doing it in a generalized model is through active manipulation of the manning variable.

Altman's conceptualization of privacy and the importance of this concept for mental health should be of much interest to the clinician-researcher. Boundary control processes are clearly involved in all interpersonal interactions and are the stuff of clinical focus.

One of the important problems in primary prevention is defining the area, and both Ansbacher and Cowen contributed to this issue. Cowen's presentation should leave little doubt what primary prevention is and how it is different from secondary and tertiary preventive efforts. Ansbacher's notion of positive mental health as the objective of both interventional programs and sound living experiences provides a more affirmative approach to these important problems.

Two interesting notions about research strategies for primary prevention were introduced in the discussion sessions. One was that when dealing with high-risk populations, we might concentrate on those who come through the period of disadvantage unscathed—that is, focus our attention on the successful rather than the unsuccessful cases—in order to find variables that might be built into a primary prevention program. The second notion was an additive versus a subtractive approach to preventive research in following up a demonstration project like Heber's. The subtractive approach would involve dropping off specific aspects of the total interventional program and showing the effects in further demonstration projects. Heber, for example, could eliminate the fifth year of his program, or replace his trained staff with volunteer help, and repeat the study. The additive approach would involve selecting, by best guess, the single intervention which would appear most likely to have significant influence on the end result. The experiment would then be done again, varying only that dimension and assessing the effect. If selected insightfully (and luckily), the full effect would obtain and the generalization of the program would be greatly simplified. If less than full effect were obtained, a second interventional variable would be added and the study repeated; and so on. Of course, several additive possibilities could be accomplished at the same time.

Appendix

Report of the
Task Panel on Prevention

During the time that Professor Forgays has been involved in the difficult task of editing this volume, particularly deciphering and editing the conference material not presented as formal papers, I have been engaged in a collaborative effort with a group working to produce a paper on primary prevention containing recommendations to the President's Commission on Mental Health.

In the spring of 1977 President Carter, fulfilling a campaign pledge, appointed a Presidential Commission to reexamine the nation's approach to problems of mental health. Dr. Thomas Bryant accepted the chairmanship, and Rosalynn Carter, who for many years has played an active role in the mental health field, agreed to serve as Honorary Chairperson.

The Commission was composed of twenty people, a majority of them not members of the traditional mental health professions but representing a wide range of backgrounds and perspectives. Early in its existence the Commission set up Committees (later called Task Panels) to survey various areas of mental health activity and provide the Commission with summaries of the important research literature and with recommendations. I was asked by Dr. Bryant to chair the Task Panel on Prevention, which consisted of ten members from a variety of disciplines and orientations who had had experience in the field of prevention. Also assisting us was Richard Millstein, J.D., an attorney with wide experience in mental health law.

Our panel met on two occasions in Washington in the summer of 1977 for discussion and for writing sessions. Both Millstein and I submitted interior progress reports, and the final reports—submitted in revised form in February 1978—incorporated the suggestions of all of the panel members who had contributed extensively.

Especially welcome was detailed assistance by Emory Cowen, Professor of Psychology, Psychiatry, and Education at the University of Rochester. Because of our report's timeliness and the summary of relevant literature it includes, Professor Forgays asked that it be incorporated into this volume. The Commission's Report to the President, with the supplementary Task Panel Reports, is scheduled to be published by the Government Printing Office in the spring of 1978.

George W. Albee, Ph.D.

Members of the Task Panel on Prevention

George W. Albee, Ph.D., Coordinator
Professor of Psychology
University of Vermont
Burlington, Vermont

Bernard L. Bloom, Ph.D., M.S. Hyg.
Professor of Psychology
University of Colorado
Boulder, Colorado

Elsie Broussard, M.D., Dr.P.H.
Professor of Public Health Psychiatry
Graduate School of Public Health
   and Associate Professor of Child
   Psychiatry
School of Medicine
University of Pittsburgh
Pittsburgh, Pennsylvania

Emory L. Cowen, Ph.D.
Professor of Psychology and
   Psychiatry and Education
University of Rochester
Rochester, New York

L. Erlenmeyer-Kimling, Ph.D.
Principal Research Scientist
Department of Medical Genetics
New York State Psychiatric Institute
New York, New York

Ernesto Gomez, M.S.W.
El Centro del Barrio
San Antonio, Texas

Donald C. Klein, Ph.D.
Consultant
Ellicott City, Maryland

Roy Menninger, M.D.
President, The Menninger Foundation
Topeka, Kansas

Vera S. Paster, Ph.D.
Acting Director
Bureau of Child Guidance
New York City Board of Education
New York, New York

John Reilly, J.D.
Partner
Winston and Strawn
Washington, D.C.

Vivian K. Rubinger
Founder
Palm Beach County Comprehensive
   Community Mental Health
   Center, Inc.
West Palm Beach, Florida

Acknowledgments

The Task Panel wishes to express special appreciation to Richard A. Millstein, J.D., Staff Liaison to the Task Panel, for his extraordinary contributions to the work of the Panel and his invaluable assistance to Panel members.

The Task Panel also wishes to acknowledge the invaluable assistance of the following persons in the preparation of this report: Esther R. Prince, Support Staff, President's Commission on Mental Health, Washington, D.C.; Stephen E. Goldston, Ed.D., M.S.P.H., National Institute of Mental Health, Rockville, Maryland.

SUMMARY

Western society's approach to persons with mental disorders has progressed in a series of steps. Each step has been characterized by increasingly humanitarian concern. For thousands of years the insane were reviled, feared, and rejected. Two hundred years ago, in the first mental health "revolution," they were led by Pinel out of the fetid dungeons, up into the light and into more humane treatment. A second revolution, led by Freud, greatly increased our understanding of the continuity between the insane and the sane. Half a century later, a third revolution was dedicated to providing care in a single comprehensive center accessible to all those at high risk. Now, less than a quarter century later, we are on the threshold of a fourth and most exciting mental health revolution. Its goal is to prevent emotional disorders.

Although each revolution has drawn strength from, and built on, earlier ones, we have come more and more to recognize that widespread human distress can never be eliminated by attempts—however successful—to treat afflicted individuals. We shall continue to do everything we can for persons in pain. But we are also determined to take action to reduce the identifiable causes of later distress, and thereby decrease the incidence of emotional disturbance and disorder.

Primary prevention means lowering the incidence of emotional disorder (1) by reducing stress and (2) by promoting conditions that increase competence and coping skills. Primary prevention is concerned with populations not yet affected by individual breakdown, especially with groups at high risk. It is proactive: it often seeks to build adaptive strengths through education and reduce stress through social engineering.

We have identified a number of sources of resistance, and barriers, to primary prevention efforts. We have identified problems in setting priorities where choices must be made among programs of demonstrated effectiveness affecting relatively few people; programs with high (estimated) potential for greater numbers of people based on limited but encouraging research efforts; and programs involving broad social efforts not traditionally associated with the field of mental health but with potentially positive impact for very large numbers of people.

We have reviewed several representative research areas to show that a solid research base exists for primary prevention. As illustrative examples we have focused especially on competence training programs for those at risk by virtue of natural and life crises and the effects of social climate on mental health.

An important "paradigm shift" must be considered in focusing attention on research in primary prevention. There are good reasons to believe that just as an emotional disorder may result from any of several background factors and life crises, so can any specific intense stressful event precipitate any of a variety of mental and emotional disorders. Different life histories and different patterns of strengths and weaknesses among different individuals can and do lead to different reactions to stress. This new paradigm requires that we recognize the futility of searching for a unique cause for every emotional disorder. It accepts the likelihood that many disorders can come about as a consequence of many of the varieties of causes. This paradigm leads to the acceptance of the argument that successful efforts at the prevention of a wide variety of disorders can occur without a theory of disorder-specific positive causal mechanisms.

Our recommendations include a focus on a coordinated national effort toward the prevention of emotional disorder with a Center for Primary Prevention within the National Institute of Mental Health, with primary prevention specialists deployed in each of the ten USPHS Regional Offices, with the establishment of State-level efforts, and with the creation of field stations and model demonstration centers. Because many other relevant government agencies can, and should, be concerned with prevention, we are recommending the coordination of efforts through the proposed

NIMH center that is to have convening authority. We are recommending that first priority in primary prevention be directed toward work with infants and young children (and their social environments). We give a number of illustrations of the kinds of programs we have in mind. We take special note of the urgent need to reduce societal stresses produced by racism, poverty, sexism, ageism, and the decay of our cities. We make certain suggestions about funding and about a broadly competent citizen's committee to have a continuing advisory role.

PREAMBLE

The *first* revolutionary change in society's approach to the mentally ill and the emotionally disturbed was the humanitarian concern exemplified by Philippe Pinel who, in 1792, removed the chains binding the insane in the fetid dungeons of Paris. He brought those victims up into the sunlight and showed the world that kindness and concern were defensible and appropriate.

The *second* revolutionary change in our attitudes and values had its origin in Freud's work that stressed the continuities between the sane and the insane, the mind of the child and the mind of the adult, the world of dreams and the world of reality.

The *third* revolution was the development of intervention and treatment centers serving all persons needing help—comprehensive community mental health centers—where, through a single door, everyone could seek and find skilled help for the whole range of human mental and emotional problems.

Unlike political revolutions, each of these mental health revolutions drew strength and inspiration from the earlier ones.

We believe we now stand on the threshold of a *fourth* revolution. Like its predecessors, this revolution will not attempt to displace or replace progress already achieved. The new revolution will involve major societal efforts at *preventing* mental illness and emotional disturbance. It will apply the best available knowledge, derived from research and clinical experience, to prevent needless distress and psychological dysfunction. It will, in the best public health tradition, also seek to build strengths and increase competence and coping skills in populations and thereby reduce the incidence of later disturbance. This fourth revolution, if it happens, will identify our society as a *caring society*—one that both holds out its hand to its unfortunate members and does all it can to prevent misfortune for those at risk.

In speeches at the 1977 World Federation for Mental Health in Vancouver, both Rosalynn Carter, Honorary Chairperson of the President's Commission on Mental Health, and Bertram Brown, until recently Director of the National Institute of Mental Health, elaborated a theme of Margaret Mead about the moral dimensions of mental health services. Dr. Mead has suggested that if we select for first consideration the most vulnerable among us, then our whole culture is humanized (1977). Mrs. Carter believes, as does Dr. Mead, that ". . . our value as individuals, our success as a society, can be measured by our compassion for the vulnerable." Dr. Brown asserts that "The system that serves the largest collection of this diverse, oppressed, and needful group is mental health. Mental health services . . . increasingly represent the court of last resort for the poor, the ill, the underprivileged, the hungry, and the disenfranchised" (1977, p.4).

The Task Panel on Prevention applauds the sentiments expressed in these statements and goes further to suggest that an additional template be applied in judging a society: its devotion to the prevention of those tragedies that lead to the creation of society's unfortunate members. Thus the Panel takes as its point of departure the conviction that *a society must also be measured by the steps it takes to prevent every form of preventable misfortune.* Barrington Moore said much the same thing: "Human society ought to be organized in such a way as to eliminate useless suffering" (1970, p. 5).

Increasingly, the ranks of those who seek to emphasize the potential of prevention are growing. President Carter has suggested that "the most important improvement in the quality of health care" would be to make available "additional resources for primary and preventive care, nutritional services, and occupational and environmental health initiatives" (1977). Dr. Julius Richmond, Assistant Secretary for Health in the Department of Health, Education, and Welfare, says "I feel very keenly that we must move to bring our knowledge to the area of prevention" (1977). He stresses the importance of behavioral research in learning how our society "can enlist people in preventive activities for the promotion of their own health." And the Institute of Medicine of the National

Academy of Sciences has in process a major document on Strategies for Promotion of Health and Prevention of Disease in the United States.

The Fourth Revolution is an idea whose time has come.

INTRODUCTION AND RATIONALE

The development and application of primary prevention programs in the field of the emotional disorders is the great unmet mental health challenge of our time. From both a moral and ethical point of view, preventive intervention has the potential for reducing human suffering associated with emotional disorder and the impact of that suffering on family and friends. From an economic point of view, effective primary prevention programs promise to be less expensive in the long run than the direct (fiscal) and indirect (human) costs to society of not providing such services.

The term "primary prevention" refers to a group of approaches that share the common objectives of (1) lowering the incidence of emotional disorders (i.e. the rate at which new cases occur) and (2) promoting conditions that reinforce positive mental health. Primary prevention, in concentrating its efforts on promotion and maintenance of competence, is distinguished from traditional mental health services designed to identify, treat, or rehabilitate persons already disturbed (Kessler and Albee, 1975; Albee and Joffe, 1977; Cowen, 1977; Bloom, 1977; Klein and Goldston, 1977).

One way in which primary prevention works in the mental health field is to eliminate the causes of disorders of known or discoverable etiologies (e.g. cerebral syphilis). Equally or perhaps more important, primary prevention involves building the strengths, resources, and competencies in individuals, families, and communities that can reduce the flow of a variety of unfortunate outcomes—each characterized by enormous human and societal cost. Because primary prevention approaches can be applied flexibly in a variety of situations, they are an especially attractive means for reaching vulnerable, high-risk groups.

Primary prevention activities have two main justifications: (1) the body of evidence supporting the efficacy of these approaches in their own right; and (2) the growing sense of dissatisfaction, as the gap widens between demonstrated need for help and the costly, often unavailable, human resources to meet that need, with mental health's past exclusive reliance on corrective measures.

From a logistical point of view, there can never be a sufficient number of skilled health care providers to meet unchecked intervention needs. And, in any case, no major disorder in a population has ever been eliminated by providing one-to-one treatment, however comprehensive.

Historically, the mental health field has always been unswerving in its definition of mandate, i.e. to understand the complexities of psychological aberration and to contain or minimize dysfunction when called on to engage it. However constructive that mandate is, the service systems developed to meet it cannot be expected to resolve society's mental health problems. Thus, today (1) there are too few resources to deal with mental health problems as defined, (2) distribution of those limited resources is inequitable, following the ironic rule of where help is most needed it is least available, and (3) mental health energies are disproportionately allocated to the exacting and costly task of trying to overcome already rooted, crystallized, "end state" conditions—precisely those that most resist change.

The history of public health in the past century provides ample evidence that programs designed to prevent disease and disorder can be effective and reasonably economical. Infectious diseases that can now be prevented include smallpox, malaria, typhus, cholera, yellow fever, polio, and measles. An equally impressive group of nutritional disorders, including scurvy, pellagra, beriberi, and kwashiorkor, is now also understood and preventable. Imagine what our health bill would be if those diseases were not preventable and society therefore needed to bear the costs of supporting state malaria hospitals, state pellagra hospitals, and state hospitals for polio victims.

Preventive measures have proved to be a vital extension of health care practices in physical health. The mental health field, however, has yet to use available relevant knowledge to develop comparable efforts systematically. Public health approaches offer a sound conceptual and operating framework for undertaking primary prevention in the mental health field.

Primary prevention approaches, on logical, humanitarian, and empirical grounds, thus offer an attractive, sorely needed extension of existing mental health practices that hold promise for reducing the eventual flow of emotional disorder.

In the history of medicine, the response to disease illustrates the relationship between the state of knowledge and what physicians actually do. At a time when few normal physiological processes, let alone the pathological ones, were understood, physicians had to be content with describing what they saw and paltry efforts at palliation. Only with the advance of medical knowledge was it possible to refine descriptions into diagnoses and, with an understanding of etiology, to prescribe disease-specific treatment. As we have become more sophisticated about the nature of illness, efforts to prevent illness have also increased. For diseases with specific etiologies, i.e. in which the pathogenic relationships between causative agent and disease came to be fully understood, prevention efforts were often dramatic. But as most diseases have multiple causes, they required more complex strategies for prevention as well.

Most mental conditions lack the single etiology or definitive understanding of pathogenesis needed for dramatic prevention efforts. That very fact has led many people to despair of *ever* preventing mental disturbance and to continue to advocate an exclusive emphasis on diagnosis and treatment as the only scientifically justifiable approach to mental illness. This broad kind of denial of the possibiltities of prevention has led to widespread indifference toward it both by the medical profession and within society at large. We have thus lived through an era of greater and greater expenditures for treatment and rehabilitation without a much-needed corresponding attention to existing possibilities for prevention.

Prevention in the field of mental health can properly be seen as an integrating perspective that can fuse our best understandings of the etiology of mental disorder, personal and family relationships, and individual psychodynamics on the one hand with a recognition, on the other, of the salient social forces and pressures that combine to produce the individual and collective disorganization we call emotional illness.

The belief that our thinking must be reoriented away from the past exclusive focus on diagnosis and treatment is not new. More than one hundred years ago, Lemuel Shattuck and his coauthors of the 1850 *Report of the Sanitary Commission of Massachusetts,* stated:

We believe that the conditions of perfect health, either public or personal, are seldom or never attained, though attainable:— that the average length of human life may be very much extended, and its physical power greatly augmented:—that in every year, within this Commonwealth, thousands of lives are lost which might have been saved:—that tens of thousands of cases of sickness occur, which might have been prevented:—that a vast amount of unnecessarily impaired health, and physical debility exists among those not actually confined by sickness:—that these preventable evils require an enormous expenditure and loss of money, and impose upon the people unnumbered and immeasurable calamities, pecuniary, social, physical, mental, and moral, which might be avoided:—that means exist, within our reach, for their mitigation or removal:—and that measures for prevention will effect infinitely more than remedies for the cure of disease. (Quoted by Jonathan E. Fielding, in "Health Promotion: Some Notions in Search of a Constitutency," AJPH 67: 1082, November 1977.)

More recently, a major national effort in the field of mental health—the work of the Joint Commission on Mental Illness and Health (JCMIH) (1961)—also acknowledged the need for prevention. However, the JCMIH placed major emphasis on early case finding and early treatment, i.e. *secondary* prevention. That emphasis underscored the fact that emotionally disturbed people needed immediate help using resources from their own communities, a recognition that led ultimately to the creation of the community mental health centers system.

Despite its acknowledgment of the need for prevention, the Joint Commission's report and recommendations continued to reflect a powerful emphasis on treatment, with little indication of a concern for the importance of *primary* prevention. The following statement from the JCMIH's final report, *Action for Mental Health* (1961), clarifies its priorities:

A national mental health program should recognize that major mental illness is the core problem and unfinished business of the mental health movement, and that the intensive treatment of patients with critical and prolonged mental breakdowns should have first call on fully trained members of the mental health professions.

The President's Commission on Mental Health, established in 1977, set up the Task Panel on Prevention with a charge to study, report, and recommend efforts at prevention. The purposes of this present Task Panel on Prevention, therefore, are: (1) to identify and develop the conception of primary prevention in mental health; (2) to examine current strategies and program possibilities in this area; and (3) to propose specific recommendations for primary prevention to the President's Commission on Mental Health.

Charge to the Task Panel on Prevention

In its deliberations the Task Panel has attended to the following charge from the President's Commission on Mental Health:

In recent years increasing attention has been paid to methods for reducing needless mental and emotional disorder. The Commission is establishing a Task Panel on Prevention to marshal information demonstrating whether or not prevention is feasible, set forth options for future courses of action, and indicate sources of funding from which programs of prevention can be supported. Specifically, it will be the task of this Panel to:

- *Review current definitions of the term "prevention" and, given the state of the art and fiscal and other constraints, develop an operational definition of primary prevention; and, within the confines of that definition, review various services and programs and determine which are or are not successful;*

- *Identify barriers which interfere with the ability of the consumer to obtain and receive needed preventive services and with the capacity of community institutions to provide these services;*

- *Assess the national need for prevention services and programs and the manpower and research needs which the effectuation of a national prevention strategy will require; and*

• *Report to the Commission by January 15, 1978, setting forth materials inventorying what works and in what settings, citing suggested practical models of preventive programs which can be utilized by States, local governments, community mental health centers, and other community institutions.*

DEFINITIONS: WHAT PRIMARY PREVENTION IS AND IS NOT

Primary prevention in mental health is a network of strategies that differ *qualitatively* from the field's past dominant approaches. Those strategies are distinguished by several essential characteristics. This brief section highlights primary prevention's essences using the direct contrast style of saying *what it is* and *what it is not.*

(1) Most fundamentally, primary prevention is *proactive* in that it seeks to build adaptive strengths, coping resources, and health in people; not to reduce or contain already manifest deficit.

(2) Primary prevention is concerned about total populations, especially including groups at high risk; it is less oriented to individuals and to the provision of services on a case-by-case basis.

(3) Primary prevention's main tools and models are those of education and social engineering, not therapy or rehabilitation, although some insights for its models and programs grow out of the wisdom derived from clinical experience.

(4) Primary prevention assumes that equipping people with personal and environmental resources for coping is the best of all ways to ward off maladaptive problems, not trying to deal (however skillfully) with problems that have already germinated and flowered.

WHAT DO WE SEEK TO PREVENT?

We believe there is sufficient evidence to encourage further development of strategies for the prevention of a wide variety of conditions, such as: the psychoses, especially organic psychoses, neuroses and other social disorders, learning disabilities, child abuse, and other behavioral, emotional, and developmental deviations that fall within the broad range of mental health problems.

One key difference between the human organism and lower animals is the much longer period of time during which the human infant and child must depend on others for survival and support. During that long growth process, successful development can be interfered with by an unusually large number of factors at any point. Thus, under certain unfortunate circumstances, all infants are at risk for subsequent emotional and developmental deviations. Scientific advances have markedly reduced the mortality and morbidity of childbirth. Never before in our history have infants had as good an opportunity as they now do to be born healthy and to thrive. Unfortunately, however, the delivery of a biologically healthy full-term infant does not guarantee smooth psychosocial development forever after. Precisely because interference with optimal development is known to occur with high frequency, and to exact a heavy toll, it is imperative that programs for primary prevention be developed. It is essential to establish priorities, to select infants and children at particularly high risk, and to develop programs to assure optimal continuing development for such target groups. We firmly believe that efforts directed toward infants and young children will provide maximum return in successful prevention.

The Task Panel advocates the establishment of programs designed to prevent persistent, destructive, maladaptive behaviors, i.e. those unfortunate "end states" that result from identifiable stresses for which the individual lacks the necessary coping skills and the adaptive competencies to handle constructively. That critical goal suggests the need to identify (1) agreed-upon behavioral conditions that pose a serious threat to others because of the damage they cause; (2) patterns of behavior that are so distasteful for the affected person that he cries out for relief; or (3) emotional states that lead to withdrawal from meaningful social participation. Clearly, many such traits or conditions require social value judgments about what is desirable or undesirable behavior, acceptable and unacceptable styles of living. Some of these decisions, in short, may present dangers to liberty and to the freedom of people to follow their own drummers, to be unconventional, and even to be damned fools. There are many historical examples of the tyranny of the majority enforcing patterns of approved behavior and lifestyles, and too many deviants who have been punished, excommunicated, or even killed, for nonconformity. Clearly, preventive efforts must be directed toward those end states that cause either genuine harm to others or genuine unwanted suffering in affected individuals.

Attempts to classify mental conditions have turned out to be far more complex than was originally thought. The exciting successes of medicine and biology during the nineteenth century in classifying physical illnesses were viewed as models that might lead ultimately to successful classification of mental diseases. Indeed, the discovery of specific physical causes for certain mental conditions—the role of the spirochete, and the relationship of untreated syphilis to the subsequent appearance of a serious mental illness called general paresis; relationships between vitamin deficiency and pellagral psychosis; the serious social and behavioral consequences of oversecretion and undersecretion of certain endocrine glands such as the thyroid and the adrenals—each served to strengthen the belief that, eventually, all disturbed behavioral states would be found to have an underlying pathologic organic cause. That view persists even today. Some experts accept Nobel Laureate Linus Pauling's view that there can be no insanity in a healthy brain (1968). Another world famous chemist, Ralph Gerard, said much the same thing: "There can be no twisted behavior without a twisted molecule." Unfortunately, life is not so simple; indeed many everyday observations contradict that view. For example, soldiers under extreme combat stress often show serious emotional disturbances; children of disturbed parents often exhibit serious emotional problems; many persons undergoing naturally occurring life stresses, such as sudden widowhood or marital disruption, experience extreme personal anguish and depression. Yet each of these conditions is reversible. The critical point to be understood is that while all behavior has an underlying physiological *basis*, disturbed behavior need not imply an underlying pathological organic *process*. In short, people react emotionally to stress; they learn to withdraw, to attack, or to distort their relationships with others through normal physical mechanisms.

The Task Panel on Prevention thus advocates a broad-gauged effort in primary prevention directed ultimately to reducing the incidence of the major aberrant conditions and end states that have for years occupied the attention of, claimed the efforts of, and been sources of exasperation to the mental health field: the major childhood behavioral and developmental disabilities, the functional and organic psychoses, symptom and character neuroses, and profound psychosocial disorders such as delinquency and addiction. The Task Panel advocates a vigorous national effort to build health and competencies in individuals from birth, so that each person may maximize his chances for a productive, effective life.

We note especially that any serious national effort at prevention of mental disorders and promotion of mental health must also be addressed to those social-environmental stressors that significantly contribute to the pathology of prejudice. Racism is a particularly noxious influence. Likewise, bias against ethnic minorities, sexism, and ageism must be recognized as placing significant portions of the population at high risk of mental disorder merely by membership in these groups and from the environmental stress that such membership attracts. While outside the direct purview, or immediate special competence, of mental health specialists, elimination of institutionalized and other forms of racism and other biases must continue to be a priority for primary prevention as well as for other aspects of our national interest.

BARRIERS TO PRIMARY PREVENTION EFFORTS

However sensible or rational primary prevention is, however critical it is as a key future strategy for the mental health fields, it is an approach that must surmount powerful barriers, including the following:

(1) Our society is crisis-oriented; we react to here-and-now pain, blood, and visible suffering. Because primary prevention is future-oriented, many see it as postponable—or if not that, then certainly as having low priority. Because it is oriented so heavily to strengthening people's resources and coping skills rather than addressing current casualty, it lacks a constituency and political clout.

(2) The history, traditions, and past values of the mental health professions have been built on the strategies of repairing existing dysfunction. People are attracted to mental health with that image in mind; moreover, they are trained

and they practice in the same mold. That image of self and way of behaving professionally is reinforced because it serves such human needs as the need for status and economic gain and the (understandable) gratifications involved in the process of being personally helpful to distressed others. The question is whether it serves society equally well.

(3) Primary prevention in mental health is threatening to some because its very nature may raise sensitive issues of social and environmental change and/or issues about people's right to be left alone.

(4) Existing mechanisms to support certain mental health activities (e.g. funds for third-party reimbursement, treatment staff, hospital beds) are not geared to primary prevention activities. Accordingly, primary prevention proposals are viewed by some not only as threatening to rooted ways and vested interests but also as competing for resource dollars.

(5) The past lack of recognition of primary prevention as an accepted way in mental health that differs qualitatively from past approaches leaves a series of *Catch-22* residues:

(a) Fiscal allocations for primary prevention dollars rarely exist, or are at best pitifully small.

(b) We lack appropriate administrative structures charged with the responsibility of promoting the development of primary prevention.

(c) Personnel trained in the ways of primary prevention are in extremely short supply. Moreover, they tend to be the last hired and the first fired.

(d) Few professionals are assigned to primary mental health activities on a sustained, full-time basis.

(e) Activities that are labeled primary prevention often, in fact, are not that at all.

(f) There has been virtually no support for research in primary prevention; yet, ironically, critics argue that the field lacks sufficient evidence to warrant programmatic action. One indication of the difference in attitudes toward treatment and prevention is that treatment efforts are mandated even without adequate effectiveness data, whereas prevention efforts are discouraged because of "lack of evidence." With respect to treatment of already identified cases, the social mandate is to "try to be helpful." No such mandate has existed for prevention efforts.

Problems such as the above cannot be engaged, much less resolved, until primary prevention is accorded a place of visibility and importance, backed by leadership with the mechanisms and resources needed to achieve true viability, rather than tokenism.

PRIORITIES

Our Task Panel was asked to order our priorities among a range of prevention interventions and among the variety of target groups for whom primary prevention efforts are possible. It is not easy to set such priorities; indeed, decisions about them could well vary as a function of the weights given to social value judgments versus scientific criteria.

We can try to illustrate the kinds of choices we considered in setting priorities among the large variety of primary prevention programs the Task Panel reviewed. We found ourselves considering:

(1) Programs with high potential for success that affect relatively few people, e.g.

  (a) Genetic counseling of persons with a family history of Huntington's Disease, PKU, or Down's Syndrome;

  (b) Intensive intervention with blind infants (based on the fact that such children are known to be at high risk for psychosis).

(2) Programs with significant research effectiveness demonstrated on small samples but with good prospects for reaching large numbers, e.g.

  (a) Competency training in pre-school settings and early school grades;

(b)   Widow-to-widow self-help counseling groups.

(3)   Programs with strong *theoretical* promise for success affecting potentially large numbers of people, e.g.

(a)   Helping groups for people who experience sudden or extreme stresses such as infant death, job loss, or marital disruption.

(4)   Programs aimed at improving broad social situations with potentially great impact on millions of people. Because such conditions are not usually considered part of mental health's purview, considering them might give the Commission the set that the Task Panel has too wide a range of things, i.e. *everything* is primary prevention! Candidly, too, such considerations may involve sufficiently controversial social values that it would be politically wiser to avoid them. Examples include the potentially damaging mental health consequences of:

(a)   Unemployment, discrimination, and lack of job security;

(b)   Boring and/or dangerous work;

(c)   The national epidemic of teen-age pregnancies, unwanted births, premature parenthood;

(d)   Smoking and the use of drugs, including alcohol; their effects on unborn children;

(e)   Ethnocentrism—racism, sexism, ageism; the damage wrought, the self-fulfilling prophecy, the damaged self-esteem of the persecutor and the persecuted.

Priority-setting may be premature. One rational, possible approach would be to base priorities on three sources of judgment:

(1)   Epidemiological information on prevalence of distress;

(2)   Value judgments solicited from affected groups, e.g. minorities, the aged, the impoverished—all at high risk; and

(3)   Research and demonstrations of effectiveness.

STRATEGIES RESTING ON A RESEARCH BASE

Members of the Task Panel, pulled between the choice of an overinclusive need to cite every relevant study done on primary prevention and the clear realization that brevity and readability were essential, opted for the latter. Somewhat self-consciously, we regarded ourselves as being among the nation's experts on primary prevention. We thus hoped that we might have enough credibility with the members of the Commission to be able to say firmly that the existing evidence indeed supports a major shift in emphasis toward primary prevention. For Commission members who already have the vision that mental health's major new thrusts must be toward the prevention of distress and the building of competence in the citizenry, we need cite only enough data to be reassuring that a broad capability for such an effort truly exists.

At the risk of sounding apocalyptic, the Task Panel believes that a firm, enthusiastic recommendation by the President's Commission for a genuinely accelerated national effort in primary prevention would be a major step forward for humankind. Symbolically, this would mark acceptance of our role as our brothers' and sisters' keepers. It would say that relevant mental health activities must go beyond the here-and-now and would thus move to center-stage a long-term view of benefiting all humankind.

Primary prevention's defining characteristics and mandates necessarily structure its main strategies. With proaction, health and competence-building, and a population orientation among its core qualities, it follows virtually automatically that primary prevention programs must be heavily oriented to the very young. Although the Panel's discussions of programs and strategies have ranged across all developmental stages, we agreed that major primary prevention efforts must be focused on the prenatal, perinatal, infancy, and childhood periods.

The National Association for Mental Health has developed a detailed program of primary prevention that guides efforts from conception through the first months of life. In our recommendations we list a number of other efforts that can be applied at prenatal, perinatal, and subsequent childhood levels. Again, we reemphasize our agreement about the importance of an approach that follows the developmental sequence. In this section, however, we will illustrate the research base with just a few brief programmatic examples.

Let us give a detailed example that involves efforts with children beginning with the pre-school years. Such an approach, consistent with the spirit of primary prevention, has yet to be harnessed systematically by the mental health fields. At the same time, a rapidly growing body of evidence demands that it be taken into serious account.

It has been known for some years that performance on an interrelated group of skills known collectively as interpersonal cognitive problem solving skills (ICPS) consistently discriminates between maladapted clinical or patient groups of children (and adults) and healthy normals (e.g. Spivack and Levine, 1963; Platt, Altmann, and Altmann, 1973; Spivack, Platt, and Shure, 1976; Spivack and Shure, 1977). Such ICPS skills as the ability to "sense" problems, to identify feelings, to use alternative-solution thinking, means-end thinking, and consequential thinking apparently provide a useful cognitive and emotional technology for engaging interpersonal problems effectively. Those who have and use those skills effectively appear to others in interpersonal relations as well adjusted behaviorally. Those who lack or are deficient in such skills are seen as maladjusted—sometimes even with clinically-significant conditions such as neuroses, psychoses, problems of delinquency, antisocial behavior, or addiction. ICPS skills can thus be thought of as mediating effective behavioral adjustment. If that is so, the challenge it presents for primary prevention is to find ways to equip children, as early and effectively as possible, with those skills. The model of ICPS skill-training well illustrates primary prevention's defining attributes: it is health-building, proactive, mass-oriented, and educational. The main theoretical constraint on the ICPS approach is the human organism's limit to profit developmentally from such training. Once that developmental point is reached, only the formats and mechanisms of ICPS training, not its goals, need change for different groups who can be exposed to the approach.

Several research teams have implemented ICPS training programs directed to different target groups that are quite diverse in terms of age, prior history, and sociocultural and ethnic background. Their findings have been instructive—indeed, exciting.

Spivack and Shure (1974) developed one such program consisting of 46 "lessons," given over a ten-week period, for four-year-old Head-Start children. Not only did children in the program acquire the key ICPS skills, but as that happened their behavioral adjustment was also found to improve. Particularly interesting was the fact that the initially most maladapted youngsters both (1) advanced the most in ICPS skill-acquisition and (2) improved the most behaviorally. Spivack and Shure also demonstrated direct linkages between the amount of gain in ICPS skills—particularly in the ability to generate alternative solutions—and improvement in subsequent adjustment. Follow-up of program youngsters a year later, when they had gone on to new class-settings, showed that program improvements were maintained over time (Shure and Spivack, 1975a). In a closely related project (Shure and Spivack, 1975b), it was shown that inner-city mothers given special training in the ICPS method were successful in training their own children in those skills—again with positive radiation to the adjustment sphere. Thus, a potentially powerful primary prevention tool was shown to have coequal applicability in the two settings that most significantly shape a child's early development: home and school.

Several other groups, working within the same general framework, have provided further demonstrations of the applicability and fruitfulness of the ICPS training model as a strategy for primary prevention (Stone, Hinds, and Schmidt, 1975; Allen et al., 1976; Gesten et al., 1977; Elardo and Caldwell, 1976; Elardo and Cooper, 1977). It is beyond the scope of this brief summary to review that body of work in detail. Indeed the main reason for providing the citations is to establish that the efficacy of the approach is not confined to the inputs and wisdom of a single team, working with a particular target group, in a special setting; rather, because the approach has been shown to have generality across diverse settings and age, sex, and ethnic and socioeconomic levels, it stands as an example of a promising generalized strategy for primary prevention.

Findings based on the ICPS approach are in the same research tradition as an earlier set of demonstrations growing out of Ralph Ojemann's pioneering programs (1961, 1969) to train children to think causally. Other workers (Bruce, 1968; Muuss, 1960; Griggs and Bonney, 1970) have shown that successful mastery of causal thinking skills is accompanied by significant gain on measures of (decreased) anxiety, (increased) security and self-concept, and improved overall adjustment status in children.

This broad competence training strategy is limited primarily by its newness and by the minimal investment that has gone into it so far. Thus, the broad range of its potential has scarcely been explored. By broad range is meant the fact that many other competencies besides those that make up the ICPS group may be clearly shown to contribute significantly to behavior adjustment. Examples might include such qualities as healthy curiosity behavior, altruism, role-taking, and the ability to set realistic goals. A promising recent study by Stamps (1975) provides evidence in support of the basic argument. Working with fourth-grade inner-city children, Stamps developed a curriculum, based on self-reinforcement techniques, designed to teach realistic goal-setting skills. Program children learned those skills readily. As their goal setting skills developed, they showed parallel improvements in achievement, in behavioral adjustment, and on personality measures. At the end of training, teachers judged them to have fewer behavior problems than demographically comparable nonprogram controls. Moreover, they showed improvement on measures of openness, awareness, and self-acceptance.

The importance of early competence acquisition can be illustrated at a somewhat different level, i.e. in relationship to a rapidly developing body of knowledge about the efficacy of enrichment stimulation programs for young disadvantaged children (Gottfried, 1973; Horowitz and Paden, 1973; Jason, 1975). Among the most impressive program efforts in the area is that of Heber (1976) and his associates, in Milwaukee—a ten-year longitudinal program with dramatic and exciting findings. Heber's program, directed to the high risk children of mothers with IQs of 75 or less, started immediately after the child was born. An intensive, saturated program emphasizing continual skill training was conducted at a day care center where the children spent all day every day for the first five years of life. Each family was also assigned a home teacher who taught mothers child-rearing and other life skills. Careful comparisons of the program children to matched nonprogram controls, over a ten-year period, have uncovered some remarkable findings. For example, this initially high-risk program sample has not only far outpaced controls, cognitively and linguistically (e.g. at age 7 they had a mean IQ of 121, versus 87 for controls), but they have also run well ahead of expectancies for a normal population of age-peers at large. The key message from this impressive demonstration is that systematic early competence acquisition seems to pave the way for effective later adaptations in key life spheres.

The main sense of the program development and research efforts we are describing here is as follows: We now know that several pivotal competencies, on the surface quite far removed from mental health's classic terrain, can be taught effectively to young children and that their acquisition radiates positively to adaptations and behaviors that are, indeed, of prime concern to mental health. Symptoms and problem behaviors are reduced after acquisition of these skills. Health has been proactively engineered, so to speak, through skill acquisition. This is a message we cannot afford to repress; it is both a paradigmatic example and further mandate for intensified primary prevention efforts.

However promising the competence training approach to date has been, it should be seen as just one model—not as a bible. We urgently need a fuller and clearer understanding of the nature of core competencies in children—how they relate to each other and, even more important, how they may radiate to interpersonal adjustment. We need to understand what changes take place with development in the nature of essential competencies. As competencies that radiate to adjustment are identified, curricula and methods for helping young children acquire them must be developed. The effectiveness of those curricula, as well as their actual behavioral and adjustive consequences, must be carefully evaluated. That is a complex and time-consuming challenge, one that must be met by a concerted effort and not by small, isolated programs or small research grants. The costs will be substantial, but so is the potential reward: a healthier, happier, more effective, better adjusted next generation, on the positive side, and a decrease in the flow of those types of emotional dysfunctions and behavioral aberrations that are at once socially draining, degrading, costly, and destructive of human beings.

Competence training, though unquestionably a powerful tool for primary prevention, is not the only one. A second strategy, also with high potential, is the analysis and modification of social systems. It can be applied at multiple levels, from broad to narrow. It rests on the view that people's (especially children's) development, adaptation, and effectiveness are significantly shaped by the qualities of a relatively few high-impact environments in which they live (e.g. families and schools and communities). Environments can be many things. One thing they cannot be is neutral. Whether planned or by default, they are factors that either facilitate or impede the growth and adaptation of their inhabitants. The following section illustrates research-based efforts to change environments, including social environments, constructively. The first and most impactful social system is the infant-caregiver relationship.

Broussard (1976) has demonstrated, under careful research conditions, negative later outcomes in first-born children whose mothers perceived them negatively shortly after birth and a month later. In those cases in which the mother reported negative attitudes toward the infant at birth and also a month later, follow-up studies through age 11 have shown a high risk of emotional disturbance in these children. Broussard is now engaged in an intervention study with a sample of these high risk infants and mothers using family interviews, home visits, and mother-infant groups up to two years following birth. Preliminary results show significantly better developmental scores for the Intervention children than for Intervention-refused and comparison groups. This set of studies again is illustrative. Viewed together with the Klaus and Kennell studies (1976) showing the critical importance of early bonding experiences between mother (and/or other caregiver) and infant, certain implications for preventive intervention emerge. Conditions designed to maximize optimal positive social perception of the infant are important to the development of a sense of self-esteem and self-worth.

The demonstration of relationships between characteristics of environments and the emotional well-being of people is not at all limited to the infancy period. Indeed, there are examples of such work involving children of all ages during the school years. Illustratively, Stallings (1975) developed a comprehensive framework for assessing class environments for young school children in Project Follow Through. She reported clear relationships between environmental properties and positive outcomes, academic as well as interpersonal (e.g. cooperativeness, curiosity, persistence). Moos and his colleagues at Stanford (Moos, 1973, 1974a, 1974b; Moos and Trickett, 1974; Insel and Moos, 1974) have pioneered the development of measures of a variety of social environments (e.g. hospital wards, schools, military companies, and work units) and have shown consistent relationships between environmental properties and how people feel and behave in those environments. Environments that score high in such relational qualities as involvement and mutual support, compared to their opposites, appear to have occupants who are less irritable and depressed, more satisfied and comfortable, and have higher self-esteem. Specifically, for high schools, Trickett and Moos (1974) demonstrated that students from classes with high perceived student involvement and close student-teacher relationships reported greater satisfaction and more positive mood states than their opposites.

Although qualities of social environments clearly affect what happens to their occupants, it oversimplifies things to assume that those effects are constant for all people. Several observers have stressed the importance of "ecological-matches," i.e. environments that are facilitative for one person can strangle another (Hunt, 1971)—a point that has been documented empirically in several studies (e.g. Grimes and Allinsmith, 1961; Reiss and Dyhdalo, 1975). Especially relevant is the extensive work reported by Kelly and his colleagues (Kelly, 1968, 1969; Kelly et al., 1971, 1977). who have examined, longitudinally, the nature of adaptive behavior in fluid (high annual pupil-turnover) and stable (low annual pupil-turnover) high school environments. Their main finding was that what is adaptive in one environment was not in the other. For example, new students integrated much more readily in fluid environments, where personal development was highly valued. By contrast, status and achievement were more important in stable environments. Insel and Moos (1974) bring the ecological-match question an important step closer to mental health's prime terrain with the following observation: "A source of distress and ill health is in the situation in which a person attempts to function within an environment with which he is basically incompatible."

The purpose of the preceding brief summary is simply to establish that there is already a body of data showing that social climate variation relates to person outcomes on variables of central interest to mental health; moreover, such outcomes may differ for different people. Although we still lack a full understanding of those complex relationships, enough is in place to pinpoint future challenges for primary prevention: What *are* the high-impact dimensions of the important social environments that shape children? How are they best *assessed*? What are the *relationships* between environmental properties and person outcomes, i.e. which qualities facilitate or impede development, and for whom? Ultimately, the goal for primary prevention is to help engineer social environments that optimize development for all people.

Research and demonstration strategies based on impactful social systems must rest on prior or concurrent efforts to provide a sound foundation of good health care and nutrition. Good health care before and at the time of birth has preventive impact. At the time of childbirth, many preventable traumata occur, both physiological and psychological, that can affect the later mental health of the child. Prolonged and difficult births often involve anoxia (lack of oxygen) for the infant. Because low birth weight is known to increase the risk of later difficulties, hospital nurseries must be available for premature infants to prevent damage. Psychologically, support from family members and others is important for the woman at the time of childbirth.

Promoting the health of the expectant mother and child during and after pregnancy, together with sound health care to avoid the complications of pregnancy, including prematurity, can materially reduce the incidence of future mental problems.

Clinical observation of many disturbed people documents the important role played by identifiable environmental social system stresses in precipitating emotional breakdown. Situations involving unusual and intense distress often serve as a kind of "natural experiment" establishing this relationship. Thus, children of parents involved in disrupted marriages, and children moved from foster home to foster home, show a high frequency of emotional disturbance. Adults who lose a job, or who experience the loss of a spouse or child, often show psychological, physiological, and psychosomatic disturbances. (See Holmes and Rahe, 1967; Dohrenwend and Dohrenwend, 1974.)

Although individuals differ in their resistance to environmental pressure, the reduction of environmental stress clearly reduces emotional disturbance. A considerable amount of recent research has related life stresses to subsequent emotional disturbances. The death of a spouse, the loss of a job, going on vacation, marriage, the birth of a child—all are environmental events that may lead to both physical and psychological disturbance.

The individual's social support system is a key factor in determining his or her response to a stressful environmental event. (Caplan and Killilea, 1976; Collins and Pancoast, 1976; Gottlieb, 1976.) We can point to members of identifiable groups and predict a higher than random chance of their later serious emotional disturbance. Children of adults labeled schizophrenic or alcoholic are more likely to be identified later as emotionally disturbed. Primary grade children who are seen by teachers or peers as having adjustment difficulties have been shown to have higher rates of later emotional problems (Cowen et al., 1974, 1975; Robins, 1966; Werner and Smith, 1977).

Research on *stress reduction* is voluminous. Interventions can range from effective sex education for school-age children to anticipatory guidance or emotional inoculation to modeling and/or abreactive approaches before predictable stresses such as elective surgery, all the way through the life cycle to widow-to-widow self-help groups during and following bereavement (Silverman, 1976, 1977). Relationships between stress and emotional disturbance are often much less visible or direct than those between environmental toxins and physical illness. But there are exceptions to this rule, one of which is documented more fully in the paragraphs to follow.

Of all social variables that have been studied in relation to the distribution of psychopathology in the population, none has been more consistently and powerfully associated with this distribution than marital status (Bloom, 1977). Persons who are divorced or separated have repeatedly been found to be overrepresented among the emotionally disturbed, while persons who are married and living with their spouses have been found to be underrepresented. In a recent review of 11 studies of marital status and the incidence of mental disorder reported during the past 35 years, Crago (1972) found that, without a single exception, admission rates into psychiatric facilities were lowest among the married, intermediate among the widowed and never-married adults, and highest among the divorced and separated. This differential appears to be stable across different age groups (Adler, 1953), reasonably stable for each sex separately considered (Thomas and Locke, 1963; Malzberg, 1964), and as true for blacks as for whites (Malzberg, 1956). Supportive evidence of these differentials was provided by Bachrach (1975), who noted that "utilization studies [of mental health services] have generally shown that married people have substantially lower utilization rates than nonmarried people and that the highest utilization rates occur among persons whose marriages have been disrupted by separation or divorce."

Not only are highest admission rates to mental hospitals reported for persons with disrupted marriages, but the differential between those rates and similarly calculated rates among the married is substantial. The ratio of admission rates for divorced and separated persons to those for married persons is on the order of 18:1 for males and about 7:1 for females for public inpatient facilities. In the case of admissions into public outpatient clinics, admission rates are again substantially higher for separated or divorced persons than for married persons. Ratios of these admission rates are nearly 7:1 for males and 5:1 for females (Bloom, 1977).

Although data documenting the adverse mental health correlates of marital disruption are especially extensive and compelling, that is by no means the only area in which linkages between life-stress and emotional upheaval have been shown. Other prominent examples include bereavement, natural disaster, loss of a child, e.g. as in the Sudden Infant Death Syndrome (Goldston, 1977), and job loss. It has been said, with good reason, that life stresses and crises involve both danger and opportunity. Such crises are frequent. They menace—often disrupt—the victim's well-being. They have potentially long-term debilitating effects. The challenge for primary prevention is to develop new program models for at-risk victims of life stresses—programs that minimize the dangers of stress situations and maximize the opportunities they offer for learning effective new ways of coping.

The Task Panel reviewed a very large number of studies of social systems and life events that produce high degrees of stress in large numbers of people. It is important, as noted above, to point out that social stress (from child abuse and marital disruption to racism, discrimination, and unemployment) increases the probability of physical and mental breakdown or disturbance. At the same time, because there are no clear-cut cause-specific connections between single identifiable stresses and a subsequent disturbance, the primary prevention strategist cannot always "produce the convincing evidence" of direct linkages of cause and effect so often demanded by research funding agencies.

It should perhaps be stated explicitly that the Panel's proposals for program development and research in primary prevention involve what philosophers of science call a major new "paradigm shift" (Kuhn, 1970; Rappaport, 1977). The area of social stress illustrates the point. The history of efforts to prevent organic disease shows that one particular research paradigm has been remarkably successful in giving us a sound research base for developing preventive methods. That traditional paradigm may be outlined as follows: (1) define a disease or condition that is judged to be in need of prevention and then develop procedures for reliably identifying persons with the condition; (2) study its distribution in terms of time, place, or person characteristics in the population in order to identify factors that appear to be causally related to it; (3) mount and evaluate experimental prevention programs to test the validity of the hypotheses generated by the previous observations.

That paradigm has been enormously successful; it was used, for example, to develop highly effective preventive programs for smallpox and cholera in the nineteenth century and for rubella and polio in the twentieth century. In the case of the emotional disorders, general paresis is now preventable, as is psychosis following pellagra—both as a result of this approach.

But there are good reasons to believe that new paradigms are now needed. One such reason is that many emotional disorders do not seem to have specific biological causal basis; indeed, most result from a multiplicity of interacting factors. Hence, a paradigm that represents a major departure from the earlier model outlined above is now having a much greater impact on our knowledge base. Its steps may be summarized as follows: (1) identify stressful life events or experiences that have undesirable consequences in a significant proportion of the population and develop procedures for reliably identifying persons who have undergone or who are undergoing such events or experiences; (2) study the consequences of those events in a population by contrasting subsequent illness experiences or emotional problems with those of a suitably selected comparison population; (3) mount and evaluate experimental prevention programs aimed at reducing the incidence of such stressful life events and/or at increasing coping skills in managing those events.

This new paradigm assumes that just as a single disorder may come about as a consequence of a variety of stressful life events, any specific stress event may precipitate a variety of disorders, as a result of differing life histories and patterns of strengths and weaknesses in individuals. For example, an unanticipated death or divorce, or a job loss, may increase the risk of alcoholism in one person, coronary artery disease in another, depression and suicide in a third, and a fatal automobile accident in a fourth. That is, this new paradigm begins by recognizing the futility of searching for a unique cause for every disorder. It accepts the likelihood that many disorders can come about as a consequence of any of a variety of causes. With this acceptance comes the realization that successful efforts at the prevention of a vast array of disorders (particularly emotional disorders) can take place without a theory of disorder-specific causative mechanisms.

This section has presented a brief distillation of some of the current knowledge base in three main areas of primary prevention in mental health: (a) competency training emphasizing developmental approaches, (b) the impact of social systems on individual development, and (c) the reduction and management of naturally occuring life development stresses. All three areas already have substantial, promising knowledge bases that not only justify accelerated primary prevention efforts for the future, but point specifically to areas in which such efforts may be most useful at once.

RECOMMENDATIONS IN PRIMARY PREVENTION

Initiating a significant national effort in primary prevention of mental and emotional disturbances requires that key decisions be made about (1) the necessary optimizing *structures*, (2) the needed *program emphases*, (3) *funding mechanisms*, and (4) ways of *monitoring* such efforts to ensure that balance and relevance are maintained.

The Task Panel's recommendations, though constrained by time pressures, relate to each of the above key components in a national program for primary prevention.

Recommendation 1 (Structural)

A coordinated national effort is required if significant progress toward the prevention of emotional disorders is to take place. The components of that effort must include:

(a) *A Center for Primary Prevention within the National Institute of Mental Health.*

(b) *Primary Prevention Specialists assigned to each of the ten USPHS Regional Offices.*

(c) *Offices of Primary Prevention in each State-level mental health agency.*

(d) *A small number of Primary Prevention Field Stations— "model" centers for training, demonstration, and research—strategically located in representative communities and/or universities.*

(e) *Legislative authorization for earmarked grants available to local agencies including, but not limited to, community mental health centers on a competitive basis for establishing and evaluating primary prevention programs, perhaps paralleling Section 204 (Grants for Consultation and Education Services) of PL 94-63.*

(f) *Significant expansion of professional training and research opportunities in primary prevention.*

Discussion of Recommendation 1 A Center for Primary Prevention within NIMH should have the necessary (1) authorizations, (2) monetary resources, and (3) staff to carry out the following functions:

(a) Serve as the "lead agency," with *convening authority*, to bring together representatives of other Federal departments to discuss, plan, and implement primary prevention activities in which overlapping interests exist;

(b) Prepare and disseminate critical reviews of theory, programs, and research in the area of primary prevention. Such reviews should include periodic surveys of the state of the art and of practitioner needs; the assembling of available knowledge; the preparing of curriculum materials and teaching aids; the identifying of promising areas for applied research and field trials; and promising leads for new research and program development;

(c) Convene conferences and workshops bringing together appropriate persons to discuss, and review research and practice issues in, primary prevention;

(d) Assist in the development of State-level Offices of Primary Prevention;

(e) Award, with its own review committee mechanism, contracts and grants for research and training in primary prevention. High priority should be given to the allocation of funds for post-professional, public-health-oriented education for established mental health professionals who can then provide leadership for program development at both State and local levels, and who would be in a position to train and supervise others in the field;

(f) Help institutions of higher education to develop curriculum materials for training in primary prevention;

(g) Develop priorities and policy recommendations for program development in primary prevention; and

(h) Publish a professional-level scientific journal in primary prevention.

In order to carry out these objectives, the proposed Center for Primary Prevention should establish an Advisory Group composed of representatives of all relevant agencies and institutions. The Advisory Group should include, but not be limited to, mental health professionals.

The recommendation that a Center for Primary Prevention be established within NIMH does not preclude establishing similar centers within other appropriate Federal agencies and an inter-agency mechanism for coordinating Federal efforts by all relevant departments.

Primary Prevention Specialists in USPHS Regional Offices should provide the impetus for program development within each Region and should serve as the major link between State-level Offices of Primary Prevention, local community mental health centers, and other agencies interested in primary prevention program development and training on the one hand and the NIMH Center for Primary Prevention on the other. Such linkages would provide an excellent mechanism for alerting staff within the Center for Primary Prevention about issues of regional concern, needs for specific curriculum materials, and difficulties in implementing programs or research studies.

State-level Offices of Primary Prevention should be responsible for maintaining an overview of each State's governmental structure in order to encourage the development of primary prevention programs. As states have a variety of organizational structures, in terms of relationships of mental health and general health care, public health, welfare, and education, State-level Offices of Primary Prevention should be designed to provide wide-ranging interaction with all of the human service components of State government. State-level Offices of Primary Prevention should seek to provide consultation and financial inducements to local communities interested in developing or expanding primary prevention activities.

It may be necessary, at least initially, to subsidize State-level Offices of Primary Prevention through a Federal funding or matching mechanism.

Primary Prevention Field Stations should function as one key component of the NIMH Center for Primary Prevention's research and demonstration program. They should have clear administrative linkages in the Center.

Field Stations should be able to join with the NIMH Center in publishing a professional level scientific journal in primary prevention. They should provide ongoing training in the practice of primary prevention and in primary prevention research for persons charged with such responsibilities in institutions and agencies across the country.

Field stations should not only conduct basic research on ways to reduce significantly the incidence of emotional disorders, but should also foster long-range field trials to evaluate preventive strategies and to develop feasible dissemination mechanisms for those shown to be effective.

Recommendation 2 (Structural)

There should be a legislative mandate and Executive Order to the relevant government agencies (such as the Office of Education, the Office of Child Development, the National Institutes of

Health, and other relevant components of the Department of Health, Education, and Welfare, the Departments of Agriculture, Labor, and Housing and Urban Development) setting up appropriate mechanisms, supported by funding, to develop primary prevention programs. As indicated earlier, the NIMH Center for Primary Prevention should be authorized as the convenor of such groups to coordinate and provide technical assistance for their efforts. There should be an annual reporting to appropriate review agencies of the accomplishments of this effort.

Discussion of Recommendation 2. Primary prevention activities often involve agencies other than traditional mental health systems. Preventive intervention is frequently organized to provide assistance to normal children and adults in developmental age-appropriate tasks. Many of these prevention efforts are directed toward ensuring a nurturant environment, physically and psychologically, for the fetus, infant, and child. Many Federal agencies have important and relevant areas of responsibility for such preventive efforts.

Recommendation 3 (Emphases)

Top priority for program development, training, and research in primary prevention should be directed toward infants and young children and their environments, particularly including efforts to reduce sources of stress and incapacity, and to increase the competence and coping skills in the young.

Discussion of Recommendation 3 Both the logic and the evidence of primary prevention support the position that "earlier is better." Although serious effective efforts to reduce distress and emotional disorder can, and should, be developed for the entire life span, and especially for known stress periods, the Panel agrees that helping children to develop soundly from the start, and to maintain good mental health, must be our first priority. Listed below are several proposed program initiatives to promote the mental health of infants, children, and others throughout the life span, with a focus on developmental, on-going processes:

(1) *Promoting maternal-infant bonding and facilitating posi-*

tive maternal perceptions of the newborn child. Needed strategies in this area include prenatal parent education; group programs (post-delivery) to enhance the mother's sense of competence and self-esteem in her new role; adaptation of hospital environments and regulations to create conditions that favor positive mother-child bonding.

(2) *Developing systematic educational programs in such preventively-oriented areas as:* (a) education for marriage and parenthood, beginning in the early school years and continuing through adolescence; (b) prenatal parent-education programs, including information on exercise and nutrition during pregnancy, and family planning programs, based on collaboration between mental health and public health workers; (c) school-based educational programs from kindergarten to sixth grade and beyond, to encourage responsible interpersonal relationships, including but not limited to sexual relationships; (d) parenting programs that focus on age-appropriate content as children develop; (e) genetic counseling, permitting the development of screening programs including amniocentesis and selective (and optional) terminations of pregnancy in cases of clear-cut damage or defect in the fetus.

(3) *Utilization of existing program knowledge and development of further programs for building competencies in young children.* Examples of relevant competencies include interpersonal problem solving, realistic goal setting, role-taking and curiosity (question-asking) behaviors.

(4) *Analyzing and understanding the nature of social environments* such as primary grade classrooms, and their effects on young children's educational and personal development, with the ultimate goal of creating environments that maximize the development of all children's potential.

(5) *Programs designed to prevent the stressful effects of life crises experienced by high risk groups such as:* (a) parents of premature babies; (b) parents who lose a child through death; (c) surviving siblings when a child dies; (d) parents of malformed children; (e) parents who must leave their infants in the hospital beyond the discharge of the mother, or those who must rehospitalize an infant. A related

example is the development of specific programs to prevent post-partum reactions in parents.

(6) *Programs that deal with the mental health needs of children hospitalized for physical conditions.* Approaches must be developed that (a) prepare children for hospitalization by reducing the stress-potential of such experiences; (b) reduce parents' own anxieties about a child's hospitalization and also provide them with skills to help the child cope successfully with the experience; (c) modify hospital procedures so as to reduce the trauma of hospitalization for both children and parents.

(7) *Programs designed to reduce stresses associated with such major later life-crises as* (a) bereavement; (b) marital disruption (including particularly its negative effects on children); (c) job loss; (d) natural disaster; (e) premature parenthood.

(8) *Promoting the development of helping networks and mutual support groups* that deal preventively with both everyday crises and extraordinary crisis situations. Examples of such programs include (a) identifying and working supportively with natural "neighborhood helpers"; (b) widow-to-widow programs for the recently bereaved. Closely related is the need to support the naturally-occurring everyday help-giving efforts of first-line community "caregivers" who interact continually with interpersonally distressed people (e.g. beauticians, bartenders, divorce attorneys).

(9) *Establishing new initiatives and directions in training a wide variety of professionals, including those in mental health,* as for example in (a) public health theory and practice, including epidemiology; (b) human growth and development as these relate to prevention efforts.

(10) *An increasing focus on the mental health aspects of nutrition.* Nutritional disturbances (e.g. under- and/or over-nutrition) are known to relate directly to such classical mental health conditions as obesity, school maladjustment, and school failure. We need conjoint nutritional programs and mental health designed to cut down the flow of such adverse end states.

Recommendation 4 (Emphases)

The national effort to reduce societal stresses produced by racism, poverty, sexism, ageism, and urban blight must be strengthened as an important strategy for primary prevention.

Discussion of Recommendation 4 The Task Panel recognizes that the President's Commission on Mental Health has no magical power to eliminate the above sources of societal stress. That does not, however, deter us from taking leadership in pointing clearly to them as factors capable of producing profound emotional distress in individuals. Thus, the Panel strongly supports efforts to reduce racism and related forms of prejudice as important aspects of a comprehensive national program for primary prevention.

The Task Panel was often reminded that mental health services are disproportionately available to relatively more affluent, educated, privileged members of the white majority whose first language is English. We are thus compelled to underline the fact that many correlates of emotional distress are economic and cultural. Programs aimed at reducing injustice and discrimination must take into account different linguistic, cultural, and social factors.

Recommendation 5 (Funding)

If primary prevention is to be a major priority in mental health, funds to support new initiatives in training, program development, and research must be increased at least to $12–$15 million immediately and rise gradually to approximately $20–$25 million by 1985.

Discussion of Recommendation 5 According to our best current information, the estimated total annual expenditures of NIMH for primary prevention is about $2–$3 million. There is no special NIMH primary prevention program, and only one mental health professional is specifically designated as responsible for such work there. Clearly, primary prevention has *not* been a significant activity at NIMH. Equally clearly, constructive change requires a significant funding increase with specific instructions that such monies be spent to increase program development, training, and research in this field.

Recommendation 6 (Management and Review)

We recommend that the proposed Federal program in primary prevention be mandated for at least a 10-year period. This new program should be overviewed by a citizens' advisory committee to include experienced persons in the several professions concerned with primary prevention as well as "consumer" and minority group representatives. Such an advisory group should be concerned with both program emphases and management.

Discussion of Recommendation 6 Primary prevention efforts are directed toward groups of persons who are not showing individual patterns of distress or disturbance; such efforts often are designed to strengthen competence and coping skills, not to excise weaknesses. The Task Panel seeks to ensure that primary prevention funding be directed to a wide range of programs. In the past, mental health efforts, because of the health-illness model of individual treatment, have been largely restricted to illness-oriented interventions. We believe, most urgently, that effective primary prevention efforts will be more social and educational than rehabilitative in nature and recommend that a citizens' advisory committee be created to ensure that emphasis.

REFERENCES

Adler, L. M. The relationship of marital status to incidence of and recovery from mental illness. *Social Forces*, 1954, *32*, 185–194.

Albee, George W., and Joffe, Justin M. (Eds.). *Primary prevention of psychopathology. Vol. 1: The Issues.* Hanover, N.H.: The University Press of New England, 1977.

Allen, G. J., Chinksy, J. M., Larcen, S. W., Lochman, J. E., and Selinger, H. V. *Community psychology and the schools: A behaviorally oriented multi-level preventive approach.* Hillsdale, N.J.: Lawrence Erlbaum Associates, 1976.

Bachrach, L. L. *Marital status and mental disorder: An analytical review.* Washington, D.C.: U.S. Government Printing Office, DHEW Pub. No. (ADM) 75–217, 1975.

Bloom, B. L. *Community mental health: A general introduction.* Monterey: Brooks-Cole, 1977.

Broussard, Elsie. Neonatal prediction and outcome at 10/11 years. *Child Psychiatry and Human Development*, 1976, *7*. Winter

Brown, Bertram S. Remarks to the World Federation for Mental Health, Vancouver, British Columbia, August 24, 1977.

Bruce, P. Relationship of self-acceptance to other variables with sixth-grade children oriented in self-understanding. *Journal of Educational Psychology*, 1958, *49*, 229–238.

Caplan, G., and Killilea, M. (Eds.). *Support systems and mutual help: Multidisciplinary explorations.* New York: Grune and Stratton, 1976.

Carter, Jimmy. Hospital cost containment. *National Journal*, 1977, *9*, 964–965.

Carter, Rosalynn. Remarks to the World Federation for Mental Health, Vancouver, British Columbia, August 25, 1977, p. 1.

Collins, A. H. and Pancoast, D. L. *Natural helping networks: A strategy for prevention.* Washington, D.C.: National Association of Social Workers, 1976.

Cowen, E. L., Pedersen, A., Babigian, H., Izzo, L. D., and Trost, M. A. Long-term follow-up of early detected vulnerable children. *Journal of Consulting and Clinical Psychology*, 1973, *41*, 438–446.

Cowen, E. Baby-steps toward primary prevention. *American Journal of Community Psychology*, 1977, *5*, 1–22.

Cowen, E. L., Trost, M. A., Lorion, R. P., Dorr, D., Izzo, L. D., and Isaacson, R. V. *New ways in school mental health: Early detection and prevention of school maladaptation.* New York: Human Sciences Press, Inc., 1975.

Crago, M. A. Psychopathology in married couples. *Psychological Bulletin*, 1972, *77*, 114–128.

Dohrenwend, B. S. and Dohrenwend, B. P. (Eds.). *Stressful life events.* New York: John Wiley and Sons, 1974.

Elardo, P. T., and Caldwell, B. M. The effects of an experimental social development program on children in the middle childhood period. Unpublished.

Elardo, P. T. and Cooper, M. *AWARE: Activities for social development.* Reading, Mass.: Addison-Wesley, 1977.

Gesten, E. L., Flores de Apodaca, R., Rains, M. H., Weissberg, R. P., and Cowen, E. L. Promoting peer related social competence in young children. In M. W. Kent and J. E. Rolf (Eds.), *Primary prevention of psychopathology. Vol. 3: Promoting social competence and coping in children.* Hanover, N.H.: University Press of New England, 1978.

Goldston, S. E. An overview of primary prevention programming. In D. C. Klein and S. E. Goldston (Eds.), *Primary prevention: An idea whose time has come.* Washington, D.C.: U.S. Government Printing Office, DHEW Pub. No. (ADM) 77–447, 1977, pp. 23–40.

Gottfried, N. W. Effects of early intervention programs. In K. S. Miller and R. M. Dreger (Eds.), *Comparative studies of Blacks and Whites in the United States: Quantitative studies in social relations.* New York: Seminar Press, 1973.

Gottlieb, B. H. Lay influences on the utilization and provision of health services: A review. *Canadian Psychological Review*, 1976, *17*, 126–136.

Griggs, J. W., and Bonney, M. E. Relationship between "causal" orientation and acceptance of others, "self-ideal self" congruence, and mental health changes for fourth- and fifth-grade children. *Journal of Educational Research*, 1970, *63*, 471–477.

Grimes, J. W. and Allinsmith, W. Compulsivity, anxiety, and school achievement. *Merrill-Palmer Quarterly*, 1961, *7*, 247–261.

Heber, R. Research in prevention of socio-cultural mental retardation. Address presented at the 2nd Vermont Conference on the Primary Prevention of Psychopathology. Burlington, Vt., 1976.

Holmes, T. H., and Rahe, R. H. The social readjustment rating scale. *Journal of Psychosomatic Research*, 1967, *11*, 213–218.

Horowitz, F. D., and Paden, L. Y. The effectiveness of environmental intervention programs. In B. M. Caldwell and H. Ricciuti (Eds.), *Review of child development research.* Vol. 3. New York: Russell Sage Foundation, 1973.

Insel, P. M., and Moos, R. H. The social environment. In P. M. Insel and R. H. Moos (Eds.), *Health and social environment.* Lexington, Mass.: Lexington Books, 1974.

Jason, L. Early secondary prevention with disadvantaged preschool children. *American Journal of Community Psychology*, 1975, *3*, 33–46.

Joint Commission on Mental Illness and Health. *Action for Mental Health.* New York: Basic Books, 1961.

Kelly, J. G. Towards an ecological conception of preventive interventions. In J. W. Carter (Ed.), *Research contributions from psychology to community mental health.* New York: Behavioral Publications, 1968.

Kelly, J. G. Naturalistic observations in contrasting social environments. In E. P. Willems and H. L. Raush (Eds.), *Naturalistic viewpoints in psychological research.* New York: Holt, Rinehart, and Winston, 1969.

Kelly, J. G., et al. The coping process in varied high school environments. In M. J. Feldman (Ed.), *Studies in psychotherapy and behavior change.*

No. 2: *Theory and research in community mental health.* Buffalo: State University of New York, 1971.

Kelly, J. G., et al. *The high school: Students and social contexts in two mid-western communities.* Community Psychology Series, No. 4. New York: Behavioral Publications, Inc., 1977.

Kessler, M., and Albee, G. W. Primary prevention. *Annual Review of Psychology,* 1975, *26*, 557–591.

Klaus, M. H., and Kennell, J. H. Maternal-infant bonding. St. Louis: C. V. Mosby Co., 1976.

Klein, D. C., and Goldston, S. E. *Primary prevention: An idea whose time has come.* Washington, D.C.: U.S. Government Printing Office, DHEW Pub. No. (ADM) 77–447, 1977.

Kuhn, T. S. *The structure of scientific revolutions.* 2nd ed. Chicago: University of Chicago Press, 1970.

Malzberg, B. Marital status and mental disease among Negroes in New York State. *Journal of Nervous and Mental Disease,* 1956, *123*, 457–465.

Malzberg, B. Marital status and incidence of mental disease. *International Journal of Social Psychiatry,* 1964, *10*, 19–26.

Mead, Margaret. Conversation with Mrs. Rosalynn Carter, The White House, June 28, 1977, as reported by Mrs. Carter, remarks to the World Federation for Mental Health, Vancouver, British Columbia (August 25, 1977), p. 1.

Moore, Barrington, Jr. *Reflection on the causes of human misery and upon certain proposals to eliminate them.* Boston: Beacon Press, 1970.

Moos, R. H. Conceptualizations of human environments. *American Psychologist,* 1973, *28*, 652–665.

Moos, R. H. *The social climate scales: An overview.* Palo Alto: Consulting Psychologists Press, Inc., 1974. (a)

Moos, R. H. *Evaluating treatment environments: A social ecological approach.* New York: John Wiley and Sons, 1974. (b)

Moos, R. H., and Trickett, E. J. *Manual: Classroom Environment Scale.* Palo Alto: Consulting Psychologists Press, Inc., 1974.

Muuss, R. E. The effects of a one and two year causal learning program. *Journal of Personality,* 1960, *28*, 479–491.

National Association for Mental Health. Primary prevention of mental disorders with emphasis on prenatal and perinatal periods. Action Guidelines. Mimeographed, undated.

Ojemann, R. H. Investigations on the effects of teacher understanding and appreciation of behavior dynamics. In G. Caplan (Ed.), *Prevention of mental disorders in children.* New York: Basic Books, 1961.

Ojemann, R. H. Incorporating psychological concepts in the school curriculum. In H. P. Clarizio (Ed.), *Mental health and the educative process.* Chicago: Rand-McNally, 1969.

Pauling, Linus. Orthomolecular psychiatry. *Science,* 1968, *160*, 265–271.

Platt, J. J., Altman, N., and Altman, D. Dimensions of real-life problem-solving thinking in adolescent psychiatric patients. Paper presented at Eastern Psychological Association Meetings, Washington, D.C., 1973.

Rappaport, J. *Community psychology: Values, research and action.* New York: Holt, Rinehart, and Winston, 1977.

Reiss, S., and Dyhdalo, N. Persistence, achievement and open-space environments. *Journal of Educational Psychology*, 1975, *67*, 506–513.

Richmond, Julius. Remarks made at his swearing-in ceremony as Assistant Secretary of Health, Department of Health, Education, and Welfare, Washington, D.C., July 13, 1977.

Robins, L. *Deviant children grown up.* Baltimore: Williams and Wilkins Co., 1966.

Shattuck. L., et al. Report of the sanitary commission of Massachusetts. Quoted by Jonathan E. Fielding, in Health promotion: Some notions in search of a constituency. *American Journal of Public Health*, 1977, *67*, 1082.

Shure, M. B., and Spivack, G. *A preventive mental health program for young "inner city" children: The second (kindergarten) year.* Paper presented at the American Psychological Association, Chicago, 1975. (a)

Shure, M. B., and Spivack, G. *Training mothers to help their children solve real-life problems.* Paper presented at the Society for Research in Child Development, Denver, 1975. (b)

Silverman, P. R. The widow as a caregiver in a program of preventive intervention with other widows. In G. Caplan and M. Killilea (Eds.), *Support systems and mutual help: Multidisciplinary explorations.* New York: Grune and Stratton, 1976, pp. 233–244.

Silverman, P. R. Mutual help groups for the widowed. In D. C. Klein and S. E. Goldston (Eds.), *Primary prevention: An idea whose time has come.* Washington, D.C.: U.S. Government Printing Office, DHEW Pub. No. (ADM) 77–447, 1977, pp. 76–79.

Spivack, G., and Levine, M. Self-regulation in acting-out and normal adolescents. Report M–4531, National Institutes of Health, 1963.

Spivack, G., Platt, J. J., and Shure, M. B. *The problem-solving approach to adjustment.* San Francisco: Jossey-Bass, 1976.

Spivack, G., and Shure, M. B. *Social adjustment of young children.* San Francisco: Jossey-Bass, 1974.

Spivack, G., and Shure, M. B. Preventively oriented cognitive education of preschoolers. In D. C. Klein and S. E. Goldston (Eds.), *Primary prevention: An idea whose time has come.* Washington, D.C.: U.S. Government Printing Office, DHEW Pub. No. (ADM) 77–447, 1977.

Stallings, J. Implementation and child effects of teaching practices on follow-through classrooms. *Monographs of the Society for Research on Child Development*, 1975, *40* (Serial No. 163).

Stamps, L. W. *Enhancing success in school for deprived children by teaching realistic goal setting.* Paper presented at Society for Research in Child Development, Denver, 1975.

Stone, G. L., Hinds, W. C., and Schmidt, G. W. Teaching mental health behaviors to elementary school children. *Professional Psychology*, 1975, *6*, 34–40.

Thomas, D. S., and Locke, B. Z. Marital status, education and occupational differentials in mental disease. *Milbank Memorial Fund Quarterly*, 1963, *41*, 145–160.

Trickett, E. J., and Moos, R. H. Personal correlates of contrasting environments: Student satisfaction in high school classrooms. *American Journal of Community Psychology*, 1974, *2*, 1–12.

Werner, E. E., and Smith, R. S. *Kauai's children come of age*. Honolulu: University of Hawaii Press, 1977.

Name Index

Numbers in parantheses indicate the location of a chapter in this volume. Italicized numbers indicate the location of a name in a list of references.

Adler, A., 5, *6*
Adler, L. M., 87, *102*
Agrawal, K. C., 83, *103*
Albee, G. W., 8, 10, 11, *23*, 196, *198*
Albizu-Miranda, 67
Alexander, N. Y., 139, *150*
Allen, G. J., 18, *22*
Allinsmith, W., 15, *22*
Altman, I., (110–111), (133–151), 34, 130, 134, 139, 140, *150*, 152, 154, 155, 164, 165, *178*, 186, 189–191, *198*, 204
Ansbacher, H. L., (3–6), 65, 106, 195, 204
Aponte, J. F., 96, *102*
Arthur, R. J., 90, *104*
Asche, S. E., 192, *198*
Asher, S. J., 85, *102*

Bachrach, L. L., 85, *102*
Badger, E. D., 70, *76*
Baguador, E., 91, *102*
Baird, L. L., 174, *178*
Banks, C., 123, *128*
Barker, L. S., 172, *178*
Barker, R. G., 12, 16, *22*, 153, 165–173, 175, *178*, 181, 189, 191, *198*, 203
Bauman, G., 152
Beardsley, E. L., 143, *150*
Bennet, E. M., 10, *24*
Biber, B., 14, *23*, *198*
Birley, J. L. T., 97, *102*

Blank, S. S., 19, *22*
Blashfield, R. K., 16, *23*
Bloom, B. L., (81–105), (152–153), 10, *22*, 27, 28, 85, 88, 91, 95 *102*, 106, 107, 110, 111, 155, 181, 186, 188, 195, 199, 201, 202
Bodenheimer, B. M., 92, *102*
Boll, E. S., 139, *150*
Bossard, J. H. S., 139, *150*
Bourestom, N., 126, *128*
Braehha, R. G., 96, *104*
Branch, J. D., 83, *103*
Briscoe, C. W., 93, *102*
Broman, M., 90, *104*
Broussard, E., 30
Brown, G. W., 97, *102*
Bruner, J. S., 71, *76*

Caldwell, R. A., 91, *102*
Calhoun, J. B., 124, *128*, 160, *163*
Canter, D., 140, *150*
Canter, S., 140, *150*
Caplan, G., 8, 9–10, *22*, *23*, 96, *102*
Carp, F. M., 125, 126, *128*
Carter, J. W., *22*
Cedrone, A. R., 91, *102*
Chandler, C. A., 17, *23*
Chapman, J. W., 143, *150*
Chase, A., 64, *76*
Cherlin, D. L., 10, *24*
Chermayeff, S., 139, *150*
Chesy, J. J., 90, *102*

Chinsky, J. M., 18, *22*
Clarizio, H. P., *23*
Clayton, P. J., 90, *105*
Cline, D. W., 90, *102*
Cochrane, R., 97, *102*
Coelho, G. V., 13, *22*
Conry, J., 42 (figure)
Covington, M., 19, *22*
Cowen, E. L., (7–24), 3, *6,* 8–10, *22,*
    24, 33–35, 64, 106, 186, 195,
    196, 201, 203, 204
Crago, M. A., 87, 93, 94, *102*
Crissey, M. S. *See* Skodak
Crosson, J. E., 42

Darwin, C., 65
Davenport, C. B., 64
Davidson, W. S., 19, *23*
Delong, W. B., 97, *103*
Demone, H. W., Jr., 90, *105*
Dennis, W., 67, 69
Dever, R. B., 42 (figure)
Dohrenwend, B. P., 84, 97, *102*
Dohrenwend, B. S., 84, 97, *102*
Doll, E. A., 5, *6*
Donne, J., 121
Dorr, D., 9, *22*
Dupont, R. L., 94, *103*
Dwinnel, J., 90, *105*
Dye, H. B., 63, 73, *76*
Dyhdalo, N., 15, *23*
Dytryck, Z., 100, *104*

Edwards, D. W., *23*
Eisdorfer, C., *23, 24*
Ellis, N. R., *76*
Ensminger, M. E., 83, *103*
Erlich, J. L., 17, *24*
Etzioni, A., 122, *128*
Evans, D. R., 19, *22*

Fatke, R., *23*
Fairweather, G. W., 17, *22*
Farberow, N. L., 88, 89, *103, 104*
Feldman, M. J., *23*
Felipe, N., 138, *150*
Festinger, L., 192, *198*

Forgays, D. G., (201–204), 131,
    132
Fraiberg, S., 30
Freedman, J. L., (159–163), 124,
    128, 131, 159, 160, *163,* 180,
    189–192, *198,* 203
Freud, S., 4, *6*
Friesen, W., 173, *178*
Fuller, R. B., 117, *128*

Gagné, R. M., *198*
Galton, F., 64
Gardner, E. A., *24*
Gardner, R. A., 93, *103*
Gaskin, F., 93, *102*
Geertz, U. W., 140
Gesell, A., 50–52
Gesten, E., 35
Glick, P. C., 84, 86, *103*
Gobineau, Count Joseph Arthur de, 64
Goddard, H., 64
Goffman, E., 143, *150*
Golann, S. E., *23, 24*
Goldenberg, I. I., 10, *24*
Goldston, S. E., (25–32), (106–109),
    36, 186, 194, 195
Goodall, K., 125, *128*
Gordon, T. A., *23*
Gove, W. R., 96, *103*
Grant, M., 64
Gravel, M. L., *198*
Gregor, T., 140, 141, *150*
Grimes, J. W., 15, *22*
Gross, H., 143, *150*
Gross, M. M., 90, *104*
Grunebaum, H. U., 94, *103*
Guetzkow, H., *198*
Gump, P. V., 12, *22,* 170, 172, 173,
    175, *178, 179*
Guze, S. B., 90, *105*

Hall, E. T., 138, 140, *150*
Hamerlynck, L. A., 42
Haney, C., 123, *128*
Harris, T. O., 97, *102*
Hartley, W. S., 16, *22*
Hebb, D. O., 66, *76*

Heber, F. R., (39–62), (180–181), 42 (figure), 64–69, 71, 73–80, 129, 131, 132, 155, 161, 180, 186–188, 192, 193, 195, 199–204
Herrnstein, R. J., 187, *198*
Hess, R. D., 55
Hill, J. P., 123, *128*
Hodges, W. F., 91, *102*
Holmes, T. H., 90, *103*
Hornstra, K., 97, *103*
Hudgens, R. W., 96, 97, *103, 104*
Hunt, J. McV., (63–76), 34, 35, 66, 68, 70, 71, *76*, 77, 186, 201–203
Hunt, M. M., 93, *103*

Insel, P. M., 15, *22*
Isaacson, R. V., 9, *22*
Ittelson, W. H., 135, *150*
Izzo, L. D., 9, *22*

Jahoda, M., 195, *198*
James, J. W., 139, *150*
Jensen, A. R., 129, 187, *198*
Johnson, C., 87, *104*
Jones, M. R., *178*
Jourard, S. M., 139, 143, *150*

Kaplan, B., *178*
Kellam, S. G., 83, *103*
Kelly, J. G., 7, 11, 15, 16, *22, 23*
Kennedy, J. F., 83
Kessler, M., 8, 10, 11, *23*, 196, *198*
King, M. G., 139, *150*
King, S. H., 120, *128*
Kira, A., 139, *150*
Klassen, D., 97, *103*
Klaus, M., 30
Koestler, A., 115–118, *128*
Kohlberg, L., 100, *103*
Koran, L. M., 117, *128*
Kozol, J., 15, *23*
Krantzler, M., 93, *103*
Kraus, R. M., 9, *22*

La Crosse, J., 100, *103*

Langnor, T. S., 105
Lantz, H. R., 93, *103*
Larcen, S. W., 18, *22*
Lett, E. E., 139, *150*
Levine, M., 10, *24*
Lewin, K., 129, 130, 153, 154, 181, 190, 192, *198*
Lewis, E., 90, *104*
Lewis, O., 139, *150*
Lippitt, R., 192, *198*
Litman, R. E., 89, *103*
Lochman, J. E., 18, *22*
Locke, B. Z., 87, *105*
Loevinger, J., 195, *198*
Lorion, R. P., 9, *22*

Malenowski, B., 90, *104*
Malthus, P., 64
Malzberg, B., 87, *103*
Martell, R., 15, *23*
Marton, S., 93, *102*
McBride, G., 139, *150*
McClintock, S. K., *23*
McCormack, A., 118
McGee, D. P., *23*
McKean, J. E., Jr., 90, *104*
McMurray, L., 89, *103*
Mehler, A., 175, *179*
Menninger, K., 118
Mering, O. von, 120, *128*
Michael, S. T., 105
Miller, F. T., 96, *102*
Mindey, C., 93, *103*
Minuchin, P., 14, *23*, 195, *198*
Mitchell, A., 19, *23*
Mitchell, C., 99, *104*
Moore, B., Jr., 101, *104*
Moos, R. H., 13–16, *22, 23, 24*, 154, 201
Morrison, J. R., 96, *104*
Mullens, S., 137, *150*
Murphy, L. B., 17, *23*
Murphy, R. F., 138, 141, *150*

Nelson, P., 139, *150*
Newman, B. M., *23*
Newton, M. R., 170, *178*

Ojemann, R. H., 17, *23*
Opler, M. K., 105

Page, E. B., 65, 67, *76*, 77, 78, 186, 187
Parad, H. J., 96, *104*
Paraskevopoulos, J., 74, *76*
Patterson, M. L., 137, *150*
Pennock, J. R., 143, *150*
Perry, H. S., *198*
Piaget, J., *70*
Plato, 65
Porter, L. C., *23*
Prehm, H. J., 42
Price, R. H., 16, *23*
Prokopek, J., 100, *104*
Proshansky, H., 135, *150*

Rahe, R. H., 90, *104*
Rapoport, A., 135, 138, *150*
Rappaport, J., 19, *23*
Raush, H. L., *22*
Redick, R. W., 87, *104*
Reid, D. D., 84, *104*
Reiss, S., 15, *23*
Rennie, T. A. C., 105
Rice, R. R., *23*
Ricks, D., 100, *103*
Riessman, F., 19, *24*
Ripin, R., 69
Rivlin, L. G., 135, *150*
Roberts, J. M., 140, 141, *150*
Robertson, A., 97, *102*
Robins, E., 93, 97, *102*, *103*
Rohner, L., 93, *104*
Roistacher, R. C., *23*
Romano, J., 137, *150*
Rosenblatt, S. M., 90, *104*
Rosenzweig, M. R., 23
Roth, A., 97, *103*
Rothman, J., 17, *24*
Rubenstein, E. A., 13, *22*
Rubin, J., 116, *128*
Rubin, Z., 99, *104*
Rutledge, A. L., 92, *104*
Ryder, R. G., 94, *103*

Sanders, D. H., 17, *22*
Sanford, N., 3, *6*, 8, *24*
Sarason, S. B., 10, 17, *24*
Scarr, S., 68, *76*
Scarr-Salapatek, S., 68, *76*
Schneidman, E. S., 88, *104*
Schoggen, M., 165, 170, *178*
Schoggen, P., (164–170), 16, *22*, 130, 165, 168, 170–172, 175, *178*, 181, 189–191, 193, *198*, 203
Schuller, V., 100, *104*
Schwartz, B., 135, 139, *150*
Scriven, M., 166, 191, 192, *198*
Selinger, H. V., 18, *22*
Selzer, M. L., 97, *105*
Shapiro, E., 14, *23*, *198*
Sherif, M., 192
Shipman, V., 55
Shockley, W., 129
Shure, M. B., 17, 18, *24*, 34, 35, 201
Silverman, P., 32
Simmel, G., 135, *151*
Skeels, H. M., 63, 73, *76*
Skinner, B. F., 117
Sklair, F., 97, *102*
Skodak, M. Crissey, 69
Smilansky, M., 74, *76*
Smith, J. B., 93, *102*
Smith, M. B., (185–198), 36, 185, 191, 193, *198*
Snyder, E. C., 93, *103*
Sommer, R., (115–128), 77, 78, 118, *128*, 129, 130, 132, 138, *150*, *151*, 160, 181, 190–192, 199, 203
Spanier, G. B., 98, *105*
Specter, G. A., 17, *24*
Spencer, H., 64
Spivack, G., 17, 18, *24*, 34, 35, 201
Srole, L., 93, *105*
Stamps, L. W., 19, *24*
Steiner, I., 110
Stewart, C. W., 91, *105*
Strong, E. K., Jr., 5, *6*
Sullivan, H. S., 194, *198*
Susskind, E. C., 19, *24*
Syme, S. L., 94, 95, *105*

Systra, L., 91, *102*

Tars, S., 126, *128*
Teresa, J. G., 17, *24*
Theorell, T., 90, *105*
Thomas, D. S., 87, *105*
Thum, D., 90, *105*
Todd, D. M., *23*
Tornatzky, L. G., 17, *22*
Trickett, E. J., 14, *24*
Trost, M. A., 9, *22*
Turner, R. J., 93, 94, *105*
Tyhurst, J. S., *32*, 107
Tyler, L. E., 194, *198*
Tyler, R. W., *198*

Uzgiris, I. C., 66, 70, 71, *76*

Vallance, T. R., 12, *24*
Vinokur, A., 97, *105*

Wechsler, H., 90, *105*
Weinberg, R. A., 68, *76, 178*

Weiss, R. S., 93, *105*
Weissman, M. M., 98, *105*
Westin, A., 134, 135, 138, 140, 142, 143, *151*
White, R. K., 192, *198*
White, S. W., 85, *102*
Wicker, A. W., 170, 174, 175, *179*
Wilkerson, D. A., *76*
Willems, E. P., *22*, 173, 174, *179*
Wilson, M. N., 19, *23*
Wolfe, M., 125
Wolman, B., 6
Wood, F., *178*
Woodruff, R. A., Jr., 90, *105*
Wright, H. F., 165, 170, 172, *178*

Yarrow, L., 70

Zax, M., 3, *6*, 8, 10, 17, *24*
Zigler, E., 67, *76*
Zimbardo, P., 123, *128*
Zimiles, H., 14, *23, 24, 198*

Subject Index

Abortion, 10, 64
Accident, 26, 28; motor vehicle, 89
Achievement: academic, 15; motivation, 49; tests, 19, 61
ADAMHA. *See* Alcohol, Drug Abuse, and Mental Health
Adaptation, 11–13, 15, 17, 20; maladaptation, 27. *See also* Adjustment, Maladjustment
Adjustment, 11, 12, 17–19, 21, 34, 61, 101, 108; criteria of, 34; interpersonal, 17; radiation, 34, 35. *See also* Adaptation
Advantaged, disadvantaged, 111, 122, 204
Affection, 65
Aged, 196, 199; housing studies, 125–126; problems, 108
Alcohol, Drug Abuse, and Mental Health (ADAMHA), 28
Alcoholism and Marital Disruption, 90
American College Test, 174
American Orthopsychiatric Association, 29
American Psychiatric Association, 29, 30
American Psychological Association, 81, 189; Task Force on Health Research, 29, *32*, 108
American Public Health Association, 29; Program Area Committee on Mental Health, 26, *32*
Anorexia nervosa, 32
Antipollution, 10
Architects, 10, 12

Assessment: context of privacy and mental health, 145–147; holism, 145, 147, 149; interpersonal process, 146–147; regulation of social interaction, 145–147; system effectiveness, 146–147; system efficiency, 146–147
Attitude, 154; change, 181; institutionalized, 181; theory, 154
Auto-instruction, 19
Autonomy, 14, 18
Awareness, 116, 117

Bank Street study of progressive and traditional schools, 195–196
Behavior: child, 165; disorders, 4, 201; levels, 144, 145, 148, 154, 155; mechanisms, 144, 149; modeling, 80; modification, 118; motor, 49, 69; non-task-oriented, 48; social, 144; verbally informative, 48, 57. *See also* Behavior setting
Behavior setting, 13, 121, 154, 165, 167, 171, 172, 175, 176, 190; in churches of varying size, 174–175; definition, 168; description, 167–168; as ecological unit, 169; and mental health, 177; method, 168; milieu parts, 168–169, 190; overmanned, 172, 176; in schools of varying size, 173–174; standing patterns of behavior, 168–169, 190; study examples, 170; survey, 168, 170, 190; as synomorphic relation, 168; theory, 172–176; undermanned, 172, 174–176

Berko Morphology Test, 52
Biofeedback, 115–117, 119
Birth weight, 65, 78; and intelligence, 78; and other comparisons, 78
Black: "English," 52, 55; high-risk children, 202; marital disturbance, 87; persons, 19, 30, 46, 50, 68, 78
Boulder County, Colorado, 91, 111; separation data, 91
Bureau of the Census, 85

Cattell Test, 57
Causation, 110, 155, 202; difficulties, 132, 153; epidemiological approach, 153; evaluation model, 129; linear model, 110–111; perpetuating, 83; precipitating, 83; predisposing, 83; social and physical, 123–124
Child: guidance clinic, 9; naturalistic observation, 167; research methods, 167. See also Children
Child Welfare Research Station, 69
Children, 15, 17–19, 33, 35; adopted, 68, 73; charming and attractive, 73; disturbed, 9, 201; of divorce, 32, 90–91, 100, 108; group homes, 10; high-risk, 33, 186, 202; home-reared, 70, 72, 74, 75; hospitalized, 32; kibbutz-reared, 74; looking after younger children, 5; losing parent, 108; marital disruption and, 90–93; motor behavior of, 69, 75; naturalistic observation of, 167; number of, 45; orphanage, 66, 69, 72, 74, 77; pampered, 5; slum-dwelling, 41, 187. See also Child
CMH. See Community mental health
Cognition, 65
Cognitive dissonance, 192
Commissar approach, 115, 118, 120, 127, 131, 191, 195; changes produced by, 122; environmental change, 117; environmental psychology, 116, 121; token economy, 115
Community mental health (CMH), 11, 31, 84, 107; facilities, 11, 32, 180; personnel, 11

Community Psychology Action Center (CPAC), 19
Community, 16, 20, 26, 27, 31, 36, 47, 60, 77, 82, 86, 107, 111, 120, 121, 199; action, 106, 181; growth-inducing, 112; organization, 36, 181; psychology, 11, 36
Competence, 16–21, 27, 28, 33, 35, 65–67, 74, 78, 99, 194, 195; acquisition, 35; pathology prevention and, 200, 204; training, 20, 21, 34, 201
Competition, 14
Conation, 65
Conceptual: analysis, 111, 121, 133, 134–136, 185; framework, 25–28, 31, 134, 146, 147, 194, 195; Newtonian approach, 162, 166, 191–192; scheme, 193
Conference, 29–32, 164, 185, 189–192, 194; evaluation, 201–204
Consciousness raising, 10
Construction of object relations in space, 71, 72
Coping, 27, 28, 31, 32, 109; failure, 107; mechanisms, 145
Counseling, 27, 99, 109; divorce, 28, 92; genetic, 64
CPAC. See Community Psychology Action Center
Crisis, 27–31, 33, 96, 107, 188; family, 47; intervention, 27, 31, 60, 99, 109; life, 32, 108, 109; normative, 83, 108
Curiosity, 19
Crowding, 121, 159, 162, 165, 189, 190; evaluation of studies, 160; sex difference, 159, 162; short term, 124
Curriculum, 17, 18; for children of mentally retarded mothers, 48, 49; for mentally retarded mothers, 47

Density, 121, 162; high-density living, 160, 190
Department of Health, Education, and Welfare (DHEW), 28, 29, 78, 84, 85

Dependence, 5

Depression, 27, 28

Deprivation: of opportunity, 40; social, 40, 41, 46

Desired environmental events, development of means for obtaining, 71, 72

Development, 20, 27, 50; cognitive, 48, 49, 78, 129; critical periods in, 33; intellectual, 41; language, 48–51; personal, 13–15, 17; personnel, 20; psychological, 68, 69, 75, 202; sensory-perceptual-motor, 48, 49, 70, 71–75; social, 48

DHEW. See Department of Health, Education, and Welfare

Diet, 10, 28

Disadvantaged. See Advantaged

Disease, 26, 28; duration of, 82; incidence of, 82; morbidity and marital disruption, 90; pre-germ theory, 81; prevalence, 82; prevention, 81

Divorce, 83, 84, 108, 199; books on, 93; counseling, 92; "good," 92; incidence of, 85; laws regarding, 85–86; motor vehicle accidents and, 89–90; psychopathology and, 93; rate of, 93, 100; relative to marriage, 85; without separation, 100

Draw-A-Man Test, 67

Early experience, 69, 74, 195, 199, 202–203; adult adjustment and, 100–101; audio-visual enrichment, 70, 72, 74

Ecology, 13, 15, 118; psychology and, 165

Education, 116, 117; affective, 27; compensatory, 122, 186; death, 27, 30; family life, 27, 28; parent, 27, 68; primary prevention, 107; privacy, 147, 148; sex, 27. See also Educational

Educational, 17, 27, 194; day care, 67, 76, 202; engineering, 57; intervention, 63–65, 69, 75, 76, 79;

model, 4, 27; psychology, 20; settings, 14. See also Education

Ego, 14, 27, 28, 31; development, 195

Emotional distress, 27, 31, 81–83, 194; and marital disruption, 86, 87, 92–94, 97, 98, 202

Environment, 3, 6, 14–16, 26, 33, 49, 50; educational, 14, 15, 48; health-promoting, 13, 16, 69, 130; learning, 48; marriage as a protective, 95–96; mental hospital, 118, 120, 162; physical, 12, 154, 162, 180, 190, 199; social, 12–16, 21, 45, 46, 154, 201. See also Environmental

Environmental: activism, 118; analysis difficulties, 159–162; behavior, 137; change, 117, 120, 122, 160; change evaluation, 161; conditions, 119, 159; design, 119; determinism, 4; psychology, 116–118, 121–125, 127, 130, 160, 181, 186, 188–191, 201, 203; quality, 127; reinforcement contingencies, 117; research strategies, 159–162; shaping of behavior, 117. See also Environment

Epidemiology, 31, 62, 83, 195; approaches, 106; causation in, 153; data, 40, 202; of marital disruption, 91

Etiology, 26–28, 32; of mental retardation, 40, 45

Eugenics, 64

Euthenics, 65

Evaluation model, 125–126, 129–130; criteria, 125; effectiveness determination, 125, 160; importance of timing, 126; short- and long-run studies, 126

Evaluation research, 125–126, 192–193; formative, 192–193; summative, 192–193

Evolution, 65

Family: annual check-up, 94, 152; conflict, 60, 61; medicine, 152;

Family *(continued)* planning, 32
Fathers, absent, 43, 44, 47, 60
Follow-up, 77, 78, 173, 186, 203;
    data, 60, 61; marital, 99; need for,
    64, 79, 132, 187–188, 199

Gesell Test: data, 50; language scale,
    52; norms and schedules, 50, 51
Goals, 19
Grammatical Comprehension Test, 52
Group homes: for children, 10; for
    the mentally retarded, 181
Guaranteed annual wage, 10
Guidance, 27, 28; counselors, 119;
    vocational, 80

Habitat-claims, 171, 172; definition,
    171
Happiness, 11, 14
Hawthorne Effect, 161
Head Start, 18, 123, 129, 186
Health, 30; promotion, 8
Helplessness, learned, 108
Hereditary mechanisms, 64–66, 68,
    73, 187; heritability, 131
Historical determinants, 4
Homicide, 89; marital disruption and,
    89; race and, 89; sex differences
    and, 89

Id, 4
Illinois Test of Psycholinguistic
    Abilities (ITPA), 52, 55, 56; mean
    length of utterance, 52, 53
Imaginativeness, 15
Imitation, 70, 71; gestural, 72; pseudo,
    71; vocal, 70–73
Immaturity, 4–6
Independence, 20
Individual differences, 12, 68;
    ethnic/racial, 64, 68
Infants, Infancy, 29, 49, 65, 68;
    caretaker behavior, 70; center, 47;
    intervention program for, 46–48,
    63, 70–72
Infection, 26, 28
Institutional failure, 77

Intelligence, 5, 66; decline in, with
    age increase, 43; maternal, 41, 45,
    46, 62, 79; tests, 41, 50, 65, 67,
    68
Intelligence Testing, 57. *See also*
    Cattell Test, IQ, Stanford-Binet
    Test, Wechsler Adult Intelligence
    Scale, Wechsler Intelligence Scale
    for Children
Interdisciplinary collaboration, 36
International cartels, 10
Interpersonal relations, 14, 47
Intervention, 26, 60, 107; community
    programs, 107; context of privacy
    and mental health, 147–149; in
    marital disruption, 92–93, 99,
    100, 101, 106; massive, 161, 187;
    programs, 48, 57, 60, 61, 69–71,
    92, 201; social, 180
Intervention context of privacy and
    mental health, 147–149; education
    and training, 147, 148; flexibility
    in system, 148; use of privacy regu-
    lation mechanisms, 147
IQ, 41, 43, 44, 46, 55, 57–60, 65–69,
    72, 73, 75; child's, as related to
    parents', 43, 66–68; of a couple,
    152; declining pattern of, 60;
    mothers with low, 43, 46, 64, 66;
    paternal and maternal, 43, 44;
    practice gain in, 66
ITPA. *See* Illinois Test of Psycho-
    linguistic Abilities

Javanese, 140; privacy behaviors,
    140
Joint Commission on Mental Illness
    and Health, *198*

Language: acquisition of, 52, 71;
    aptitude, 55; comprehension,
    52; development, 48–51, 71;
    performance, 51, 54, 55, 61;
    syntactic structures in, 55, 71
Law Enforcement Assistance Admin-
    istration, 33
Learning: capacities, 62; learned help-

Learning *(continued)* lessness, 108;
  studies in the laboratory, 124, in
  the school, 124–125; tasks, 50;
  theory irrelevance, 124–125, 127
Literacy, 48
Los Angeles County, 88; suicide
  rates in, 88

Maladaptation. *See* Adaptation
Maladjustment, 17, 18, 27, 35, 99,
  107, 111
Man-environment relationship, 115–
  127, 129, 153, 154, 164, 189;
  under natural conditions, 165–
  166; strategies of research on,
  129, 131
Marriage: age and, 86; couples, 9,
  94, 111; counseling, 92; duration
  of, 85; history of, and disorder,
  95–96; incidence of, 85; as a
  protective environment, 95–96;
  satisfaction, 98; sex roles in, 98;
  trial, 86
Marital disruption, 27, 28, 83, 84,
  86, 107, 112, 155, 188; alcoholism and, 90; children of, 90–93;
  as consequence, 93; consequences
  of, 85–87, 91, 92; death rates
  and, 90; disease morbidity and,
  90, 95, 106; epidemiology of,
  91; as high-risk group, 84; homicide and, 89; hospital admission
  rates and, 87, 88, 106; hypotheses
  about, 93–96, 202; illness and,
  94; intervention in, 92–93; marital role performance and, 98;
  mortality and, 94–95; motor
  vehicle accidents and, 89, 106;
  physical and emotional disorder
  and, 93, 94, 98; psychiatric disorder and, 87, 93, 94, 96–97, 98;
  research in, 86, 108, 155; separation in, 91; suicide and, 88; as
  undesirable change, 97
Marxism, 117, 118
Massachusetts General Hospital, 90
Maternal-infant: affectional bonding,

32; interaction, 47, 48, 50, 55,
  60; intervention, 46–48, 60
Maturity, 4–6, 65, 106, 194, 195
Medical evaluation, 50
Medical model, 4, 26, 195
Meditation, 115–117, 122
Mehinacu, 140–142; privacy behaviors of, 140–141
Mental disorder, 3, 33, 84, 100;
  amelioration of, 111; cure of, 5;
  as immaturity, 4, 6; prevention of,
  8, 26, 81, 197
Mental health, 3, 6, 8–12, 15–16, 18,
  20, 27, 28, 30, 31, 33, 35, 64, 65,
  76, 107, 191, 204; childhood behavior and adult, 100–101; definition, 4, 6, 194–195; education in,
  27, 82; marital disruption and, 97;
  as maturity, 4, 5; organizations,
  29–31; outcomes, 12, 181; privacy
  and, 134, 144–149; personnel,
  10–12, 16, 20, 21, 26, 29, 31, 33,
  36, 81; problems, 106; roles of
  personnel in, 107, 108, 194, 196–
  197, 202
Mental Health Authorities, State and
  Territorial, 29, 32
Mental illness, 3, 26–28, 31, 84, 100
Mentally retarded mothers, 50; attitudes of, 47, 48
Mental retardation, 40, 41, 45, 46, 67;
  adolescent, 79; facilities for, 180;
  foster homes in, 120; genetic determinants of, 40, 41, 45, 46; institutions for retardates, 120; maternal,
  45–47; prevention of, 46, 62, 64,
  65, 185, 187; research in, 161;
  sociocultural (cultural familial), 40,
  41
Metera Center (Athens), 74
Midwest, Kansas (Oskaloosa), 167,
  170, 172, 173, 175, 189
Midwest Psychological Field Station,
  165
Milwaukee, 41, 47, 66, 76, 181; Project, 40, 60, 61, 63–65, 67, 78,
  186

Minorities, racial/ethnic, 40
Misery, 27, 28, 107
Motivation, intrinsic, 69, 71
Motor vehicle accidents, 89; marital disruption and, 89; race and, 89; sex differences and, 89
Mutual-help groups, 32, 36, 107

National Association for Mental Health, 29
National Center for Health Statistics, 85, 86, 89, 91, *104*
National Council of Community Mental Health Centers, 29
National Institute of Mental Health (NIMH), 5, *6*, 28, 29, 32, 65, 108, 109
Needs, social-emotional, 49
Neurosis, 4
NIMH. *See* National Institute of Mental Health
Nutrition, 26, 28; mental health and, 32

Object permanence, 70–72, 74, 75
Office of Education, 65
Operational causality, 71, 72
Operator: approach, 166, 193; psychologist as, 166
Oral fluency, 15
Orphanage of the Farah Pahlavi Charity Society, 69, 75, 186, 202
Oskaloosa, Kansas, 165, 167, 170–173, 175, 189
Overmanned settings, 172, 191, 203; surplus manpower in, 176, 181

Parent: competence, 79; effectiveness training, 10; intelligence of, 39–62, 64, 66–69. *See also* IQ
Parent and Child Center (Illinois), 70, 75
Participant observer method, 167, 170, 194
Pathology, 21, 35, 69, 194, 199; central nervous system, 40; prevention of, and competence, 200;

in utero, 64
Peabody Quotient, 44; maternal, 44; paternal, 45
Persistence, 15
Personal space, 134, 136, 138, 165; distance zones in, 138; intrusion of, 138; violation of distance zones in, 139
Personality, 19; behavior and, 153; characteristics of, 167–168; psychology of, 167; research methods in, 167
Physical health/disorder, 31, 107; marital disruption and, 86, 87, 93, 94, 97, 98, 202
Picture Morphology Test, 52
PLQ. *See* Psycholinguistic Quotient
Poison, 26, 28
Policy makers, 10, 12, 30
Politics, 30, 33, 116, 118
Poor, poverty, 40, 41, 45, 64, 84, 117, 118, 162; psychopathology linked to, 84
Postpartum disturbances, 32
Premarital counseling, 28
Prenatal clinics, 10
Primary prevention of psychopathology, 3, 4, 6, 7, 9–12, 14, 16–21, 25–29, 31, 32, 34, 69, 76, 81, 82, 84, 194; in adults, 33; causation, 153; community and, 36; conceptualization of, 186, 194; cost of, 132; definitions, 8–12, 204, difficulties, 8–11, 196–197, 204; efforts at, 33, 64, 109, 200; environmental psychology and, 186, 190, 191, 199; intervention in, 107; marital disruption and, 96, 186, 188; methodologies of, 31; practice of, 31; privacy and, 145–149; program development in, 29–31, 33; research strategies in, 31, 131, 204; state programs in, 31, 32, 36
Primary Prevention Publication Series, 29, 31, 32
Prisons: architecture of, 118; importance of staff in, 118–119; improvements in, 118–119, 121–122;

Prisons *(continued)* simulation of, 123

Privacy, 133–149, 154, 155, 164, 165, 190; anonymity, 135; assessment context and mental health, 145–147; conceptual analysis of, 134–136; definition, 134; desired vs. achieved, 136; dialectic nature of, 135, 145–149; input and output processes, 136; intimacy, 135; invasions of, 143; mechanisms of, 133, 137–141; mental health and, 134, 144–145, 204; optimization nature of, 135; as pancultural universal, 165; regulation of, 138–140, 144–145, 146–148, 153, 155; reserve, 135, 140; as self-other boundary control process, 133–136, 141, 142, 191, 204; solitude, 134; units of, 134–135. *See also* Privacy mechanisms, Privacy regulation functions

Privacy mechanisms, 133, 137–141, 145, 147; culturally based practices as, 139–142, 144; environmental, 138–139, 140, 144, 147, 165; nonverbal, 137–138, 139–141, 144, 147, 149; verbal, 137, 140, 144, 147, 149

Privacy regulation functions, 142–144; interface of self and world and, 142; interpersonal nature of, 142; self-definition of, 142–144

Psycholinguistic Quotient (PLQ), 55

Psychological bulletin, 81

Psychology, 110; approaches to, 191; definition, 110; ecological, 165–177, 181, 189; environmental, 116–118, 121–125, 127, 130, 160, 181, 186, 188–191, 201, 203; relevant to the public, 180; social, 20, 127, 152, 154, 189

Psychopathology, 27, 28, 82, 83; behavior settings and, 177; marital disruption and, 93, 97, 98; marital status and, 87; needless, 108; social class and, 84

Psychosexual development: genital stage, 4; other stages, 5

Psychosocial disabilities, 29

Psychotherapy, 116–118, 122

Public health, 26, 31, 107, 195; concepts of, 106; training in, 153; values in, 106

Public relations, 78

Pueblo, Colorado, 88; marital disturbance data from, 88, 95

Quality of life, 10, 11, 21

Rehabilitation, 46, 47; educational, 46; facilities for, 180; vocational, 46–48, 180

Relating to objects, development of schemes for, 71, 72

Relational factors, 13, 14

Remarriage: age and, 86; rates of, 86; sex differences in, 86

Research, 87, 106; action model, 107, 129, 130, 201, 203; additive vs. subtractive approach to, 131, 204; applied vs. basic, 110, 126–127, 129, 152, 160, 180; control (baseline) group in, 132; correlational studies, 124, 132, 162, 202; cross-national, 100; cross-sectional, 66; demonstration studies in, 192, 199; designs in marital disruption, 94, 97; and development, 187; difficulties in, 159–162; evaluation model in, 125–126, 192–193, 203; experimental model, 124, 125, 166, 191; future, 200; grants and contracts, 108, 109; longitudinal, 66, 79, 94, 196; methodological problems in, 97, 161, 166, 186; naturalistic model of, 166–167; parametric, 192; quick-and-dirty, 126, 130, 132, 193; short- and long-run, 126, 187, 203; systematic, 162; wave design, 69, 72–75

Response stereotypy, 51

Rice, 10

Risk: groups at, 21, 63, 106, 108, 109,

Risk *(continued)* 186; high-, 80, 83, 84, 145, 199, 202

Schizophrenia, 27, 194
School(s), 15, 16, 18, 19; character-
    istics of, 121; conflict with, 60,
    61; design of, 122; environments
    in, 119; improvements of, 77,
    119; integration in, 10; malad-
    justment in, 9, 15, 60, 61; mental
    health services in, 9, 18, 32, 33,
    201; open vs. self-contained, 14,
    15; operant conditioning studies
    in, 124–125; performance in, 68;
    progressive vs. traditional, 195–
    196; research in the, 77; small
    vs. large, 12, 173–174, 181; as
    unchanging institutions, 181
Secondary prevention of psycho-
    pathology, 3, 9, 81, 82, 201, 204
Security, 11
Self-: definition, 134, 142–144;
    esteem, 14, 47, 92; evaluation,
    142; image/identity, 11, 12, 14,
    15, 19, 143; other, 133–134;
    realization, 143
Semantic mastery, 70, 71
Sentence Repetition Tests I, II, 52
Separation, 91, 99, 107, 108; housing
    and, 100; length of, 91; time of,
    100
Sesame Street, 10
Sibling comparisons, 57, 60
Sierra Club, 117–119, 129
Skill, 16–20, 21, 35, 40, 49
Skinnerian approach, 117; reinforce-
    ment contingencies in, 117, 122
Slums, 41, 43, 45, 46
Social: action, 106; behavior, 144;
    change, 16, 115, 116–117, 119,
    120, 127, 129, 130, 181; deter-
    minants, 4; experiences and mari-
    tal disruption, 92; physical vs.,
    121–123, 139; problems, 117;
    psychology, 20, 127, 152, 154,
    189; reinforcement, 19; responsi-
    bility, 106; skills, 17–19, 34, 60,

68; studies, 47; supports, 111–
    112; systems, 4, 13, 20, 21, 34, 35,
    94, 111, 149, 187, 188; units, 110,
    144–147, 152, 154, 155; variables,
    87; work, 36
Social climate, 13, 14
Social Ecology Laboratory, 13
Social usefulness, uselessness, 5, 6
Society, 5
Spatial behavior, 121, 134, 137; intru-
    sions in, 138
Stanford-Binet Test, 57, 67
Statistical effects, 190; main effect,
    15; third-order and higher inter-
    actions, 125, 159
Stress, 107; environmental approach
    to, 124; laboratory created, 123;
    life changes as, 97; marital disrup-
    tion and, 91, 96, 98–100, 108;
    mental illness and, 123; reduction
    of, 82, 92; among unmarried
    couples, 99; vulnerability to, 82,
    87
Strong Vocational Interest Blank, 5
Sudden Infant Death Syndrome, 30,
    31, 108; mental health aspects of,
    107
Suicide, 9, 28; age and, 89; marital
    disruption and, 88–89; sex differ-
    ences and, 89
System maintenance, 13, 14, 16;
    properties of, 16

Task-orientation, 14, 50
Teacher: -child relationship, 49;
    experimental, 46; importance of,
    119; as model, 80; mother's ability
    as, 57; reports by, 61
Territoriality, 134, 136, 138, 139,
    165
Tertiary prevention of psychopathol-
    ogy, 3, 82, 204
Theory: ecological model, 130;
    humanistic model, 130; impor-
    tance of, 110, 130–131, 191; lack
    of, 164; learning model, 124–125,
    127, 131; levels of, 111, 131;

Theory *(continued)* perspectives
of, 146; refutable propositions
in, 152; self-actualization model,
130
Titanium paint, 10
Token economy, 115
Training, 20; home and child care,
46, 47, 80; need for, 32; privacy,
147, 148
Transducer: approach, 165, 167,
193; psychologist as, 165–166,
193
Treatment, 13, 33; specificity of,
77, 78
Tuareg, 138, 141, 142; privacy
behaviors of, 141–142; use of
veil by, 141

Undermanned settings, 172, 174,
191, 203; consequences of, 175,
181; functional identity in, 176;
functional importance of persons
in, 175; insecurity in, 176; responsibility in, 176; sensitivity to
individual differences in, 175
Urban planners, planning, 10, 12, 119
U.S. Bureau of the Census, 84, 85,
105
U.S. Department of Health, Education, and Welfare, 28, 29, *32*,
84, 85, *105*
U.S. Government, 28
Utopia, 111, 119; mouse, 124

Values, 20; public health, 106
Variability, 67, 68, 76, 155, 162,
190; in IQ scores, 66–74; 203
Variables, 15, 18, 34, 41, 192, 201,
202, 204; critical, 123, 162,
203, demographic, 125; depen-

dent, 11, 12, 20, 71, 75, 195;
environmental, 3, 6, 13, 14, 162,
201; independent, 11, 16, 21, 82,
122; manipulation of, 131–132;
social, 87
V.D., 10
Vermont Conference on the Primary
Prevention of Psychopathology,
30, 32, 69, 201
Vineland Social Maturity Scale, 5

WAIS. *See* Wechsler Adult Intelli-
gence Scale
Washington, D.C., 28, 78
Wechsler Adult Intelligence Scale
(WAIS), 48, 152
Wechsler Intelligence Scale for
Children (WISC), 57, 59, 60
Well-baby clinic, 16
Well-being, sense of, 10, 11, 13, 21,
97, 98
Westinghouse Learning Corporation,
186, *198*
White House, 29
Widowed persons, 86, 89
WISC. *See* Wechsler Intelligence Scale
for Children
Woodlawn Mental Health Center,
Chicago, 83

Yagua, 138
Yoga, Yogi approach, 115–118, 120,
127, 131, 191, 195; biofeedback
training as, 115–117, 119; changes
produced by, 122; education as,
116, 117; meditation as, 115–
117; psychotherapy as, 116–118
Yoredale, England, 170–173, 175

Zoom, 10